THE PASSING OF ARTHUR

THE GARLAND REFERENCE LIBRARY
OF THE HUMANITIES
(VOL. 781)

THE PASSING OF ARTHUR

New Essays in Arthurian Tradition

edited by

Christopher Baswell
and
William Sharpe

GARLAND PUBLISHING, INC. · NEW YORK & LONDON
1988

Library of Congress Cataloging-in-Publication Data

The Passing of Arthur: new essays in Arthurian tradition /
  [edited by] Christopher Baswell and William Sharpe.
    p.   cm. — (Garland reference library of the humanities; v.
781)
  Papers originally presented at 8th Annual Barnard College
Conference on Medieval and Renaissance Studies, Barnard College,
Nov. 15, 1986.
  Includes index.
  ISBN 0–8240–8097–1 (alk. paper)
  1. Arthurian romances—History and criticism—Congresses.
I. Baswell, Christopher. II. Sharpe, William. III. Barnard
College. IV. Barnard College Conference on Medieval and Renaissance
Studies (8th: 1986) V. Series
PN685.P28 1988
809'.93351—dc19   87–32441
                                                        CIP

Printed on acid-free, 250-year-life paper
Manufactured in the United States of America

TABLE OF CONTENTS

PREFACE

The essays collected in this volume are based on papers delivered at "The Passing of Arthur," the Eighth Annual Barnard College Conference on Medieval and Renaissance Studies, November 15, 1986. One contributor, M. Alison Stones, spoke at the conference but prepared a specially commissioned paper for the book. Roberta Krueger's essay was also commissioned for inclusion here. We are grateful to M. Victoria Guerin for translating Charles Méla's article, and for traveling to Geneva to adapt it with his cooperation. W. W. Norton and Co. has kindly given permission to quote from Marie Borroff's verse translation of *Sir Gawain and the Green Knight*.

The editors are grateful to Barnard College for funding the conference. We are indebted to Dean Charles Olton for his assistance, and to Jean McCurry and Eileen Macholl for their invaluable logistical support. Finally, we wish to thank our colleagues in the English Department, and especially Professor Anne Lake Prescott, for their encouragement.

Christopher Baswell and William Sharpe
Barnard College
October 1987

INTRODUCTION:
REX QUONDAM REXQUE FUTURUS

Christopher Baswell and William Sharpe

Yet some men say in many parts of England that King Arthur is not dead, but had by the will of our Lord Jesu into another place; and men say that he shall come again, and he shall win the Holy Cross. Yet I will not say that it shall be so, but rather I would say: here in this world he changed his life. And many men say that there is written upon the tomb this:
HIC IACET ARTHURUS REX QUONDAM REXQUE FUTURUS
—Sir Thomas Malory

I

There is no Arthurian "now." At every stage of the Arthurian tradition, the narrative moment, the moment of the tale's telling, hesitates between a past irrevocably lost and a future return forever awaited. As in almost any story, the Arthurian narrator speaks of a finite moment that has ended; yet this same narrator also lives before a vaguely predicted messianic return of the king. Such narration hovers then between its historic past and its apocalyptic future.

Even in the narrated present, as opposed to the narrator's present, there is no Arthurian "now." No Arthurian story is experienced without some foreknowledge of its end, an awareness which the text at once acknowledges and avoids through any of a complex range of methods: echo, deferral, revisionism. To take just one example, *Sir Gawain and the Green Knight*—a tale of the early and unspoiled Arthurian realm—is ominously bracketed by references to the fall of Troy, England's genealogical forebear, and its plot centers around a first encounter with the terrors of human mortality and the danger of sexual temptation—both elements which will later contribute to Camelot's downfall. Even the vast French cycles, the bulk of which have little overt reference to Arthur's death, could be said to put off their ending by extensions and repetitions of knightly adventure.

From this perspective, all such narratives concern the passing of Arthur. The narrator and reader live in the empty if long moment between loss and return, and the story is always aware of the loss that is to come. In Tennyson's version, even Arthur himself is not fully present:

For there is nothing in it [Camelot] as it seems
Saving the King; tho' some there be that hold
The King a shadow, and the city real.
            ("Gareth and Lynette")

In ways other than the historical, too, it is difficult to establish an Arthurian "presence": certainty about the status of morality, of women, of signification, passes constantly out of our grasp. Thus Spenser's *Faerie Queene*, built around an exposition of moral virtues wholly embodied by Arthur, depicts its hero only in brief flashes, literally in passing.

But if there is no Arthurian "now"—as present or presence—there most certainly is Arthuria*nism* now, and this volume is dedicated to that critical present. Where is Arthurianism today? The story of Arthur and his world has captured the imagination of the West from its first major appearance in the twelfth century to recent popular books like Marion Zimmer Bradley's *The Mists of Avalon* (1983). At the same time, many other resources which have traditionally provided our culture with a sense of continuity are falling away from us. Classical literature is radically less studied today than in the past. Similarly, the great religious texts of the Western tradition, like the Bible, are less and less known. But the figure of Arthur and the Round Table's model of social concord, simultaneously idealized and endangered, no sooner achieved than corrupted, continue to fascinate contemporary readers.

The appeal of the Arthurian legend to anyone caught in the cycle of seasons, between birth and death, is evident. The Christian "man in the middest," for whom the final Revelation and judgment are always deferred, must necessarily be fascinated by a story whose structure is coextensive with that of the Bible, a story which describes the Eden of Camelot, the fall into woe brought about by a woman, and the promise of a resurrected king and a new city at some imminent yet unknown time in the future.

This popularity has generated a vast scholarship on Arthurian literature and legend. A major problem among Arthurians, however, is the tendency to divide into highly specialized subfields between which there has too often been inadequate communication. This is as true within traditional disciplines, with their boundaries of language and period, as it is among exponents of conflicting methodologies. And recent work which attempts to cross disciplinary boundaries has also created divisions. For all their richness, many new theoretical approaches, using discourses that can approach the hermetic, have limited their audiences to specialists of yet another kind.

Nonetheless, much work has been devoted of late to bridging these gaps, if only by collecting and organizing the various sources of Arthurian study, and by creating forums for exchange among Arthurians of varied period and persuasion.[1] *The Passing of Arthur* was conceived as an attempt to extend and broaden this encouraging development. The volume presents a wide range of contemporary Arthurian studies, and offers a series of essays, textual and iconographic, which explore both the historical passing of the Arthurian present and, in a theoretical sense, the inevitable passing of an Arthurian presence.

Though the book begins and ends with Arthur's death, there are texts whose inclusion or exclusion here may surprise readers, if they regard the title only in the sense of Arthur's dénouement. On the one hand, no essays focus on the stanzaic or alliterative *Morte Arthure* or on Malory. On the other hand, considerable attention is paid to a Middle English poem about the youthful Arthurian court, *Sir Gawain and the Green Knight*, and to *The Faerie Queene*, whose Arthur is still a prince. Yet, as suggested above, even such early episodes contain foreshadowings of Arthur's fall, and those texts which promise to deal most explicitly with his death do not exhaust the meanings of his end and return. Indeed, in addressing certain high points of the Arthurian tradition, especially in England, the contributors bring a whole series of other senses of "passing" to bear on the story.

II

Common to every corner of the tradition is the knowledge that Arthur will pass away, although this is not always synonymous with dying. All Arthurian texts are haunted by a sense of the realm's pastness—a persistent, almost elegiac note of ideal worlds under threat in their own time and long lost by the time the artist recalls them. This endangerment and nostalgia, often merely implicit in the earlier cyclic narratives, becomes more striking as Arthurianism develops in the Renaissance, and is a dominant theme in its nineteenth-century manifestations. As Alison Stones shows, illustrations of the final episodes in Arthur's life, as told in *La Mort le roi Artu*, focus attention on the moment of the king's death. But even in an early episode like *Sir Gawain and the Green Knight*, as Marie Borroff demonstrates here, the court and its premier knight must face the challenge which mortality poses to their moral and political virtues. The gentleness of the judgment finally passed on Gawain includes an acknowledgment of how desirable life is, how frightful its passing.

In Victorian times, the images of Arthur's passing expressed the culture's deep fascination with death and dying. John D. Rosenberg points out how Tennyson's *Idylls of the King* represented, in part, the poet's lifelong effort to come to terms with the early death of his close friend Arthur Hallam, the "other Arthur" whose loss also inspired the era's most revered poem, *In Memoriam*. Transforming his personal grief into an epic of a model society doomed from its inception by moral weakness, Tennyson voiced the religious and social fears of his generation. Victorian painters no less than poets were preoccupied with the death of the king, as William R. Fredeman demonstrates. But while many artists depicted his passage to Avalon and the comatose twilight of his recuperation there, none ventured to sketch his return. Both Tennyson and his illustrators dwelt, not on the future king, but on his dying, his "onceness."

This obsessive, elegiac attention to narrative passing, however, rarely lacks some promise of renewal or restoration, of passing onward at the moment of disaster. The epigraph with which this Introduction begins refers to the central myth of Arthur's return, but the idea of renewal is also present elsewhere. Bertilak's sparing of the hero, as Marie Borroff argues, includes a certain approval for Gawain's visceral wish to go on living. Charles Méla shows how *La Mort le roi Artu* contains hints of regeneration, both by echoing moments in the Round Table's glorious past and by rehabilitating Lancelot as a figure of spiritual rather than worldly accompishment. In Tennyson's *Idylls*, too, Arthur's future kingdom is displaced from this world to that other, better world in which he will most fully emulate his symbolic alter-ego, the figure of Christ.

But as the title of this book implies, the passing *on* of the Arthurian legacy, its literary transmission from era to era and country to country, forms an equally integral part of its meaning. A number of essays in this volume trace the reinscription of past Arthurianisms by later eras, and several propose new networks of transmission. M. Victoria Guerin demonstrates how early the parallels between Arthur and King David were established in the tradition, and how persistent was the exploration and elaboration of this parallel. Judith H. Anderson makes the strongest argument yet offered for Spenser's exploitation of the first Middle English Arthurian text, Laȝamon's *Brut*. In a revolutionary proposal, A. Kent Hieatt argues that Spenser's deep knowledge of Malory led him to envision Arthur's future conquest of Rome in the projected second twelve books of *The Faerie Queene*, as a previously misunderstood reference in the Book of Briton Moniments intimates. And if the Arthurian legend lay largely dormant after Spenser, John Rosenberg notes how Tennyson's poem sparked an Arthurian revival that prompted no less than a literary second coming of Arthur in Victorian times. The phenomenon then extended into the visual arts and into the very fabric of society in the modern codes of chivalry and gentlemanliness.

The Arthurian narrative does not just pass forward chronologically, however, from one period to the next. Individual Arthurian narratives also make referential "passes" over their own pasts or futures, folding back upon or scanning themselves, and proposing, through choice of version or literary echo, alternative senses of the story they tell. In Sheila Fisher's reading of *Sir Gawain and the Green Knight*, for example, the tale is seen as a revisionary version of the beginning of Arthur's realm, a version that attempts, by marginalizing such apparent threats as sexual temptation or feminine power, to create a Camelot that might never have passed. At the opposite end of the Arthurian story, in *La Mort le roi Artu*, Méla describes a series of echoes that imply not disaster but spiritual regeneration.

But this narrative passing, back to the past or toward the future, is not always *in bono*. As Fisher points out, the revisionary marginalization of feminine power in *Sir Gawain and the Green Knight* is nothing more than a temporary, nostalgic attempt: it does not work. Hieatt's proposal, that Spenser planned an Arthurian conquest of Rome, envisions a (wholly fictive) past that would recover England's own post-Trojan, Latin origins. But Arthur only visits upon his "past" (the nation of his Trojan ancestors) the same disaster of conquest which will later strike his "future" (the England which, according to Geoffrey of Monmouth, will be conquered by the Anglo-Saxons). Arthur therefore inscribes on the empire founded by his genealogical forebears the crisis which his nation's fate will mirror.

Even individual narrative moments in the Arthurian corpus, then, are always threatening to disappear into the pasts whose weights they bear or the futures they adumbrate. Several of essays presented here explore another, related dynamic, the tendency of a whole range of "presences," or apparently fixed points of reference, to pass away into uncertainty. In Arthurian as in other texts, a destabilizing dynamic affects the categories of authority—moral and social, linguistic and historical.

Parody, for instance, undermines the dominant exemplars of virtue in Spenser's *Faerie Queene*. As Judith H. Anderson argues, the lustful Argante presents disturbing parallels to the chaste Belphoebe, thereby distantly undermining the moral idealization of his queen; and Arthur's perfection is similarly called into doubt both by hints of pride in his description, and by his placement between limitless *moral* potential and the fact of his *historical* fall. The structure of familial order and fidelity is similarly unsettled in Charles Méla's reading of *La Mort le roi Artu*, with a literal son in revolt against his father even as a symbolic son abandons a lifetime of rebellion. While Arthur's life and kingdom are being destroyed by Mordred, Lancelot spares Arthur's life and returns his wife to him. Thus one son usurps paternity and the other, simultaneously, affirms it.

If moral and social certitudes are endangered in these works, recent critics have also questioned the very reliability of textual signs and the reader's ability to recover fully their "presence," their meaning and historical situation. In "The 'Syngne of Surfet' and the Surfeit of Signs in *Sir Gawain and the Green Knight*," R. Allen Shoaf shows how Gawain moves from being the knight of the pentangle to knight of the girdle, and thus from an uninterpretable and inimitable emblem of behavior to a different kind of sign, one that admits the indeterminacy of human interpretation and the limits of human virtue. Jonathan Freedman stresses how Victorian attempts to translate the Arthurian legend into the modern times reveal instead the irrecoverable quality of the past, and the groundlessness of the present. The world of Tennyson's *Idylls* is so remote that his envisioning of the returned Arthur as a contemporary gentleman seems ludicrous; yet William Morris' bold retelling of Guenevere's trial to suit the moral purposes of the present succeeds only at the expense of history.

Finally, this collection addresses the passing of women into the margins both of texts and of the social world that created those texts. The problematic interaction of authority and "presence" are approached from feminist perspectives in a sequence of essays covering each period. These represent an important new kind of attention being paid to the texts, and to the literary and social problems they pose—questions of paternal authority both textual and historical.

Roberta M. Krueger discusses the subversion of apparent feminine power in both the patroness and the heroine of *Le Chevalier de la Charrete*. Initially, it appears that Marie de

Champagne dictates the "sense" of the tale, but her authority disappears (as does the narrator who undertakes to obey her) when the romance closes in the voice of another narrator whose announced loyalty is to Chrétien. Similarly, the powerful if (to Lancelot) incomprehensible Queen Guenevere is made to regret her initial folly, and fades from the text. The *Gawain*-poet also tries to disenfranchise women, as Sheila Fisher shows in "Leaving Morgan Aside." The revisionary program she discovers in the poem can succeed only by suppressing or marginalizing women of power, thereby minimizing their inherent threat to Arthur's realm. As Sheila Cavanagh writes of *The Faerie Queene*, "Women are rarely truly 'present' in the epic." Even where they are encountered, moreover, they arouse responses of such ambivalence and even violence in the Spenserian heroes that they seem to subvert the very virtues those heroes are intended to embody.

This danger does not leave Arthurian women always at the margins, however. For the Pre-Raphaelites, Carole Silver finds, the very threat of women makes them desirable alternatives to Arthur's passivity (so much more remarkable, to these poets and painters, than his passing). Taking their text from Southey's Malory rather than Tennyson's *Idylls*, Rossetti and Morris find their most vital subjects in the sexually charged figures of Guenevere, Vivien, and other Arthurian women. Not "fallen" but triumphantly risen from her bed of adultery, the Guenevere of Morris' painting emblematizes for Silver how the Pre-Raphaelites sought to recenter the powerful spellbinder amid the rigid paternalism of the Victorian world.

III

In its most radical sense, the Passing of Arthur is not discussed in this book, since there can be only silence about what is irrevocably lost. No essay can be written about the complete *Tristan* of Thomas d'Angleterre, which despite its medieval popularity descends to us only in fragments. Even the Arthuriana of the nineteenth century are disappearing, as witnessed by the number of objects listed as "not located" in William E. Fredeman's Appendix on the visual representation of the death of Arthur.

The loss is correspondingly greater for the Middle Ages. It is not only interpretive certainties, then, that slip from us as we approach the Arthurian tradition. The very phenomena upon which we train our attention constantly pass from us through the notorious agencies of textual corruption and physical decay.

Those materials that do remain also threaten to elude us if we fail to approach them as broadly as possible, both in terms of the intellectual methods we bring to them, and the media—textual and visual—in which they come to us. We have already tried to suggest the wide variety of critical approaches employed in this volume, and the rich resonances they call forth. But as much as we may need theoretical amplitude, we also need to study both text *and* icon to pursue the Arthurian "presence" in the present moment. The interplay between the essays on *La Mort le roi Artu* by Charles Méla and Alison Stones, and those on Tennyson by John Rosenberg and William Fredeman, suggests how richly these media illuminate one another. The irrecoverable Arthurian present can be most fully approximated by our willingness to read all the signs available, in all the ways available, to make sure that the Arthur who is always passing will never finally pass.

NOTE

1.   Central to this effort has been the recent publication of *Arthurian Legend and Literature: An Annotated Bibliography* (New York: Garland, 1984), by Reiss, Reiss, and Taylor, as well as other bibliographies, and the *Arthurian Encyclopedia* (New York: Garland, 1986) under the general editorship of Norris J. Lacy, who also laments the "partitions" separating Arthurian scholars (p. viii).

The Passing of Arthur

Arthur in Medieval France

Life in *La Mort le roi Artu*

Charles Méla

La Mort le roi Artu[1] is not a story about death; or, at least, death's function there is to bring about the birth of a new, internalized *merveille*,[2] when the enchantments of the realm of Logres have come to an end. After *La Queste del Saint Graal*, and when the adventures of Arthur's court had all been told, to begin a new tale was a risky endeavor: except by a return to the chronicle of feudal wars,[3] a literature without *merveilles* seemed scarcely conceivable. The solution was to insert them in *mise en abîme* in a text otherwise empty of them so that, at the point when the whole feudal structure is threatened with ruin, evidence of a new *merveille* appears. The post-Grail text reveals, at last, the internal order which gives meaning to the whole long sequence of adventures preceding it.

With *La Mort le roi Artu*, Lancelot's real life begins. He no longer, as in the earlier texts, sees himself reflected in his friend and fearful alter-ego, the giant Galehot, or in Galaad, the hero's son whose name and destiny were Lancelot's own at birth, before Lancelot's love for the queen led him to follow another path. Both the giant and the Grail knight showed him what he might have been; henceforth he will belong only to himself. In *La Mort Artu*, Lancelot is presented in opposition to, and in radical distinction from, the adulterer Mordred, at once the product and the perpetuator of Arthur's incest. This autonomy is his greatest achievement, a "castle" raised by his own self-mastery and foreshadowed, through their very contrast, by the two other castles central to his life: La Douleureuse Garde, where he learned his name, and the Grail Castle, where he begat his son. When Lancelot's brother, Hestor, urges him to kill Gawain at the end of their long-delayed but inevitable battle, the nobility of the hero's reply is a sign of this change: "je nel feroie mie, fet Lancelos, car mes cuers a cui je sui ne s'i porroit acorder en nule maniere" (158:13-15).[4] Lancelot serves as model for a new meaning given to the *merveilles* of the Arthurian world: from now on, only those of the heart will matter (cf. 148:70-76).

But first the tale must be taken up again, the old story retold in a new form. This turning back upon itself is the first striking characteristic of the new text; the second is the frequency of the formula, "or dit li contes." These words, traditional in the earlier prose texts, take on a new emphasis in *La Mort Artu*; it is not the author but the "tale," the "story" itself, that speaks. The replacement of the author by an anonymous voice is made all the more striking by the other two fictitious sources of the text: the written record of the adventures which the heroes themselves recount before the court (2:9-12), and the supposed Latin original which "Gautier Map" is said to have translated at the request of Henry II (1:1-16). This false historical referent, peculiar to *La Mort Artu*, is as deceptive as the fictional one in a text thus doubly removed from its author. Its purpose and message have a life of their own, for in the end no one can claim to be master of the tale that he tells. In reaching its natural conclusion, at the point when a dearth of *merveilles* had made writing an impossible enterprise, the text recovers itself, distances itself, to reappear fulfilled and perfected in *La Mort Artu*.

Time has passed: the queen is fifty years old, Lancelot fifty-five, Gawain seventy-six and Arthur ninety-two.[5] Yet Lancelot reappears just as he was in the beginning, bearing armor borrowed from yet another newly-dubbed knight: red arms, this time, rather than the white which he wore when the Lady of the Lake first presented him at court. Their color, however, recalls the flaming red worn by Lancelot's son, Galaad, on his first visit to Arthur's court at the beginning of *La Queste del Saint Graal*.[6] But the time of "adventures" is past; this is merely a tournament. No matter! The text is obsessed by its memories. Lancelot has agreed, despite himself, to champion one of the loveliest maidens in the world, the maid of Escalot, and it falls to Gawain to remind him of his liaison with King Pelles' daughter, from which Galaad was born (30:80-83). But the manner in which the maid of Escalot tends the wounded hero, and the way that he dismisses her, recall the maiden of the poisoned fountain in the prose *Lancelot*.[7] The traditional motif of a knight wounded near a fountain inevitably recurs in this series of events linked by the love story of the Maid of Escalot (64-65), but this time in the context of a stag hunt taken from the initial episode of the *Lai de Guigemar*[8]; the arrow wound in the thigh (64:36-38) and the importance of a shirt tail (65:13-15) are borrowed from Marie de France's *lai*. Moreover, the arrival at court of the Maid of Escalot, lying dead in a boat which seems to sail by itself, is remarkably close to the scene of Perceval's sister in the mysterious boat of the *Queste*;[9] Arthur and Gawain agree that it is almost as if the adventures had begun again (70:21-25). Yet the name of Escalot does not belong to the Grail adventures, but seems rather a blending of the name *Esca*lon or *Esca*valon with the final letters of names like Lance*lot*, Gale*hot*, and Male*hot*.

The text accumulates signs of *faërie* even as it continually notes its absence. The love theme, on the one hand, persists. The hero leaves in the bedchamber at Escalot the shield which identifies him and recalls the magically divided shield given to Guenevere by the Lady of the Lake.[10] But the first part of *La Mort Artu* also presents the image of the hero as a sick or wounded knight confined to bed like the "roi méhaigné" of the Grail tradition (36:11). The new text repeats the old, inscribing the Grail adventure in a tale which the Grail itself had left an orphan. The bedchamber at Escalot, where the maiden leads Gawain in search of Lancelot, seems on fire with a great light like that of the inner room in the Grail Castle (27:5-8), but the only enchanted castle which still haunts the realm is that of Morgan, Arthur's sister. The king, lost in the forest, comes upon his sister's dwelling when he had believed her dead, like the queens that Gawain meets in the land of the dead at the end of *Le Conte du Graal*. The magnificent hall is filled with otherworldly music; two maidens appear from a chamber flooded with light, bearing golden candelabra, as in the Fisher King's palace. But this inner chamber conceals, not the Grail, but another *merveille*, "les oeuvres Lancelot" (52:1-2): a mural depicting a *mise en abîme* of Lancelot and the queen's love story. In *La Mort Artu*, the prose *Lancelot* has produced its own illuminated text, dragging the well-kept secret of the lovers' nights into the light of day. That which could not be written is told through images. This revelation has catastrophic consequences: what is seen "tout en apert" (52:8) is not the Grail, but the adulterous queen. Another sign that Logres will fall through a woman's misdeeds can be recognized, in a displaced form, in the episode of the poisoned fruit given by a new Eve, the queen, to the unfortunate knight, Gaheris, as if to foreshadow the death of Gaheriez and its fatal consequences for the destiny of Logres.

Responsible for these disasters is the "fole amour" (4:18) denounced by Agravain at the beginning of *La Mort Artu*. As if to underline this fact, the text models Lancelot's love on the events of the Tristan story. King Marc's nephew is specifically referred to (59:54-57), as if the two legends were henceforth to be united in a single text: this is, perhaps, the initial conception of the prose *Tristan*. In this new sequence, several episodes are easily identified as taken from Tristan's love story: the hall of statues (Lancelot's frescoes at Morgan's castle), the queen's equivocal oath,[11] the queen carried off then returned to the king, the lovers' indiscretion and the three perfidious barons (Arthur's three nephews in *La Mort Artu*), the hunt planned to entrap the lovers, the lovers taken by surprise, the insults addressed to the queen, the queen condemned to burn at the stake and the people's consequent grief, the rescue of the queen and the flight into the forest, and even the lovers' repentance and separation.[12]

At this point, however, everything changes, for Lancelot is not Tristan and he flees not to the forest of Morrois but to the former Douleureuse Garde, now Joyeuse Garde, closing the circle of his adventures in the castle where they began. On an earlier occasion, Bohort, hero of the *Queste*, had praised Lancelot above Tristan to the queen (59:54-84). To the topos of David, Solomon, and Samson—beauty, wisdom, and strength, all victims of a woman—he had added the names of Hector (spelled "Hestor," the name of Lancelot's brother), Achilles, and finally Tristan. He thus evokes the three sources of medieval romance: biblical,

Classical, and Breton, culminating with Lancelot as "d'entre les estoiles le soleill" and "la fleur des chevaliers del monde" (59:77-78).

Later, the army of Logres lays siege to Joyeuse Garde, the site of Lancelot's first great adventure, recalling also the episodes of Sorelois and the Terre Foreine, i.e., the *merveilles* of Galehot and the Grail King. The people of Joyeuse Garde welcome him as their king, and he holds court in a manner as rich as that of King Arthur. He thus comes to resemble Méléagant, the otherworld lord who stole the king of Logres' queen and kept her prisoner in *Le Chevalier de la Charrete*;[13] his claim to royalty seems a sign of pride or *démesure*, sounding the death knell of the chivalric world...or perhaps, rather, a final glimpse of the vanished *merveilles*.

For Lancelot's glory remains unstained: though he has usurped, in royalty, the place of "la *cort* le roi Artu" (111:37-38), he nevertheless refuses, in battle, to strike a blow against "le *cors* le roi Artu" (111:32). The king's tent is knocked down along with the image of the dragon atop it, in an ominous reminder of Uther Pendragon's death and a foreshadowing of Arthur's own, but Lancelot spares the king himself when he has him at his mercy. "Par ceste parole resqueust Lancelos de *mort le roi Artu*" (116:1-2): by sparing the king, the hero negates the very title of the work. Lancelot restores or preserves "la vie le roi," even in the murderous heat of battle.

In a symbolic gesture, the hero even takes the place of the Grail *merveilles*: after returning the queen to her husband, with the Pope's blessing, he sends his own shield to the Church of Saint-Etienne de Camaalot: "que mes escuz i soit en leu de moi" (120:22-23),[14] in order that the people "aient en remenbrance les merveilles que ge ai fetes en ceste terre" (120:18-19).[15] The shield, formerly kept in the bedchamber of Escalot, then at Joyeuse Garde, is now placed in the principal church of Camelot in a pattern which alternates profane and sacred, recalling both the split shield given to Guenevere by the Lady of the Lake and Nascien's shield, later borne by Galaad.[16] Lancelot's shield is to hang in the church choir, suspended from a silver chain like a holy relic: it has replaced the Grail as a relic of the vanished *merveilles* (121:8-10). The life of *La Queste del Saint Graal* penetrates the death theme of *La Mort le roi Artu*: Guenevere is welcomed by Arthur and his knights as if her presence legitimated the king's right to rule,[17] as if God himself had descended among them (120:3-4), perhaps a reminder of the descent of the Holy Spirit at Pentecost in the *Queste*.[18]

The relic of former *merveilles* hanging in the church of Saint-Etienne contrasts with the fresco which Arthur had had painted in that same church to commemorate his dream of Mordred as a serpent, foretelling the end of the Arthurian world.[19] Lancelot is not Tristan because he stands in opposition to Mordred, adulterer, patricide, and Arthur's incestuous son. This is the crux of the problem: at the crucial moment, out of his great love for the king (115:117-18), Lancelot stays his hand from the fatal blow, a symbolic act of patricide; in returning the queen to her husband, he places Guenevere's honor above his own desire (118:23-28). Lancelot assumes a self-imposed law as great as that which the lovers had broken. He chooses to live henceforth in a state of unfulfilled desire out of respect for the Name of the Father.

The essential achievement of *La Mort Artu* is to have integrated love for the king into Lancelot's love for the queen. By establishing a symbolic filial bond between Lancelot and Arthur the text reveals the essential problem, that of the Father, which is the key to the whole "Lancelot-Galaad" cycle. This explains the growing importance of Mordred, Lancelot's antithesis. In retrospect, Agravain's increasingly ominous role and the malevolence of the king's sister, Morgan, whose magic momentarily captures her brother's heart (50:58-64), seem to lead up to this development. It is suddenly made clear that the roots of disaster go deeper and farther back than its mere occasion, the discovery of the guilty love between Lancelot and the queen.

The text is skillfully constructed: it begins and ends with a battle at Winchester (15, 198); the queen's taking refuge at Joyeuse Garde is set against her imprisonment in the Tower of London; and above all, the story told in pictures on the walls of Morgan's bedroom (51:8-17) is balanced by the "lettres entaillées" by Merlin on the rock above Salisbury Plain (178:10-29), a prophecy of the battle to the death that will leave the kingdom of Logres "orfelins," fatherless (178:21). The reference to Merlin, and the previous revelation of the secret of Gawain's great strength in the hermit's words to King Lot at his son's birth (154), recall the guilt and secrecy associated with the births of Merlin, of Arthur, and of Mordred. The secondary guilt of the lovers is caught in the fatal web of this greater scheme. But the true fault is elsewhere and more obscure, and is linked to the question of paternity. This bond, to which Mordred bears witness by his hatred, is restored by the love of the king's other "son," Lancelot, whose Passion begins where carnal love ends. The Christological motif can be discerned at the moment when the hero justifies to Bohort his wish to spare the life of Gawain, who has become his mortal enemy:

"si est il li hom el monde qui riens ne m'est que je plus ai amé at aim encore, fors le roi solement. —Par foi, fait li rois Boorz, moult estes ore *merveillous*, qui si l'amés de grant cuer, et il vos het mortelment.—Par foi, fait Lancelos, ceste *merveille poés veoir*; il ne me savra ja tant haïr que je ne l'aime...."
(145:70-77; emphasis added) [20]

On this level, the whole text takes on a symbolic resonance and cosmic implications. The sun's path is reflected in Gawain's marvelous strength, which increases until midday. It is slightly after the hour of *nones* that the death-wound dealt by the king to his son is suddenly pierced by a sunbeam. As early as the *Historia Regum Britanniae*, a ray of light, the tail of a shooting star, was used to signify Arthur's power.[21] In the Old French text, the dying Arthur's embrace "*éteint* dessous lui" his butler, whose very name, "Lucans," signifies light (194:20-21; emphasis added), and Arthur reigns over ".XII. roiaumes" (194:24-25) like the sun amid the twelve signs of the zodiac.

At the moment of his death, Arthur is the "sun" of the world, and he sails away to Avalon, "vers la mer" (192:26), just as the sun sinks into the west.[22] The turn of Fortune's wheel was first "mere" [mother], then "marrastre" [stepmother], to the king (192:21-22), its painful rotation opposed to the turn of the heavens and to the "circuitude" of the world (176:72) symbolized by the Round Table. But in order for Arthur to reach the firmament, like the star Arcturus at the farthest pole of the world, the "bitter sea"[23] must first engulf all that remains of his glory: the moment has come to cast the precious sword, Excalibur, which the text attributes at times to Arthur, at others to Gawain, into the depths of the lake. It is impossible not to hear in the king's words, "Lors la lance el lac!" (192:80-81), the name of the sword's true addressee, Lancelot du Lac. But the magical waters close over their secret while, at the end of the tale, the beatific vision opens in its turn: Lancelot joins the company of the angels and enters the "meson Dieu" which Gawain, too, had won (176, 202). "Alon," says Bliobléris (202:230), and this journey toward heaven contradicts the king's death in "Avalon."[24] It is fitting, then, that even the title of the work changes at its conclusion: *La Mort le roi Artu* is included by "Gautier Map" in *L'Estoire de Lancelot* (204:8-9), as mortal death is subsumed into celestial life.

(Translated and adapted by M. Victoria Guerin)

NOTES

1. *La Mort le roi Artu: Roman du XIIIe siècle*, ed. Jean Frappier (Geneva: Droz, and Paris: Minard, 1964). All references to section and line number are taken from this edition.

2. Translator's note: I have left the word *merveille* untranslated throughout Méla's article since he employs it in the sense used by the author of *La Mort le roi Artu*; there is no exact English equivalent. The word has both secular and religious connotations; it can refer to Grail visions or magical events, and it is often used to describe Lancelot's extraordinary feats of strength, but also his great generosity of spirit.

3. This is the solution adopted by the authors of the Middle English alliterative *Morte Arthure* and the French *Perlesvaus*.

4. "I will not do so," said Lancelot, "for I obey my heart, which could not possibly agree to it."

5. Their longevity recalls the biblical period from which mankind has since degenerated, according to the same Walter Map to whom our text is erroneously attributed: "...a pristina forma uiribus et uirtute facte sumus degeneres...." (Walter Map, *De Nugis Curialium: Courtiers' Trifles*, ed. and trans. M.R. James, rev. C.N.L. Brooke and R.A.B. Mynors [Oxford: Clarendon, 1983], p. 4.)

6. *La Queste del Saint Graal*, ed. Albert Pauphilet (Paris: Champion, 1949), p. 7.

7. *Lancelot: Roman en prose du XIIIe siècle,* ed. Alexandre Micha (Paris and Geneva: Droz, 1978-83), vol. 4, pp. 133-59 (LXXVI: 1-38).

8. Marie de France, *Les Lais de Marie de France,* ed. Jean Rychner (Paris: Champion, 1973), pp. 5-32.

9. *La Queste del Saint Graal,* pp. 246-47.

10. *Lancelot,* vol. 8, pp. 204-07 (LVIIIa:13-16).

11. On equivocal oaths in medieval literature, see Ralph J. Hexter, *Equivocal Oaths and Ordeals in Medieval Literature* (Cambridge: Harvard University Press, 1975). On Guenevere's trials in *La Mort Artu,* see R. Howard Bloch, *Medieval French Literature and Law* (Berkeley: University of California Press, 1977), pp. 13-62.

12. All of these episodes are taken from Béroul's *Tristan* with the exception of the hall of statues, which is from the *Tristan* of Thomas d'Angleterre. (Béroul, *Le Roman de Tristan,* ed. Ernest Muret, 4th ed. rev. L.M. Defourques [Paris: Champion, 1947]; Thomas, *Les Fragments du Roman de Tristan,* ed. Bartina H. Wind [Geneva: Droz and Paris: Minard, 1960].)

13. Chrétien de Troyes, *Le Chevalier de la Charrete,* ed. Mario Roques (Paris: Champion, 1972).

14. "that my shield may be there in my place..."

15. "[that the people] may remember the marvelous deeds that I have done in this land" (see above, n. 2).

16. *La Queste del Saint Graal,* pp. 30-35.

17. In the prose *Lancelot,* when the queen is exiled to Sorelois so that the false Guenevere may take her place at the king's side, the Pope puts all of Britain under interdict and calls down God's vengeance on the guilty couple; Arthur falls ill and the false claimant dies horribly. (*Lancelot,* vol. 1, pp. 153-65 [IX:4-30].)

18. *La Queste del Saint Graal,* p. 7.

19. *Lancelot,* vol. 5, p. 221 (XCVI:25).

20. "'he is the man in the world, outside my own family, whom I have most loved and still do love, excepting only the king.' 'By my faith,' said King Boort, 'now you are indeed marvelous, to love him so whole-heartedly when he is your mortal enemy.' 'By my faith,' said Lancelot, 'you may see this marvel; he will never be able to hate me so much that I will cease to love him...'" (see above, n. 2).

21. Geoffrey of Monmouth, *Historia Regum Britanniae,* in *La Légende Arthurienne,* ed. Edmond Faral (Paris: Champion, 1929, repr. 1973), vol. 3, p. 217.

22. The word "Avalon" is itself a play on words; in Old French, "avaler" means "to descend." See Robert de Boron, *Le Roman du Graal,* ed.

Bernard Cerquiglini (Paris: Union Générale d'Edition [10/18], 1981), pp. 69, 226.

23.   Cf. Robert de Boron, *Le Roman de l'Estoire dou Graal*, ed. William A. Nitze (Paris: Champion, 1927), 43: "Marie est dite mer amere." On the *amarum mare* topos, see Angus Kennedy, "'Marie est dite mer amere' in Robert de Boron's *Le Roman de l'Estoire dou Graal*," *Bulletin Bibliographique de la Société Internationale Arthurienne* 29 (1977), 185-90.

24.   See above, n. 22.

The King's Sin:
The Origins of the David-Arthur Parallel

M. Victoria Guerin

Although the two kings were included among the traditional Nine Worthies of the later Middle Ages,[1] no medieval Arthurian text makes an explicit comparison between Arthur and the biblical King David.[2] However, the earliest version of the Arthur story, Geoffrey of Monmouth's *Historia Regum Britanniae*,[3] shows numerous points of similarity between the two. Once established by Geoffrey, the David-Arthur connection is developed and extended by the thirteenth century French Arthurian prose cycle, where it provides a continuing link among the various texts that anticipate and lead up to *La Mort le roi Artu*.

The following is a list of significant events in David's life and, whenever relevant, their parallels in Geoffrey's *Historia*. Both in the biblical text and in Geoffrey's, these events are listed in the order in which they occur.[4] Blank spaces in the right column designate episodes in David's life which have no correspondence in the *Historia* but which will be picked up by the French prose cycle.

1. David's reign is preceded by that of a sinful king, Saul. (1 Sam. 9-15)

Arthur's reign is preceded by that of a sinful king, Vortigern. (*Historia* vi.6-viii.2)

2. Israel is threatened by invasion from the Philistines. (1 Sam. 13ff.)

Britain is threatened by invasion from the Saxons. (*Historia* vi.10 to end of work)

3. Saul sins against God by sparing the conquered king of the non-Jewish Amalekites, Agag, and failing to

Vortigern sins against God by inviting the non-Christian Saxons into Britain, marrying a Saxon princess sacrifice to God the animals taken during the war. (1 Sam. 15)

and making alliance with his enemies. (*Historia* vi.10-16)

4. David, a child of non-noble parentage, is chosen king by the prophet Samuel. (1 Sam. 16:1-13)

5. David slays the giant Goliath. (1 Sam. 17)

Arthur slays the giant of Mont Saint Michel. (*Historia* x.3)[5]

6. David possesses a wonderful sword, that of Goliath, taken from behind the Ephod by the priest Ahimelech. (1 Sam. 21:8-9)

Arthur possesses a wonderful sword, Caliburn (later, Excalibur). (*Historia*, ix.4, ix.12, x.11)

7. David leads the Israelites in battle against the Philistines and defeats them. (2 Sam 5:17-25, 8:1-14)

Arthur leads the Britons in battle against the Saxons and defeats them. (*Historia*, ix.1-5)

8. David unites the kingdoms of Israel and Judah and builds a city which is a great center of wealth, culture and magnificence (Jerusalem). (2 Sam. 8:15-18)

Arthur unifies Britain and establishes a court which is a great center of wealth, culture, and magnificence (situated, later, variously at Carduel, Caerleon, and Camelot). (*Historia*, ix.11)

9. David catches sight of Bathsheba, wife of his captain, Uriah the Hittite. He sends Uriah to certain death in battle and marries his widow, who is already pregnant by David. (2 Sam. 11)

10. The prophet Nathan rebukes David in God's name, telling him, "The sword shall never depart from your house." Evil will come from his house, and his wives will be publicly given to others. David repents, and Nathan says that God will spare him but that the child which Bathsheba carries will die. (2 Sam. 12:1-14)

11. Another of David's sons, Amnon, commits incest by raping his half-sister, Tamar. (2 Sam. 13:1-19)

12. David's son, Absalom, rebels against his father.[6] He wins the hearts of the Israelites, sleeps with a number of David's concubines, gathers an army, and marches against him. (2 Sam. 15-16)	Arthur's "nephew," Mordred,[7] rebels against his "uncle." He wins the hearts of the Britons, marries Arthur's wife, Guenevere (or, in some later versions, seeks to do so), gathers an army, and marches against him. (*Historia*, x.13)
13. David's army and Absalom's fight, and Absalom is killed. David survives. (2 Sam. 17-18)	Arthur's army and Mordred's fight, and Morded is killed, as is Arthur. (*Historia*, xi.1-2)
14. After David's death, his son Solomon falls into the sin of idolatry and is denounced by God. In punishment, the kingdom is taken from his descendants. A series of evil kings follows. (1 Kings 11-2 Kings 25)	A series of evil kings follows Arthur's death, and the kingdom is lost to the Saxons. Geoffrey, on God's behalf, denounces the British for the sins of jealousy and pride. (*Historia*, xi.3-9)

Although points 9-11 do not have direct counterparts in Geoffrey's *Historia*, there are two possible parallels. Soon after he is crowned king, Arthur's father, Uther Pendragon, catches sight of Igerna, wife of his war leader Gorlois of Cornwall, and is overcome with desire for her. He besieges Gorlois, who is killed in battle against Uther's men, and marries Igerna, already pregnant by Uther thanks to Merlin's ruse in giving the king the face and form of the lady's husband.[8]

While there is no public denunciation of Uther for this sin, the next words in the text are, "As the days passed and lengthened into years, the king fell ill with a malady which affected him for a long time." Uther never recovers from this illness and, since he can no longer ride into battle, the land of Britain is soon laid waste by the Saxons. The king then accompanies his men in a horse-litter, and dies when the only well from which his illness lets him drink is poisoned by Saxon spies. The juxtaposition of Uther's shameful end and his sin with Igerna suggests a causal relationship which makes clear

Geoffrey's condemnation of the deed. But Uther and Igerna's adultery is the necessary condition for Arthur's birth, just as David's sin with Bathsheba and the death of their child make possible the birth of their second son, Solomon.[9]

The main difficulty with the Uther-Igerna affair as a parallel to David's sin with Bathsheba is that, since it involves Arthur's own conception, it does not correspond to the point in his life analogous to David's adultery. There is, however, a second possibility. I have argued elsewhere that there are indications that Geoffrey and his public were familiar with the story of Arthur's incestuous relationship with his sister, as described in the twelfth-century prose cycle.[10] The motif of a great hero who is secretly the son of his maternal uncle had already been associated with Charlemagne and Roland,[11] and it may well have entered Arthurian oral tradition by the time of the *Historia.* Moreover, Geoffrey's description of Mordred's treason, after referring to the traitor as Arthur's nephew, concludes with a remark to Geoffrey's patron: "De hoc quidem consul auguste galfridus monumotensis tacebit..." ("About this particular matter, most noble Duke, Geoffrey of Monmouth prefers to say nothing").[12] The "matter" in question is unclear, and I have argued that Geoffrey's public knew the incest story from oral tradition and could recognize it in his veiled allusion.

The *Historia* presents Arthur as the tragic but glorious emblem of Britain's lost Golden Age. Geoffrey may well have found explicit mention of the incest story out of keeping with his noble image of the king, yet used an oblique reference to suggest it in the minds of his public and hint at the cause of Arthur's downfall. If so, then the incest which resulted in Mordred's birth can only have occurred in the early days of Arthur's reign since Mordred is a grown man when he challenges his uncle, apparently in Arthur's prime. This would correspond to the timing of David's adultery with Bathsheba, and by introducing the incest theme it would also echo Amnon's rape of his half-sister, Tamar, which eventually provokes the treachery of her full brother, Absalom.

Throughout the Arthur portion of the *Historia,* Geoffrey establishes a pattern of sin and retribution. He is most concerned with the sin of pride, but this may take various forms. On a human scale, pride leads to acts which Geoffrey views as offenses against natural and divine law: adultery, incest, homosexuality, and the murder of family members. On a larger scale, it is the Britons' pride which makes it impossible for them to follow one leader and leads to civil war and the wasting of the land. It may also be argued that Arthur displays overweening pride in seeking to conquer France and Rome.[13] Certainly the author condemns the Britons in a long passage soon after the death of Arthur, citing civil war, jealousy, and pride as the reasons for the fall of Britain.[14]

Geoffrey is at all times conscious of biblical history as concurrent with that of his own *Historia*. At the time of Brutus' building of London, for example, Geoffrey mentions that "at that time the priest Eli was ruling in Judea and the Ark of the Covenant was captured by the Philistines."[15] He relates later events in British history to the times of the prophets Samuel, Gad, Nathan, Asaph, Elijah, and Isaiah, the kings Saul, David, and Solomon, and the apostles Peter and Mark.[16]

Although the timing of these references makes it clear that Geoffrey situates Arthur's life in post-biblical time, their very existence shows that the author sees the Britons, like the Israelites, as a people with a divinely ordained destiny including both glory and defeat.[17] The *Historia* ends with the devastation of Saxons and Britons alike by plague. An angel speaks to the Britons' exiled leader, Cadwallader, forbidding him to attempt to retake Britain: "God did not wish the Britons to rule in Britain any more, until the moment should come which Merlin had prophesied to Arthur."[18] This early reference to the so-called "Breton hope" of a messianic future, when Arthur would return to lead his people to new heights of glory, corresponds to the Jewish tradition that the messiah will come from the house of David or that David himself will return to his people.[19] The "Breton hope" is still, and perhaps most succinctly, expressed in the last medieval life of Arthur, that of Thomas Malory, who leaves us with the king's epitaph: "HIC IACET ARTHURUS, REX QUONDAM REXQUE FUTURUS": even the king's name is made to rhyme with the expression of belief in his immortality and messianic return.[20]

In the *Historia*, Geoffrey describes the British as the descendants of Trojans who have founded a new Troy in "Britain, the best of islands."[21] But like their ancestors, fugitives from the ruins of a great land, they are destined to lose their sovereignty to the Picts and Saxons. Geoffrey describes this fall from glory as divine retribution for the sin of pride,[22] a motif which recurs throughout the *Historia*. There is a strong suggestion that the British are a new "chosen people" who, like the Israelites, enjoy a special relationship with divine providence, but only so long as they recognize their debt. Once fallen they are doomed to a period of suffering to be followed, after suitable penance, by a triumphant return to glory.

There is a precedent for the association of a Christian king with David: Charlemagne was referred to in his own time and clearly saw himself as a new David, chosen by God and with religious as well as secular duties toward his people. It is not, then, surprising that Geoffrey should have replaced Charlemagne by Arthur in his concept of Britain as a new Israel, and this may have led to a transfer of the incest motif, as well, from Charlemagne to Arthur.[23]

Like David, Arthur is a king who emblematizes the golden age of his realm. Their reigns are marked by signs and portents of divine favor, and their sins mark the beginning of the disaster which will eventually engulf their realms. And both David and Arthur are associated with the idea of a messianic return. It is not difficult to see why, in assembling his Arthur story as the chief and longest episode of the *Historia*, Geoffrey consciously ordered the events of his hero's life[24] to correspond to the biblical story of Israel's finest king: as David was to Israel, so is Arthur to Britain.

Geoffrey's chronicle is the starting point and inspiration for subsequent Arthurian tradition. In translating the *Historia* into French and English, Wace and La3amon also alter its emphasis.[25] Wace adds many romance elements to Geoffrey's history, creating the Round Table and developing the courtliness of its knights, while La3amon tends more toward the creation of a nationalistic epic. Since these two *Brut* texts closely follow the plot of their original, it is not surprising that the order of events in Arthur's life remains essentially unchanged from the list given above.[26]

Neither of Geoffrey's translators preserves his eschatological time-frame, his casting of the British as a new chosen people, or his interest in divine intervention into human affairs. Wace and La3amon present a more positive image of Britain, and particularly of its heroic king; Geoffrey's criticisms are attenuated or omitted whenever possible, and it is not surprising that his chastisement of the British (see point 14 above) is absent from the two *Bruts*. The David parallel plays no role in these new interpretations of the Arthur story, and it is allowed to drop from the French and English texts.

As Arthurian literary tradition passed from Britain to the continent, Arthur himself was no longer the hero of its texts. For Marie de France, Chrétien de Troyes and the other composers of lays and episodic romances, Arthurian time was infinitely extensible by its fragmentation into a potentially endless series of individual adventures of Round Table knights.

When the concept of eschatological time reenters Arthurian literature, it is by way of the Grail story. Chrétien de Troyes' hints of a Christian message in *Le Conte du Graal* soon lead to an increasing conflation of Christian and Arthurian legend, until Robert de Boron's trilogy (*Joseph, Merlin,* and *Perceval*) finally bridges the gap between the Crucifixion and the Grail. Robert's work, in turn, is soon incorporated into a new life of Arthur, the thirteenth-century French prose cycle. Here we find a very different purpose from that of the *Historia*. Geoffrey's text makes Arthur the central figure of a British chronicle extending over centuries, where the king's life resumes in microcosm the rise and fall of his society. The prose cycle expands that life into a multi-volume framework in which Arthur is the necessary condition of chivalry, its rise and fall coterminous with his own.

Critics disagree on the number of authors and on the order of composition within the prose cycle, but at this time it seems generally agreed that the prose version of Robert de Boron's trilogy (*Joseph, L'Estoire de Merlin,* and the so-called Didot *Perceval*) were written first, followed by the major portions of *Lancelot, La Queste del Saint Graal,* and *La Mort Artu. L'Estoire del Saint Graal,* the Huth *Merlin* (*La Suite du Merlin*), and *Le Livre d'Artus,* though their subject matter precedes *Lancelot,* are thought to be of later composition.[27] It is interesting, therefore, to

note that despite the many elaborations on Geoffrey's *Historia*,
and despite the difference in scope and purpose between the
Historia and the prose texts, all the original elements of
correspondance between Arthur's life and the David story, and
more, are transferred from Geoffrey's text to the prose cycle.
Moreover, even though the prose texts were composed out of
chronological order, each new parallel with the David story is
inserted at the appropriate point in Arthur's life. This
demonstrates that the Arthur-David parallel was part of the
overall agenda for the prose cycle, however many authors may
have undertaken its writing.

Since *Joseph* and *L'Estoire del Saint Graal* describe events
well before the advent of Arthur, while *La Queste del Saint
Graal* and *Le Livre d'Artus* are only peripherally concerned with
the king, they may be omitted from consideration.[28] But Robert
de Boron's *Merlin*, and *L'Estoire de Merlin*, which extends it,
cover the period from Merlin's conception to the early days of
Arthur's reign. They include accounts of the first Saxon invasions,
Vortigern's alliance with the enemies of Britain, and Arthur's
possession of a wonderful sword; the king's resumption of the
Saxon wars is found only in *L'Estoire de Merlin*, since Robert's text
ends just after Arthur's coronation and before his first campaign.[29]
The battle with the giant of Mont Saint Michel is absent, but new
points of comparison to the David story are added. Arthur is now
helped to the throne by the prophet Merlin, who had taken him
as a baby to be raised in obscurity and ignorance of his parentage.
This corresponds to point 4 on the list given above; i.e., David's
anointing by the prophet Samuel despite his humble origins.
Moreover, *L'Estoire de Merlin* clearly articulates the portion of
Arthur's story which most closely resembles that of David, and
which is only hinted at in the *Historia*: the king's incestuous
adultery whose result will be, in other texts, an evil son destined
one day to betray his father and threaten his right to rule. (Cf.
points 9-11 on the list given above.)[30] And in what may be an
echo of David's siring both good and evil sons, among them
Solomon and Absalom, *L'Estoire de Merlin* provides Arthur with
another son, Lohot, from Arthur's brief union with the maiden
Lisanor.[31]

While David's crime is adultery alone, Arthur is unknowingly guilty of the far more serious sin of incest with his sister. Micha's demonstration that the incestuous element of the motif was probably imported from the legends of Charlemagne's begetting of Roland is a strong point in favor of the argument that it may have been applied to Arthur in oral tradition even prior to the composition of the *Historia*, circa 1136.[32] But it is added at the precise point in Arthur's life which corresponds to David's adultery with Bathsheba, and Arthur's sin leads to evil rather than good. This implies that it has been used, perhaps by Geoffrey and certainly by the prose writers, as a conscious reference to the David story. Uther's adultery with Igerna, and Arthur's own consequent birth, now become a realization of the biblical threat of "visiting the iniquity of the fathers upon the children unto the third and fourth generation."[33] Arthur is doomed to repeat, in all innocence, his father's sin of adultery in a far more serious form and, in so doing, to sow the seeds of his own downfall.

Even more striking than *L'Estoire de Merlin* is the Huth Merlin (*La Suite du Merlin*), which incorporates every one of the David parallels corresponding to the early part of the Bible story, including the giant slaying[34] and Arthur's campaign against the Saxons, absent from the *Estoire* text. The brother-sister incest is repeated in abridged form, though the birth of Arthur's second son, Lohot, is not mentioned.[35]

It is not, perhaps, surprising that *Lancelot*, which centers on the adventures of Arthur's knights rather than on those of the king himself, shows little evidence of the Arthur-David parallel. There is, however, one striking innovation which makes it clear that the correspondence was not forgotten. In *Lancelot*, immediately following Galehaut's offer of a one-year truce in his campaign against Arthur, a *preud'homme* arrives at the king's military camp and denounces him as the vilest of all sinners, prophesying that he is soon to lose all worldly honor.[36] When asked the reason for this, he replies that the king is guilty of the sin of pride: as the child of an adulterous union he has no legitimate right to the crown, which he wears only by the grace of God. He ought therefore to show particular kindness to widows and orphans and greater generosity to his vassals, both rich and poor. This is very like the prophet Nathan's condemnation of David for his sin with Bathsheba: in both cases, the king is accused of having forgotten that only God's intervention has placed him on the throne:

> tu ses bien que tu ne fus engendrés ne nes par assamblement de loial mariage, mais en si grant pechié com est avoltires: si dois savoir que nus hom mortex ne te baillast a garder la signorie que tu tiens mais que Diex seulement, et le te bailla por che que tu l'en seusses boin gré. Et tu li as faite teile garde que tu le destruis, qui garder le deusses....
>
> (Micha vol. VIII, p. 13; Sommer vol. III, p. 216.)

[you are well aware that you were conceived, not in lawful wedlock, but in so great a sin as adultery. You should know, then, that no mortal man gave the power that you hold into your keeping, but God alone, and he gave it to you so that you should be grateful to him for it. And this is the care that you have taken of it: you are destroying it, you who should have looked after it....]

And Nathan said to David...Thus saith the Lord God of Israel, I anointed thee king over Israel, and I delivered thee out of the hand of Saul; and I gave thee thy master's house, and thy master's wives into thy bosom, and gave thee the house of Israel and of Judah; and if that had been too little, I would moreover have given unto thee such and such things. Wherefore hast thou despised the commandment of the Lord, to do evil in his sight?

(2 Sam. 12:7-9)

Moreover, Nathan's parable of the poor man despoiled of his one ewe lamb[37] corresponds to the *preud'homme*'s admonition that a king must care for the poor and unfortunate of his kingdom.

In both cases, the promised punishment is the same: the loss of the worldly honors which the king has hitherto enjoyed. In both cases, he acknowledges his sin and repents. The prophet then reassures the king that, having confessed his fault, he will be spared by God. David is told that owing to his repentance, he will live, but that the child of his adultery will not survive. But Nathan's initial prophecy will indeed come true:

> "Thus saith the Lord, Behold, I will raise up evil against thee out of thy own house, and I will take thy wives before thine eyes, and give them unto thy neighbor, and he shall lie with thy wives in the sight of this sun."
>
> (2 Sam. 12:11)

These words are fulfilled in 2 Sam. 16:22 when, after usurping the loyalty of David's people and raising an army against him, Absalom lies with his father's concubines as an open act of defiance. In the prose cycle, Galehaut's love for Lancelot causes him to abandon his war against Arthur, postponing for many years the king's downfall. But Mordred's treason in *La Mort Artu* may be seen, when read in conjunction with the David story, to be a delayed retribution for Arthur's sin with his sister. The *preud'homme*'s denunciation is thus a displaced reminder of the king's other guilt: the son of Uther's adultery will come to grief through the child of his own sin of incest.

Absalom's actions are repeated by Mordred's in Robert's *Perceval* and in *La Mort Artu*: usurpation of his father's throne and bed, and murderous rebellion against a father who is also a king.[38] In the Bible, Absalom's death is a source of grief to his father, while in *La Mort Artu* the stark words, "Ainsi ocist li peres le fill, et li filz navra le pere a mort" ["Thus the father killed the son, and the son dealt the father his death wound"][39] replace the pathos of David's lament: "O my son Absalom! my son, my son Absalom! would God I had died for thee, O Absalom, my son, my son!" (2 Sam. 18:33). The element of uncanniness, however, remains: in place of Absalom's extraordinary death, suspended by his hair and struck through the heart by Joab's three darts, we find Mordred pierced by a lance so that a ray of light shines through his body.[40]

Despite the non-chronological composition of the various portions of the prose cycle, then, it preserves the order of parallels to the David story inherited from Geoffrey of Monmouth, and the elaboration of David's sin with Bathsheba into Arthur's incest with his sister. This fact argues strongly in favor of a coherent plan to the prose cycle and a single mind, if not a single author, behind it. The prose cycle parallel also argues retrospectively for Geoffrey of Monmouth's knowledge of the tradition of Mordred's incestuous birth: clearly, the hand that wrote the incest episodes into the prose cycle was a sensitive reader and interpreter of the *Historia*, and we find here an occasion for the use of a medieval critic's interpretation in support of a modern reading.

NOTES

1.   The earliest example of the Nine Worthies is Jacques de Longuyon's *Les Voeux du paon*, c. 1312. A recurring theme in medieval literature and art, the Nine Worthies are a series of three biblical, three pagan, and three Christian kings. The most common version includes Joshua, David, and Judas Maccabeus; Hector, Alexander, and Julius Caesar; and Arthur, Charlemagne, and Godfrey de Bouillon. They are frequently evoked to suggest the transitory nature of human existence and the inevitability of death. The alliterative *Morte Arthure* adapts the motif to Arthur's dream of Fortune's wheel just before his final battle against Mordred. On the Nine Worthies theme, see Roger Sherman Loomis and Laura Hibbard Loomis, *Arthurian Legends in Medieval Art* (London and New York: Modern Language Association of America, 1938), pp. 37, 40, and plates 11-15; *The Parlement of the Thre Ages*, ed. M.Y. Offord (London, New York, and Toronto: Oxford University Press for EETS, 1959), pp. xl-xlii; and *Morte Arthure*, ed. John Finlayson (Evanston: Northwestern University Press, 1971), pp. 91-92n.

2   The possibility that David may have inspired the figure of Arthur in medieval literature has been examined by Moses Gaster, Curt Leviant, and R.A. Shoaf. (Gaster, "Jewish Sources of Parallels to the Early English Metrical Romances of King Arthur and Merlin," *Publications of the Anglo-Jewish Historical Exhibition* 1 [London: Office of *The Jewish Chronicle*, 1888], 231-52; Leviant, "Jewish Influence upon Arthurian Legends," *Salo Wittmayer Baron Jubilee Volume*, English Section, vol. II [Jerusalem: American Academy for Jewish Research, 1974], pp. 639-56; Shoaf, "The Alliterative *Morte Arthure*: The Story of Britain's David," *JEGP* 81 [1982], 204-26.) However, since these scholars were chiefly concerned with Middle English Arthurian texts, they did not seek to establish the point at which the David-Arthur parallel might have entered the tradition,

or to examine its history between that point and the works which they studied.

3. Geoffrey of Monmouth, *The Historia Regum Britanniae*, ed. Acton Griscom (London, New York, and Toronto: Longman's, Green and Co., 1929). The translation cited in this article is that of Lewis Thorpe, *The History of the Kings of Britain* (Harmondsworth: Penguin, 1966). All *Historia* references apply to both Griscom's edition and Thorpe's translation.

4. Certain of these points of comparison have also been noted by Gaster (pp. 240-41), Leviant (pp. 640-47), or Shoaf (pp. 207-09).

5. This is the only instance where the two stories follow a different order and, even here, the episode is only slightly displaced.

6. It is clear from the biblical text that Absalom's hatred of his father is the direct result of events stemming from the incest committed against his sister.

7. There is some question at what point the so-called nephew was considered to be the king's incestuous son by his sister. See below., pp. 18, 22–23, 26.

8. *Historia*, viii.19-20. Cf. Leviant, pp. 640-41.

9. See below, n. 35.

10. Cf. my unpublished thesis, "Mordred's Hidden Presence: The Skeleton in the Arthurian Closet" (Ph.D., Yale, 1985), pp. 3-11.

11. Alexandre Micha, "Deux sources de la *Mort Artu*: II. La naissance incestueuse de Mordred," *Zeitschrift für romanische Philologie* 66 (1950), 371-72. The earliest text which alludes to Roland's incestuous parentage is the tenth-century *Vita Sancti Egidii* (*Saint Gilles: Essai d'histoire littéraire*, ed. E.C. Jones [Paris: Champion, 1914], pp. 108-09).

12. *Historia*, xi.1. The first two words, "De hoc...," have caused difficulty to subsequent scholars, medieval and modern. The very existence of numerous variants, however, argues in favor of the significance of this passage. See my thesis, "Mordred's Hidden Presence...," p. 5n.

13. On the role of pride in the alliterative *Morte Arthure*, see Shoaf, pp. 218-22.

14. *Historia*, xi.9.

15. *Historia*, i.18.

16. *Historia*, i.18, ii.6, ii.7, ii.9, ii.10, ii.15, and iv.15. John J. Parry points out that Geoffrey did not invent this simultaneous chronology, but rather borrowed it from St. Jerome's Latin translation of the *Chronicle of Eusebius* in the abridged version by Prosper Tito

(Prosper of Aquitaine). See "The Chronology of Geoffrey of Monmouth's *Historia*, Books I and II," *Speculum* 4 (1929), 316-22.

17.   He was not the first to do so; on the tradition of Britain as a new Israel, see Robert Hanning, *The Vision of History in Early Britain* (New York and London: Columbia University Press, 1966), pp. 53, 55, 57-58, 70, *et passim*.

18.   *Historia*, xii.17.

19.   Cf. Leviant, pp. 646-47. On the concept of the Jewish messiah from its origins to the Middle Ages, see *The Encyclopedia Judaica* (Jerusalem: Keter, 1971-72), vol. 11, cols. 1407-15.

20.   *The Works of Sir Thomas Malory*, ed. Eugene Vinaver, 2nd ed. (London: Oxford University Press, 1971), p. 717, l. 35. For an earlier example, cf. these lines from The Black Book of Carmarthen (twelfth-century manuscript): "A grave for March, a grave for Gwythur, / A grave for Gwgawn of the ruddy Sword, / Not wise (the thought) a grave for Arthur." (John Rhys, *Studies in the Arthurian Legend* [Oxford: Clarendon, 1891], p. 19.)

21.   *Historia*, i.2.

22.   *Historia*, xi.9

23.   See above, n. 17. On Charlemagne as a new David, see Peter Munz, *The Origin of the Carolingian Empire* (Dunedin: Leicester University Press and University of Otago Press, 1960), p. 1, and Heinrich Fichtenau, *The Carolingian Empire*, trans. Peter Munz (Oxford: Blackwell, 1963), pp. 71-72.

24.   Many of the elements of Arthur's life may already have existed in oral tradition, but probably not in this order and certainly not in this form.

25.   Wace, *Le Roman de Brut*, ed. Ivor Arnold (Paris: SATF, 1938), 2 vols.; Laȝamon, *Brut*, ed. G.L. Brook and R.F. Leslie (London, New York, and Toronto: Oxford University Press for EETS, 1963-68), 2 vols.

26.   However, point 5, the battle with the giant of Mont Saint Michel, is moved to precede point 13. This change will persist in later lives of Arthur; see below, n. 34.

27.   Several of these texts are represented by more than one edition. For Robert de Boron's trilogy (prose version), see *Le Roman du Graal*, ed. Bernard Cerquiglini (Paris: Union Générale d'Edition [10/18], 1981). For the prose version of Robert's *Merlin*, see also *Merlin: Roman du XIIIe siècle*, ed. Alexandre Micha (Geneva: Droz, 1979). For the extended version, *L'Estoire de Merlin*, see *The Vulgate Version of the Arthurian Romances*, ed. H.O. Sommer (Washington: Carnegie Institution, 1908-16), vols. I, II. For Robert's

Perceval, see also *The Didot Perceval,* ed. William Roach (Philadelphia: University of Pennsylvania Press, 1941). For *Lancelot,* see Sommer, vols. III-V, and *Lancelot: Roman en prose du XIIIe siècle,* ed. Alexandre Micha, 9 vols. (Geneva: Droz, 1978-83). Other texts: *La Queste del Saint Graal,* ed. Albert Pauphilet (Paris: Champion, 1923); *La Mort le roi Artu,* ed. Jean Frappier (Paris: Droz, 1936); *L'Estoire del Saint Graal* in Sommer, vol. I; the Huth *Merlin* (*Suite du Merlin*) in *Merlin: Roman en prose du XIIIe siècle,* ed. Gaston Paris and Jacob Ulrich (Paris: Firmin Didot et Cie., 1886), 2 vols; *Le Livre d'Artus* in Sommer, vol. VII. On the relative dating of these texts, see the "Tableau chronologique" in appendix to Daniel Poirion, ed., *Précis de littérature française du Moyen Age* (Paris: Presses Universitaires de France, 1983); however, many of these dates are still disputed.

28. It is, however, worth noting that Geoffrey's concept of Britain's founding by a small band of fugitives from the fall of Troy has been transferred, not without parallel, to Joseph of Arimathea (or, in *Joseph,* to his nephew), who flees Rome after the Crucifixion with a small band of disciples to found a new society in western Britain or Wales. (*Joseph,* pp. 65-71; *L'Estoire del Saint Graal,* Sommer, vol. I, pp. 208ff.)

29. Cerquiglini, pp. 183-86; Micha, pp. 268-77; Sommer, vol. II, pp. 81-84. See also the Huth *Merlin,* where there are two swords: one drawn from the stone as proof of Arthur's right to rule (pp. 134-41), the other taken from the lake (pp. 195-200).

30. *L'Estoire de Merlin* (Sommer, vol. II), pp. 128-29.

31. Sommer, vol. II, p. 124. This passage is omitted from the manuscripts edited by Micha and Cerquiglini, but it appears in the fifteenth-century English *Merlin* (ed. Henry B. Wheatley [London: EETS, 1988; 2nd ed. Greenwood, 1969. EETS vols. 10/11 and 21/36], p. 171).

32. However, Micha does not draw this conclusion.

33. Ex. 20:5; Ex. 34:7; Nu. 14:18; De. 5:9.

34. However, the text at this point follows the tradition of Wace and Laȝamon, moving the episode to fall later in Arthur's career. Since Mont Saint Michel is in France, Arthur must subdue the Saxons before extending his conquests to the continent.

35. Micha notes that while the first portion of the Huth *Merlin* is in most respects a faithful reproduction of the *Estoire* text, it contains a number of omissions or abridgments of its model. (*Merlin,* ed. Alexandre Micha, p. xliii). In *L'Estoire de Merlin,* Arthur's incest is a closer repetition of his father Uther's adultery since he enters his

sister's bed under cover of darkness, deliberately letting her mistake him for her husband. This detail is omitted from the Huth *Merlin*. However, in *L'Estoire de Merlin*, as in the Huth text, the lovers do not know that they are brother and sister. The circumstances of Mordred's conception in *L'Estoire* parallel those of Galahad's (Sommer, vol. V, pp. 108-11; Micha, vol. IV, pp. 206-11), where Lancelot is deceived into believing that King Pelles' daughter is Guenevere in order that the perfect Grail knight may be born of a stainless virgin and the finest "chevalier terrien." (Cf. Charles Méla, La Reine et le Graal: La 'Conjointure' dans les romans du Graal, de Chretien de Troyes au 'Livre de Lancelot' [Paris: Seuil, 1984], pp. 334-36). See also Mt. 16: "And David the king begat Solomon of her that had been the wife of Uriah...."

36. Micha, vol. VIII, p. 13; Sommer, vol. III, pp. 215-16.
37. 2 Sam. 12:11.
38. *Perceval*: Cerquiglini, pp. 291-301, Roach (Didot *Perceval*), ll. 2500-2646; *La Mort le roi Artu*, 134-43, 163-91.
39. *La Mort le roi Artu*, 191.
40. 2 Sam. 9-14; *La Mort le Roi Artu*, 190.

Desire, Meaning, and the Female Reader: The Problem in Chrétien's *Charrete*

Roberta L. Krueger

I. *Framing the Problem: Prologue and Epilogue*

The Prologue to Chrétien de Troyes' *Le Chevalier de la Charrete* has probably done as much as any other document of the period to stir up controversy about the role aristocratic women played in the formation of courtly literature. For Gaston Paris and many scholars after him, Chrétien's contention that he undertook the romance according to the wishes of Marie de Champagne and that she furnished both its *matière* and *sens* was proof that Marie and her female contemporaries transmitted a revolutionary concept of love to Northern France in the second half of the twelfth century.[1] This thesis has sparked lively debate about what Marie's *matière* and *sens* might have been, about how Chrétien acquitted himself of the task she imposed— with distaste or pleasure?—and about whether Lancelot exemplifies the perfect lover or a perfect fool.[2] It has also given rise to the notion that the meaning of courtly literature was shaped by powerful women to conform to their desires, despite warnings about the tenuous nature of the evidence.[3]

Most recently, literary critics have sensibly argued against the quest for a single *sens* or authorial message in a romance whose frame and narrative development are so pointedly problematic. They have drawn our attention instead to equivocations, paradoxes, and other inconsistencies in the romance as evidence of Chrétien's self-conscious literary ambiguity.[4] From this perspective, Chrétien's rhetorical display in the Prologue is as inscrutable as his performance throughout the romance; both are unreliable indices of woman's status in courtly society.

And yet, despite the truth of the ambiguity of truth in this and other Arthurian fictions, the problem of the lady's *sens* and the question of female desire remain central to our reading of the *Charrete*. The narrator inscribes his romance under the sign of Marie's wishes—"Puis que ma dame de Chanpaign / le *vialt*" ["Since my Lady of Champagne wishes"] (2)[5] in a way that has made critics ponder the unanswerable question of *what* it is that she wants.

Immediately after the narrator has announced that he undertakes the romance in the Countess' service, "com cil qui est suens antiers" ["As one who is entirely at her service"] (4), he disclaims other romancers who flatter their ladies with hyperbolic compliments. He then admits, after he disparagingly voices a flattering comparison as an example, that this compliment holds true for her: "s'est il voirs maleoit gré mien" ["Though it be true in spite of me"] (19). After asserting the truth of what he has just denied, he appropriates the feminine authority that he initially acknowledged. Although he insists that her "commandemanz" have been more important than his own "sans ne painne" ["thought or effort"] in the work's creation (21-23), he "signs" his book as he entitles it: "Del CHEVALIER DE LA CHARRETE / comance Crestïens son livre" ["Chrétien begins his book / About the Knight of the Cart"] (24-25). His equivocation about Marie's influence culminates in the baffling assertion that the Countess has given him the "matiere et san" ["The source and the meaning"] and that he scarcely adds anything but his "painne et s'antancïon" ["effort and diligence"] (27-28). Chrétien inscribes his response to Marie's "commandemanz" as the enactment of a kind of *don contraignant*, or a rash boon, where, in exchange for the gift she has given ("matiere et san li *don* et livre," 26, emphasis mine) he must perform in return under obligation.[6]

The narrator's deft manipulation of Prologue conventions effects a *mise en question* of the female privilege and influence he has ostensibly acknowledged. Chrétien undercuts Marie's alleged authority by subtly appropriating as his *own* both the *matière* and the *sens*. Although he credits Marie with the creation of his story and acknowledges her control, his rhetorical agility demonstrates to the discerning reader that he knows who pulls the strings. The effect of this strategy is double-edged: the text displaces Marie by appropriating her "san," but it also flags that displacement. By expressly creating confusion about meaning in his opening lines,[7] Chrétien invites readers to wonder—even as we know that it cannot be known—what Marie's inscrutable *sens* might be.

This problematic is starkly recast in the Epilogue, where the question we now ask is not "What did Marie want?" but "Where is she?" In the enigmatic fifteen-line conclusion, the "Chrétien" narrator has been subsumed by the voice of Godefroy de Leigni, who claims to have ended ("parfinee") the romance at Chrétien's behest, "par le boen gré / Crestien" ["with the approval / Of Chrétien"] (7106-07). Amidst considerable controversy about why Chrétien chose to end his story thus and about where Godefroy's authorship begins,[8] the significance of Marie's *absence* has been overlooked. Godefroy's problematic conclusion leaves us an ambiguous ending that erases the woman from the last lines of a romance dedicated to her. The narrative contract so personally defined between a patroness and a clerk in the Prologue has become a narrative contract between a clerk and a clerk. Godefroy promises to undertake the "matire" (7099) given him, as Chrétien has done for the Countess. No mention is made of Marie; the *Charrete's* final image of service inscribes a male-male bond.[9] More explicitly than the Prologue, the Epilogue appropriates Marie's "san" and writes the woman out of the audience. When Godefroy says, "mes nus *home* blame ne l'an mete" ["Let no one blame him,"] (7104, emphasis mine), he seems to invite the critique of another, female public. Marie's conspicuous absence makes us question the place of the female reader—and the nature of her power and her desires—in the *Charrete*.

Although it is couched in terms that are playful and ironic, Chrétien's problematization of female presence and absence in the frame invites us to scrutinize his representation of women within the ensuing narrative. The implied question "What does Marie want?" foreshadows the question of "What does Guenevere want?," which, as Charles Méla has suggested, is the underlying mystery of Lancelot's quest.[10] In the course of the hero's adventures, a succession of female figures will trouble his path with their elusive presence and their imperious desires.

II. Meaning and the Female Reader

Before we embark on an exploration of female desire in the *Charrete*, some remarks about women as readers of courtly romance are in order. Dedications to historical women appear to give evidence of female patronage; they suggest that women, as well as knights, were an intended audience for the genre.[11] But we must be extremely careful about assuming that courtly literature afforded women social equality or that it reflects their historical power.[12] Recent historical studies suggest that woman's social status under primogeniture and the new marriage system was on the wane.[13] The actual responses of romance's historical women readers are not recorded in letters, journals, or autobiographies. The vast majority of courtly texts are male-authored.[14] The central fact about historical woman in twelfth-century Old French courtly literature is that her real voice is absent and that her fictional apparitions are filtered through clerical masculine consciousness.[15] Her privilege as a literary figure is less an indication of "real" power than a male mystification of femininity, one that obscures the reality of her historical decline.

In most romances, the lady is neither the principal protagonist—the subject of the narrative's action—nor the narrator, the subject who speaks. Within the adventure, she is typically an object of exchange or an object of desire. She observes the conflicts between knights and valorizes the knights' honor with her approving presence as spectator. In the extra-diegetic sphere of the romance's transmission, the clerk's performance has a double audience: he speaks both to ladies and to knights (as well as to other clerks). If professional differences distance the clerk from the chivalric ideals of male nobles, his gender separates him more acutely from the feminine culture of noblewomen. Like her literary representations, the woman reader or listener is also an observor, sometimes the privileged dedicatee, who valorizes the clerk's performance with her presence. But the meaning of the romance for her may well be different than the meaning of the romance for aristocratic men, for she hears a discourse that casts her not as subject but as object.[16]

We cannot hope to reconstruct the actual meanings that romances may have held for their male or female audiences. But to ignore the displacement of woman in the creation and transmission of romance is to overlook one of the central tensions of the genre.[17] Historical findings about the appropriation of female sexuality to the project of primogeniture suggest that we look more closely at the tensions of gender within a genre that paradoxically privileges woman as her social status declines.[18]

Reading the *Charrete* from the perspective of the silenced female subject may seem to be reading the romance "as it was not meant to be read"; it "reads against" the dominant structure of Lancelot's love for Guenevere.[19] But Chrétien's equivocation about his implied female patron in the frame and his problematic portrayal of female characters within the romance justify such an alternative reading. As reflections of Marie's inscrutability, the anonymous damsels and the elusive Queen who loom in the landscape of Lancelot's journey invite our reflection on the place of female desire within the hero's quest.

III. The Enigma of Woman

Let us now turn to the romance proper to see how Chrétien recasts the question of woman that he framed in the Prologue. Overshadowed by the dominant mode of Lancelot's quest, by the masterfully ambiguous performance of the clerkly narrator, and by a critical tradition that celebrates the union of *clergie* and *chevalerie* in the affinity between Chrétien and his protagonist, the problem of woman has been subsumed under the dilemma of the hero's identity.

But the enigma of female desire is inscribed at the center of Lancelot's quest in the baffling scene of Guenevere's refusal. After Lancelot has performed a series of difficult and challenging exploits to rescue Arthur's queen from her abductor, Meleagant, and has incurred dishonor by accepting a ride on the shameful

Cart in order to learn her whereabouts, Guenevere, the object of his love and the reason he has put his life in peril, refuses to see him or have anything to do with him. By refusing to become the de facto prize of Lancelot's amorous adventures, as Matilda Bruckner has suggested, Guenevere creates another "delay" in romance that is characterized by deferred resolutions.[20] I would add that her refusal not only calls into question the entire code of chivalric and amorous values that have guided Lancelot's actions, but also refigures—maddeningly for the hero and enigmatically for the reader—the problem of female desire.

To put the question in terms suggested by the Prologue, What is the *sens* of Guenevere's *commandemanz*?[21] What motivates her to refuse the knight who has risked death to win her love? What (more) does this woman want? The enigma of Guenevere— the essential mystery of her sexuality—shapes a subtext of feminine desire that is elaborated in a series of puzzling female characters whom Lancelot encounters in his quest.

These secondary characters have been read as "femmes médiatrices" who dramatize the hero's desire for Guenevere,[22] as reflections of his service to the queen,[23] and as "uncanny" projections of an orginal sexual transgression.[24] Reading them as reflections of the male protagonist's identity—as vehicles for Lancelot's shame and honor, or as figures of his desire for the queen—we encounter an intriguing *conjointure* which, for all its ambiguity, is unified by the thread of the hero's trajectory.

But reading the *Charrete* "against itself" from the perspective of the displaced female subject rather than from that of the active knight, the reader encounters a troubling *disjointure* that reflects woman's displacement within the narrative of male desire. The romance's female characters form a diffuse, fragmented interlace whose common thread of meaning seems to slip ever out of grasp. These are blank figures who appear suddenly and anonymously.[25] With the notable exception of the "pucele à la mule" who returns as Meleagant's sister, their status and motivations are unexplained and they vanish from the narrative after a brief appearance.[26] Unlike the ladies in *Yvain* who enact a common pattern of helplessness, thereby allowing the hero to prove his mettle as he protects womanhood, these maidens impose a set of contradictory verbal constraints and conditions on the hero. The first damsel forbids Lancelot to sleep in the Perilous Bed and mocks his shame (471-75/430-590).[27] The "obliging damsel" extracts promises before she will indicate the paths of the Sword Bridge and the Water Bridge, "tant me porriez vos prometre" ["If you are able to promise me enough"] (614/602-709). The damsel at the ford requests the liberty of Lancelot's "prisoner" (888-91/888-927), reluctantly promising a *gueredon* in return. The "immodest damsel" imposes the "covant" that Lancelot sleep with her in return for lodging (940-45/931-2013), and later, she secures his protection under the terms of the custom of Logres (1295-301); her admiration for him throughout the episode is profuse. The "pucele à la mule" demands the "gift" of the *chevalier orgueilleux*'s head, for which she promises a *gueredon* and future help (2797-803/2779-941); when she later appears as Meleagant's sister, she frees Lancelot from his imprisonment and releases him from a constraining situation. Finally, the maidens of Noauz request from Arthur the "don" that Guenevere attend the marriage tournament (5382-96/5358-6056). After mocking his shame when Lancelot fights badly, they all desire him as a husband when he wins (6002-06). Intercalated within this last episode, the seneschal's wife demands the "covant" that Lancelot return to his prison and that he give her his love (5476-81/5436-94).

The contradictory nature of the damsels' demands seems calculated to problematize female desire. If one damsel forbids the hero a pleasurable bed, another seeks to sleep with him. While one maiden demands that Lancelot grant his opponent mercy, another asks for the rival's head. In each case, the narrative emphasizes troublesome or mysterious elements, thereby heightening their uncanny significance and provoking the reader's consternation. As in the Prologue, the narrator's "strange" presentation of woman invites our questions about her place in the narrative of male desire. In the analysis that follows, I can only sketch out Chrétien's exploration of the problem in the most striking instances. [28] Let us look first at two episodes in the first half of the romance that foreshadow the central mystery of Guenevere's reception.

In the episode of the Perilous Bed, Chrétien hints at the dark side of female power, linking it to sexual dangers that threaten male identity. The first damsel whom the hero encounters draws public attention to his shame, wondering why he is led by a dwarf as if "contret" (a crippled or disabled person) (438-39). She then imposes a restriction on the lodging she has offered. She refuses to let Lancelot sleep in the most luxurious bed, which the narrator has said possesses "tot le delit / qu'an seüst deviser an lit" ["all the perfections / One could devise for a bed "] (465-66). The damsel explains that it was not made up so splendidy for a knight who has shamed himself by riding in the Cart. Lancelot, of course, takes the forbidden bed. When a flaming lance thrusts itself down from above, grazes his skin, and nearly pins his flanks to the sheets, he confidently puts out the flame and hurls away the sword. In the readers' eyes, he has vindicated himself against the damsel's emasculating reception and has successfully defied her authority.

Curiously, the damsel's perception of Lancelot does not change because of his victory; she does not witness it. Rather, as she watches him swoon the next morning and nearly fall from the tower on seeing Guenevere in a procession below him, she says he is right to hate his life, since he has ridden on the Cart. Her harsh judgment clearly denigrates the hero's public stature, but her underlying *sens* is inscrutable. So, too, is the conversation she has held with Gauvain at the window. We do not know what she is thinking any more than we can hear what they are saying; "ne sai de quoi / ne sai don les paroles furent" ["I assure you that I / Do not know what was said"] (548-49), insists the narrator.

Just as curiously, Chrétien tells us that after she feels she has mocked Lancelot enough—the verb he uses is "gaber"—she accords him a horse and a lance, tokens of her love and respect "par amor et par accordance" ["As token of her esteem and sympathy"] (590). The conventionalism of their parting jars with the damsel's previous scorn and leaves us wondering whether she is friend or foe. Her uncanny knowledge of the hero's shame and her erratic treatment of him intensify the strangeness of this "marvelous" scene. The perils of the bed are conjoined with the powers of woman.

Lancelot explores that connection more fully in his encounter with the Immodest Damsel. In a bizarre permutation of the hospitality convention, the hero receives a night's lodging from a maiden on the condition that he sleep with her in return for her "gift." When Lancelot reluctantly seeks her after dinner to fulfill his promise, he finds her in the act of being raped by a knight while six sergeants stand guard. Instead of rushing to save her, he ponders the nature of his quest in a lengthy monologue that delays the episode's surprising revelation. Lancelot finally enters the fray against the maiden's assailants. Then, the damsel suddenly calls off her enemies and we learn that she has staged her attack! By lying next to the damsel without removing his chemise or showing any desire for her, Lancelot ultimately remains true both to his promise to her and to his transcendent love for Guenevere.

The damsel's wish to sleep with Lancelot establishes the terms of the *covant* between them, much as Marie de Champagne's *commandemanz* set the terms for Chrétien's performance; the damsel's *don* of lodging entails the *don contraignant* of submitting to *her*. Female desire determines the initial narrative frame. But, as in the Prologue, the controlling power of that desire is subtly subverted. Here Chrétien contains the threatening power of sexuality by presenting it in the form of self-willed victimization. The male fantasy of the woman who wants to be raped takes another perverse form in a lady who exploits her helplessness to obligate a man to protect her and, implicitly, to incite his desire.[29]

As the disappointed damsel requests to accompany him upon his further adventures, she is reinscribed as an object. It is she, in fact, who explains the "custom" of Logres that determines the dependent status of all women in the romance, including Guenevere. A knight cannot dishonor a woman whom he finds alone in the forest without incurring shame or blame. But if she is accompanied by another knight whose protection is contested, the victor may do what he will with her without sanction.[30] As if to exemplify the custom's crude economy, the damsel becomes the disputed object in a potential combat between Lancelot and the presumptuous knight who claims to take her as his God-given possession.

As at the Castle of the Perilous Bed, Lancelot emerges victorious against the forces of a menacing sexuality. Similarly, the female power that initiated the action is quickly contained within the trajectory of the hero's adventures. Once again, though, Chrétien's conspicuously strange presentation of female desire—here in the form of feigned sexual humiliation—raises questions about its nature and effects. Recasting the sexual tensions of the "lit perilleux," the scene foreshadows Lancelot's future reception by Guenevere.[31] Chrétien's portrayal of a damsel who exploits her sexual victimization raises the disturbing possibility that another woman, even the Queen herself, may manipulate our hero with her oppression. The equally troubling idea comes to mind that Guenevere could comply with the terms of her abduction in order to incite her lover's desire. The surprising moment when the damsel calls off her retinue and releases Lancelot presents a paradoxical image of woman, one which seems to reflect male fears and fantasies about female sexuality: even when she appears to be most abjectly subjugated, the woman wields power over men.

IV. Resistance and Subversion

Guenevere's refusal to speak with Lancelot after he has struggled so long and hard to find her inscribes the romance's most elusive instance of feminine power. When Lancelot comes to see her after his remarkable show of service in the first fight with Meleagant, instead of greeting him with joy, as we might expect, she "fet senblant de correciee, si s'anbruncha et ne dist mot" ["acted as if she were angered. / She lowered her head and said not a word"] (3940-41). She says she has no interest in seeing him and, furthermore, that she will never deny that she is *not* grateful. Lancelot, confused and chagrined, replies: "Dame, certes, ce poise moi / ne je n'os demander por coi" ["My lady, indeed this grieves me; / Yet I dare not ask your reasons"] (3963-64).

Critics troubled by Guenevere's surprising move have attempted to explain it, by suggesting that Guenevere rightly demands the absolute devotion of her lover, that she plays the coquette and deceives herself about her deepest feelings, or that she makes a mistake for which she will atone later with her anguish.[32] Our desire to know just why she has done what she has done is expressly frustrated by the narrator's refusal to provide a single answer. Lancelot, "a meniere de fin amant" ["like a perfect lover"] (3962), is stunned and reticent before his lady's mystery when she sends him away and does not ask for a reason until later. The Queen herself offers two seemingly contradictory explanations: first, that she had only meant her denial "a gas," as a joke (4204), and later, as she tells Lancelot, that it was because he had hesitated "deux pas" before stepping on the Cart (4487).

Interestingly, if we go back to the moment in the narrative when Lancelot mounts the cart, we find that the Guiot manuscript makes no mention of any hesitation and that other manuscripts which do interpolate two lines describing his hesitation may well be the result of scribal emendation, as David Hult has suggested.[33] Critics seeking coherence in the clerk's equivocal performance have seized upon these "deux pas" as the logical explanation for Guenevere's actions, because they so neatly encode the absolute devotion demanded of the courtly lover. But this explanation squares neither with her earlier contention that she spoke in jest, nor with the narrator's ambiguous presentation of female authority throughout the romance.

Guenevere's refusal and her contradictory explanations act as powerful counters to the narrative coherence of Lancelot's quest. They throw a wrench into the workings of the chivalric code and make the reader wonder about this exemplar of knighthood. By refusing to become the automatic prize in the Meleagant-Lancelot combat, Guenevere removes herself from the triangle of exchange defined by the custom of Logres. She refuses to be grateful. Her silence and her anger toward the knight who comes forward for her blessing constitute a gesture of feminine resistance to an ideology that circulates women as objects. Like the first damsel's indirection and the immodest damsel's manipulations, and like the depiction of Marie de Champagne in the Prologue, Guenevere's refusal depicts a woman who shapes or opposes chivalric values. As a narrative strategy, it transfers the determinant of the story's outcome from male to female: Lancelot submits himself to *her* will, as Chrétien has done to Marie's: "Or soit a son commandemant" ["Then let it be as she orders"] (4076), Lancelot tells Keu soon afterward, echoing the Prologue's rhetoric.

Even as Guenevere refuses and resists, however, the narrative undermines her powers in significant ways. Chrétien's account that Guenevere feigns her anger and her own admission that she was "only joking," combined with the contradictory nature of her explanations, seem, at the level of characterization, to trivialize her response. More significantly, Guenevere's refusal becomes, in the ensuing events, the condition itself for the masculine plot of desire. She provides the internal obstacle that Lancelot needs to fuel his passions. After she has recognized him (by naming him for the first time in the romance), she refuses him.[34] She then recedes from the narrative as he agonizes over her absence. As Charles Méla has described the *conjointure* of all the women in this and the preceding scenes, they project a fictive woman created by a knight so that he may subject himself to her will: "L'amant courtois a érigé une divinité impénetrable et impitoyable pour être sans fin sujet à sa demande et exposé à ses exigences."[35] Woman's "power" is a fiction of the male subject who needs her to resist so that he can desire her. If we reformulate this from a feminist perspective, woman's "impenetrable divinity" marks her displacement from the position of the desiring subject, a displacement that male desire and the enigma of woman continually enact. Insofar as the *Charrete* powerfully inscribes this displacement, it participates in a cultural mystification of woman whose effects are still with us today in the idea of femininity.

But Chrétien's remarkable narrative, which sets a pattern for future Arthurian fiction, does more than mystify the woman. From another perspective, it also demystifies her by calling attention to her very displacement. Chrétien's inscription of female desire renders it inscrutable, but his narrative presentation problematizes woman's very inscrutability. Looking closely at the romance's subtext of female desire, we come to ask, as Soshana Felman has put it, "What does the question—what is femininity—for men—mean for women?"[36]

V. The "Sens" of Absence

In the last third of the story, the narrative's subversion of female desire is even more pronounced. At the tournament of Noauz, Chrétien appears to celebrate woman's power to shape the course of narrative and pay his most brilliant hommage to Marie de Champagne. The scene portrays a queen who manipulates the hero into exemplifying the opposing poles of chivalric shame and prowess; she makes him fight "au noauz" or "au mialz" at her behest. It is precisely when the knight humiliates himself to fight at his worst that Chrétien employs the same terms to describe Lancelot's submission before Guenevere as he had to prove his own service to the Countess, "com cil qui est suens antiers" ["As one who seeks only to please the queen"] (5656).

As with the earlier scenes we have examined, a close look at the narrator's presentation reveals that he ultimately subverts female power at Noauz. Guenevere's imperious commands are framed by two female publics who are indispensable components of the episode. One consists of the young ladies of Noauz, who launch the action by calling the tournament and manipulating Arthur to ensure that Guenevere will be present. The other is the seneschal's wife, who releases Lancelot from prison so that he can attend. The women's control of narrative events and their own desires are expressly frustrated in the action that follows. When the wife decides to risk her husband's anger and release her captive if he agrees to comply with a *covant*, she knows that her wishes cannot be fulfilled. She asks Lancelot to come back and give her his love. Although Lancelot promises all the love he has on his return—"tote celi que j'ai / vos doing je voir au revenir" ["I will certainly give you / All that I have upon my return"] (5482-83)—she knows that his heart has already been "bailliee et commandee" ["assigned and given to another"] (5487).

In contrast to the surprising savvy of the seneschal's wife, the ladies of Noauz are extremely naive about the impossibility of their desires. After arranging a marriage tournament to find the best husband, and mocking the unknown knight who fights at his worst, they are frustrated when they cannot marry the knight who turns out to be the "mialz." Some of them vow that if they cannot have Lancelot's love they will not marry! No longer able to control a custom that appears to work to their advantage, the young ladies of Noauz are frustrated observors of a custom that promises them much but delivers nothing. The scene's final couplet underscores the futility of their desires: "L'anhatine ensi departi / c'onques nule n'an prist mari" ["Thus the tournament ended / Without anyone having taken a husband"] (6055-56). The Noauz episode has become a linchpin in the debates about Lancelot's valor or foolishness, about Chrétien's service to Marie, and about the general *sens* of the romance. It is telling that the narrator ends not with a celebration of Lancelot and Guenevere's reciprocal passion but with an image of thwarted feminine desire.

The hero's last feminine encounter is similarly ambivalent. When Meleagant's sister frees Lancelot from the tower where he has been imprisoned by her brother, he promises to be hers ("que je toz jors mes serai vostres" ["To be yours from this day hence"] 6589) and to do as she commands forever more ("ja mes niert jorz que je ne face / quan que vos pleira *comander*" ["Never will a day come that I will fail to do / All you may be pleased to request"], 6592-93, emphasis mine). Lancelot's grateful submission appears once again to dramatize the narrator's initial gesture before his patroness and to valorize female strength. Furthermore, Meleagant's sister is an active figure who moves autonomously. Her force and ingenuity as she frees him contrast with Lancelot's feebleness; her initiative is indispensable to the hero's survival and the narrative's continuation. Of all the female characters in this romance, the *pucele à la mule* is the only one whose motivations are clear and generous: she tells Lancelot that she has come to repay the *don* that he made her of the *chevalier orgueilleux*'s head (6579-81). She has no hidden agenda, no furtive designs.

But her remarkable strength and the clarity of her motives serve less to restore female power or to "correct" the romance's elusive image of female desire than to further the narrative of the hero. Like Lunete in *Yvain*, she acts as a kind of stand-in for the narrator as she frees the protagonist from constraints and abets his chivalric exploits.[37] Her activity liberates the hero, so that he may conclude the romance unimpeded by feminine demands. Although Lancelot offers her his "cuer," "cors," "servise," and "avoir" (6684-85) (a pledge that would compromise his service to Guenevere were he to fulfill it), the *pucele* expresses no desire of her own. She wishes only for Lancelot's honor and well-being: "que vostre enor et vostre bien / vuel je par tot et ci et la" ["For I seek that which is to your honor / And good, both now and always"] (6698-99). Despite Lancelot's promises to her, he never returns and she never reappears. With Meleagant's sister, female desire has become controlled and deproblematized. It conforms so completely to Lancelot's will for freedom and honor that the two desires have become identical.

By the romance's final scene, even Guenevere's troublesome sexuality has been tamed. In the last combat between Meleagant and Lancelot, the Queen is no longer the resisting reader or commanding force.[38] She appears as a spectator who has fully sublimated her desire to the code of courtly propriety; she makes no public show of her passion. Her "fol cuer" and "fol pansé" are contained by reason: "por ce reisons anferme et lie / son fol cuer et son fol pansé" ["Thus Reason encompassed and bound / Her foolish heart and thoughts"] (6846-47). We hear nothing more about her after Lancelot kills Meleagant.

Within that section of the narrative penned by "Godefroy," woman's desire no longer disturbs the turn of chivalric events. The female participant in the triangle of courtly desire is instead remystified as one whose "rage" (6843) and "folie" (6845)—her threatening female sexuality—are contained by the system that reinscribes her as a forbidden object of desire. Her active voice and her direct influence are conspicuously written out of the text. The woman reader is markedly *absent* in the final lines of a romance that has so often been adduced as proof of her historical presence.

As we try to piece together the disjointed interlace of female characters in the *Charrete*, we encounter a series of disappearing acts. As female desire is subverted and mystified, the female subject vanishes. This negative pattern, if one can call it a pattern, is consonant with the dynamics of the frame, where the Godefroy-Chrétien contract replaces that between Marie and Chrétien. Given what we have seen of the narrator's problematization of female desire and the romance's subversion of female influence, the disappearance of the Countess from the parting lines of a romance dedicated to her seems a calculated move. What might the female reader—modern or medieval—make of what Marie-Noëlle Lefay-Toury has called the "dégradation du personnage féminin" throughout the *Charrete* and the corpus of Chrétien's romance?[39] At the very least, we might agree with her that Chrétien expressly undermines the "courtly" structure of his material. On the basis of the romance's explicit subversion of the female influence it purports to acknowledge, we must also lay to rest—yet again—the thesis that Marie de Champagne exerted a "feminizing influence" on the ideals of chivalry in the *Charrete* or that, by extension, women shaped courtly literature to their own ends. But must we conclude that the appropriation and mystification of woman within the romance enact the same designs on its female reader?

Chrétien's explicit presentation of woman's influence and desire as a question—his problematization of female reception—resists our hasty judgment. The seams of the romance's ideological surface are not smooth; the narrator calls far too much attention to the uneasy relationship between the hero and his female dependents. Nor is the conclusion a closed case, as critical controversy still attests. Instead, Chrétien and Godefroy conspicuously call attention to the way a clerical exchange ends the romance. The narrative resolution, to adapt Nancy Miller's terminology, is "italicized."[40] The appropriation of Marie's "sens" in the Prologue, the romance's troublesome female agents, and the Epilogue's conspicuous absenting of woman are devices that sow the seeds for critical reflection in the discerning reader. They invite our questions about the uneasy relationship of the male cleric to his feminine courtly public, as well as to male aristocratic culture. If the image of female influence, power, and resistance is recuperated *within* the text, female critical reflection on the tensions of gender is pointedly invited *by* the text. *Le Chevalier de la Charrete* provides an object lesson in the dangers romance might hold for women, and, as such, it generates—and engenders—a tradition of critical reflection on sexuality and interpretation that later Arthurian fictions will continue to elaborate.

NOTES

I would like to thank Thomas Bass, Christopher Baswell, Jane Burns, Sheila Fisher, and Nancy Rabinowitz for their thoughtful comments on various drafts of this paper, and Michel-André Bossy, who invited me to present an earlier version for the Committee on Medieval Studies and the Pembroke Center at Brown University.

1. Gaston Paris, "Lancelot du Lac. *Le Conte de la Charrette.*" *Romania* 12 (1883), 459-534, esp. 516-34. For early assertions of the feminine origins of courtly love and literature, see Reto Bezzola, "La transformation des moeurs et le rôle de la femme dans la classe féodale du XI au XIIe siècle," *Les Origines et la formation de la littérature courtoise en Occident (500-1200)*, pt. 2, vol. 2 (Paris: Champion, 1960), p. 461, and Myrrha Lot-Borodine, *De L'Amour profane à l'amour sacré: études de psychologie sentimentale au Moyen Age* (Paris: Nizet, 1961), esp. pp. 16-19.

2. For a concise account of the critical controversy surrounding the *Charrete*, see Matilda Tomaryn Bruckner, "An Interpreter's Dilemma: Why Are There So Many Interpretations of Chrétien's *Chevalier de la Charrette?*" *Romance Philology* 40 (1986), 159-80.

3. See John F. Benton, "The Court of Champagne as a Literary Center," *Speculum* 36 (1961), 551-91 and "Clio and Venus: An Historical View of Medieval Love," in F.X. Newman, ed., *The Meaning of Courtly Love* (Albany: State University of New York Press, 1968), pp. 19-42. For arguments supporting the idea of noblewomen's influence on courtly literature, see, for example, Joan Kelly-Gadol, "Did Women Have a Renaissance?," in Renate Bridenthal and Claudia Koonz, eds., *Becoming Visible: Women in European History* (Boston: Houghton Mifflin, 1977), p. 146. Also see June Hall McCash, "Marie de Champagne's `Cuer d'Ome et Cors de Fame': Aspects of Feminism and Misogyny in the Twelfth Century," in Glyn S. Burgess and Robert A. Taylor, eds. *The Spirit of the Court: Selected Proceedings of the Fourth Congress of the International Courtly Literature Society* (Cambridge, England: D. S. Brewer, 1985), pp. 234-45.

4. Among these studies, see Bruckner, "An Interpreter's Dilemma" and "*Le Chevalier de la Charrete (Lancelot)*," in Douglas Kelly, ed., *The Romances of Chrétien de Troyes: A Symposium* (Lexington: French Forum, 1985), pp. 132-81; Norris J. Lacy, *The Craft of Chrétien de Troyes: An Essay on Narrative Art* (Leiden: Brill, 1980),

pp. 54-60 and 88-93; and an unpublished paper by David Hult, "Author/Narrator/Speaker: The Voice of Authority in Chrétien's *Charrete.*"

5. All quotations of the *Charrete* are drawn from *Le Chevalier de la Charrete*, ed. Mario Roques (Paris: Champion, 1972). Translations are taken from *Lancelot, or The Knight of the Cart*, ed. and trans. William W. Kibler (New York: Garland, 1984). Line references, cited in parentheses, are to the edition of Roques.

6. See my "Contracts and Constraints: Courtly Performance in *Yvain* and the *Charrete*," in Edward R. Haymes, ed. *The Medieval Court in Europe* (Munich: Wilhelm Fink, 1986), pp. 92-104.

7. As evidenced by an extensive philological debate begun by Jean Frappier and Jean Rychner. The discussion revolves around whether the "sans" that Marie gives Chrétien is the romance's "idée maîtresse" (Frappier) or whether it is merely the "inspiration" (Rychner). It hinges on the etymological and semantic difference of "sans," 23 (from the Latin *sensus*) and "sans," 26 (from the Frankish *sin), a distinction that some have argued is pointedly ambiguous. See Bruckner, "*Le Chevalier de la Charrete*," 135-38.

8. Godefroy's conclusion has provoked nearly as much discussion as the Prologue. See, for example, David A. Shirt, "Godefroy de Lagny et la composition de la *Charrete*," *Romania* 96 (1975), 27-52, and Bruckner, "*Le Chevalier de la Charrete*," 162-65. My inclination is to agree with David Hult that we read "Godefroy" as a fictional clerkly-author figure conceived by the author Chrétien. See Hult, "Author/Narrator/Speaker."

9. For theoretical discussion of literary texts as a vehicle for male bonding, see Eve Kosofsky Sedgwick, *Between Men: English Literature and Male Homosocial Desire* (New York: Columbia University Press, 1985).

10. Charles Méla, *La Reine et le Graal: La conjointure dans les romans du Graal de Chrétien de Troyes au Livre de Lancelot* (Paris: Seuil, 1984), p. 258.

11. On the female patronage of Old French and Provençal literature, see Rita Lejeune, "La femme dans les littératures française et occitane du XIe au XIIIe siècle," *Cahiers de civilisation médiévale* 20 (1977), 204-08.

12. For a cautionary statement, see Penny Schine Gold, *The Lady and the Virgin: Image, Attitude, and Experience in Twelfth-Century France* (Chicago: University of Chicago Press, 1985), pp. xv-xxi.

13. See Georges Duby, *Le Chevalier, la femme, et le prêtre: le mariage dans la France féodale* (Paris: Hachette, 1981), and Suzanne Wemple and Jo Ann McNamara, "The Power of Women Through the Family in Medieval Europe: 500-1100," *Feminist Studies* 1 (1973), 126-41.

14. This is not to deny the importance of the feminine voices of Marie de France, Héloïse, and the *trobaritz*. But even here, a problematic of absence and displacement obtains, if only in their critical context: the authenticity of the female signature has been, in each case, disputed.

15. This point has been forcefully made by Joan Ferrante in *Woman as Image in Medieval Literature: From the Twelfth Century to Dante* (New York: Columbia University Press, 1975), and in "Male Fantasy and Female Reality in Courtly Literature," *Women's Studies* 11 (1984), 67-97.

16. For a partial discussion of the object status of women, see my "Double Jeopardy: The Appropriation of Woman in Four Old French Romances of the `Cycle de la Gageure,'" in Janet Halley and Sheila Fisher, eds., *The Lady Vanishes: Feminist Contextual Criticism of Late Medieval and Renaissance Writings*, forthcoming from the University of Tennessee Press.

17. Most studies of the social function of romance have been gender-neutral in their consideration of chivalric ideology. By focusing on class tensions, on the emergence of individuality, on legal structures and kinship, or on self-conscious literary values, scholars have overlooked the genre's troublesome silencing of the female subject and its subversion of female power. Whether willingly or not, they have confirmed the concerns of clerical and chivalric male culture as romance's central problem.

18. A provocative reading of the problematic inscription of female sexuality within one of the first courtly romances, *Le Roman d'Eneas*, has been advanced by Jean-Charles Huchet, *Le Roman médiéval* (Paris: Presses Universitaires de France, 1984).

19. On "reading against" the text as a strategy of the feminist critic, see Patrocinio P. Schweikart, "Toward a Feminist Theory of Reading," in Elizabeth Flynn and Schweikart, eds., *Gender and Reading* (Baltimore: Johns Hopkins University Press, 1986), pp. 49-54.

20. Bruckner, "*Le Chevalier de la Charrete*," 162-75.

21. Although Chrétien does not refer to her refusal to see Lancelot as a "command" during the scene itself, Lancelot later uses this term to explain to Keu that he must follow the queen's wishes—"Or soit a

son comandemant" (4076). The term echoes the Countess's "commandemanz" in the Prologue (22).

22.   Moshé Lazar, "Lancelot et la `mulier mediatrix:' la quête de soi à travers la femme." *Esprit Créateur* 9 (1969), 243-356.

23.   Bruckner, *"Le Chevalier de la Charrete,"* 148-57.

24.   See Charles Méla's brilliant analysis of how the women are used to dramatize the shame and ecstasy of the hero's sexual transgression in his chapter on the *Charrete*, "L'in-Signifiance d'amour," in *La Reine et le Graal*, pp. 257-321.

25.   For a very different reading, which views these women as independent and powerful reflections of Marie de Champagne's influence, see McCash, "Marie de Champagne's 'Cuer d'Ome et Cors de Fame,'" pp. 236-38.

26.   The longest episode, the sequence of events with the "immodest damsel," comprises over 1000 lines (931-2013), but the other encounters are significantly shorter.

27.   The figures in parentheses refer to the utterance of the verbal constraint and to the boundaries of the episode, respectively.

28.   This article has been abridged from a longer study on women readers and the representation of woman in the *Charrete* and other twelfth- and thirteenth-century Old French romances.

29.   As Kathryn Gravdal has suggested in a paper delivered at the December 1986 MLA, the rape scene is a cynical extension of the "rape is what women really want" argument.

30.   Since not all knights are honorable, this means, presumably, that a woman would do well to attach herself to a champion, thereby becoming fair game in the exchange system. See my discussion of this "custom" and its implications in "Love, Honor, and the Exchange of Women in *Yvain*: Some Remarks on the Female Reader," *Romance Notes* 25 (1985), 302-17.

31.   Lexical and thematic resonances underscore the parallels between the damsel's staged rape and Guenevere's abduction. As Lancelot wonders where the damsel is after dinner, Lancelot says "Je la querrai tant que je l'ai" ["I'll seek her until I have her"] (1055), as he might for the queen. The hero specifically reflects upon his quest for Guenevere during his delaying monologue at the scene of the "crime" (1097-99).

32.   See, for example, Reto Bezzola, *Le sens de l'aventure et de l'amour* (Paris: La Jeune Parque, 1947), p. 44; Eugène Vinaver, *A la recherche d'une poétique médiévale* (Paris, 1970), p. 114; Douglas Kelly, *"Sens" and "Conjointure" in the "Chevalier de la Charrete"*

(The Hague: Mouton, 1966), p. 58; Jean Frappier, *Chrétien de Troyes* (Paris: Hatier, 1968), 130-41.

33. David Hult, "Lancelot's Two Steps: A Problem in Textual Criticism," *Speculum* 61 (1986), 836-58.

34. On the role of the "femme bonne" whose recognition and resistance affirm masculine identity in the phallogocentric order, see Hélène Cixous, "Sorties," in Catherine Clément and Hélène Cixous, *La Jeune Née* (Paris: 10/18, 1978), pp. 144-47.

35. Méla, *La Reine et le Graal*, p. 288.

36. Shoshana Felman, "Rereading Feminity," *Yale French Studies* 62 (1981), 21. I am grateful to Mary Jacobus' excellent discussion of reading the representation of women in fiction for bringing the relevance of this essay to my attention. Mary Jacobus, *Reading Woman: Essays in Feminist Criticism* (New York: Columbia University Press, 1986), pp. 13-21.

37. On Lunete's affinity with Yvain and the narrator, see my "Love, Honor and the Exchange of Women." David Hult has remarked, in discussion, that the emergence of narrative interventions in the "Godefroy" section of the poem coincides with the appearance of Meleagant's sister. Hult emphasizes the centrality of her role, which clearly deserves further attention.

38. Hult has offered another perspective on Guenevere's absence in these final lines in "A Queen is Missing: Guenevere in Chrétien's *Lancelot*," given at a session on "Woman and Old French Romance" at the International Congress on Medieval Studies, Kalamazoo, 1987.

39. Marie Noëlle Lefay-Toury, "Roman breton et mythes courtois: l'évolution du personnage féminin dans les romans de Chrétien de Troyes." *Cahiers de civilisation médiévale* 15 (1972), 193-204 and 283-93.

40. Nancy K. Miller, "Emphasis Added: Plots and Plausibilities in Women's Fictions," *PMLA* 96 (1981), 44. Miller's comments on "marking" and "italicization" in women's fiction seem applicable to any text that highlights the tensions of gender.

Aspects of Arthur's Death in Medieval Illumination

M. *Alison Stones*

The vogue enjoyed in the Middle Ages by tales of the final episodes in the story of Arthur and his knights of the Round Table is documented by its widespread inclusion in the chronicle tradition, and by the existence of several 'literary' versions that concentrate on Arthur's last exploits.[1] Illustrations appear both in the chronicle and in the literary traditions, although there is considerable chronological and regional variation in whether the texts were illustrated and, if they were, which episodes were selected for illustration.[2] How the pictorial tradition originated and developed, and to what extent the pictures reflect or add meaning to the narrative of the text, and what the illustrations reveal about the cultural context which gave rise to them, are the subjects of the present paper.

The Texts

There can be little question that the story of Arthur must have circulated most widely in Geoffrey of Monmouth's *Historia regum britanniae*, of which close to two hundred manuscripts survive from Britain and the continent: it was clearly among the most widely read of any medieval text that includes Arthur, as more MSS survive than of any of the other chronicles that mention him, and it numerically far outweighs the vernacular versions.[3] In this context the relationship between Geoffrey's popular *Historia* and the manuscript tradition of the Arthurian romances is somewhat comparable to that of the still more popular *Pseudo-Turpin Chronicle* in which the story of Charlemagne's exploits in Spain circulated much more widely than in the literary vernacular versions.[4] But Geoffrey's *Historia*, like the *Pseudo-Turpin* chronicle, was illustrated only rarely. The combat between Arthur and the giant of Mont-Saint-Michel in the twelfth-century manuscript of Geoffrey's *Historia* from Anchin is the earliest surviving Arthurian illumination, but it is the only Arthurian illustration in that, or apparently in any manuscript of Geoffrey's *Historia*.[5] Even in the more fully illustrated vernacular chronicles of the thirteenth, fourteenth, and fifteenth centuries, Arthurian subjects are represented in no more than a handful of manuscripts, only two of which include an episode from Arthur's final moments.[6]

By comparison with the enormous corpus of manuscripts of Geoffrey's *Historia*, relatively few manuscripts preserve the vernacular romance versions of Arthur's death, and still fewer of them are illustrated. The English manuscript tradition is extremely limited: only five manuscripts survive, two of Laȝamon's *Brut* and one each of the stanzaic and alliterative verse versions and of Malory's prose *Morte Arthur*, none of which is illustrated.[7] Malory's version owes its popularity to the fact that it was published by Caxton, and circulated in editions based on his; Wynkyn de Worde's editions of 1498 and 1529 contain illustrations.[8] On the Continent, there is one illustrated Italian compilation, written in 1446, that depicts Arthur's end; and Wace's Anglo-Norman verse version, *Le Roman de Brut*, includes an important account of the death of Arthur, but the most copiously illustrated manuscript of it includes only a single scene of Arthur's death.[9]

It is only the French prose version of the story, the *Mort Artu*, the last of the five branches of the Vulgate Cycle, which attributes its authorship to Walter Map writing at the behest of King Henry II,[10] that preserves an illustrative tradition that is both numerically significant and fully developed as a narrative sequence.[11] Of the 50 or so partial or complete manuscripts of the *Mort Artu*, some 34 are illustrated, and 25 contain more than one illustration.[12] The success of this version was widespread: illustrated copies of this French text were made by scribes and illuminators for patrons who lived in England, Italy, France, and

Flanders; the chronological range spreads over two centuries, from the second quarter of the thirteenth to the end of the fifteenth centuries. The case of Italy is particularly interesting as French texts were copied there, variant versions in French were composed, and Italian versions were also written, one of which is important for its illustrations.[13] Moreover, Boccaccio's inclusion of Arthur in his *De casibus virorum illustrium* also gave rise, largely through its French translation by Laurent de Premierfait, to illustrations showing Arthur's death.[14]

An examination of the illustrative treatment of the death of Arthur must necessarily be primarily concerned, then, with the manuscripts of the *Mort Artu* in French prose, and with the few further illustrations supplied by the chronicle traditions that precede and follow it, together with the illuminations in the Italian manuscript versions. Were there a body of illustrations in other media that depict the death of Arthur, one would surely wish to take it into consideration as well, but the material surveyed by the Loomises shows that the death of Arthur was not a subject favored in the sculpture, wall painting, textiles, or portable objects that have survived.[15]

Methods

The nucleus of this study is the list of *Mort Artu* manuscripts assembled in Appendix 1 from secondary sources and primary observation. The stylistic arguments that have led to the attributions of date and place cannot be presented in detail here for reasons of space, but I emphasize now how fundamental this work is to what follows here. For the MSS that emerge as the most important, either in terms of density of illustration, or for their treatment of a particular episode, or both, I include lists of manuscripts that are comparable stylistically, with major references. There is still much to be done to confirm many of the attributions, and the list is intended as a guide rather than a definitive study.

The approach I take is diachronic in the sense that, for the first time, every illustrated *Mort Artu* manuscript is taken into consideration here. The questions that emerge are those of frequency and distribution, in terms of the numbers of manuscripts produced, and the quantity of illumination they contain.

Here I examine a small component—two or three scenes— within a pictorial cycle, reserving the rest of the cycle for more detailed treatment elsewhere. The method, however, is the same as for a complete cycle, and its major purpose is to enable a range of observations and conclusions to be made about the totality of an illustrative tradition that cannot be made on the basis of "single case studies" in which one randomly selected manuscript or illustration is picked, as it were, out of a hat. Of course, the observations and conclusions based on the totality of surviving illustrations must still be provisional since we inevitably lack links in the chain of transmission, but we can only come close to reconstructing its history by taking all the surviving evidence into account.[16]

The questions that I wish to raise could be classified as largely functional: who was interested in Arthur's death, and why? To what extent do the illustrations contribute overlays of meaning that differ, or complement, those of the text? With some notable exceptions, few of the books considered here were made for patrons who are known by name, and there is much that is uncertain about the interrelations between production team and patrons, and about the process of transmitting, transforming, and inventing the illustrations. Although the names of the individuals, both producers and patrons, may in most cases remain elusive, the illustrations can inform us in large measure about what role these books played in the cultural history of the period.

For texts like the *Mort Artu*, which were illustrated with some frequency, a simple one-to-one relationship between picture and text cannot be taken for granted, although it clearly occurred at some stage in the proceedings, and often more than a single time. The exact circumstances of the production of books and their illuminations in the thirteenth century, when illustrative cycles for Arthurian texts begin, are still poorly understood. It is unclear to what extent the locus of production in the provinces was fixed, as was the case in Paris, where tax records indicate that parchmenters, scribes, illuminators, and dealers (*libraires*) lived and worked in adjacent streets, and how common was the practice of the manuscript makers working on commission at the castles of their aristocratic patrons and patronesses.[17]   Similarly we know little about just how the pictorial cycles of vernacular manuscripts, newly worked out in the thirteenth century, were devised and transmitted.   Evidence from the manuscripts themselves shows that intermediaries in the form of marginal notes and sketches aided the process of invention and transmission, and it is also likely that rubrics played a part; we rarely know how many individuals took part in the complex process of deciding upon an illustrative sequence, placing the scenes in the text, writing, decorating, and illuminating, and who was in charge of the operation.   I raise this issue here because one of the workshops whose products are discussed here—Add.10292- 4 and related books—left many traces of marginal notes both to the rubricator and to the illuminator, as I have shown elsewhere, and because the process of transmission is one that is often overlooked in discussions of text-picture relationships.[18]

Comparative examination of the picture cycles—every illustration in every manuscript of a given text, here the *Mort Artu*—shows too that the cycles were not fixed: some manuscripts have a single illustration, others have a short cycle of pictures, others have a long cycle, and the relationship between the possibilities is not altogether a chronological one.[19]   Other factors, such as the cost of each illustration, the extent to which gold was used, and the availability of suitable pictorial models, must have governed the choice, and in the absence of documents one cannot be sure of the precise circumstances that explain what appears in each particular instance.

Arthur's Death: The Mort Artu Account

The preface to the fifth and final branch of the Vulgate Cycle explains that when Walter Map had written it for his patron King Henry, he named it *La Mort le roi Artu* because it ends with Arthur's wounding at the Battle of Salebieres, and his taking leave of Girflet, after which he was never seen alive again.[20]   The preface points immediately, if cryptically, to moments that are among the most poignant in Arthurian romance: the final dialogue between Girflet (Bedevere in the English

versions) and Arthur, the speeches to the sword, the hand
receiving the sword back into the lake and Arthur sailing away
with Morgan, then Girflet's discovery of Arthur's tomb, which he
recognizes because of its splendor and its identifying inscription.[21]
Girflet dies of grief, and the story ends with Guenevere's
retirement to an unspecified convent and her death, the deaths of
the sons of Arthur's treacherous son Mordret, killed by Lancelot
and his friends at the Battle of Wincestre, in which Lionel also
dies; Hestor and the penitent Lancelot die at a hermitage,
leaving Boort, who will renounce the kingdom in the end and
follow their footsteps to a hermitage.

Omitted altogether, in the *Mort Artu*, is the idea of Arthur's
healing and ultimate return.[22] The emphasis on the Girflet's
discovery of Arthur's tomb is what aligns the *Mort Artu* with the
late twelfth-century Latin accounts composed in England by
Gerald of Wales and Ralph of Coggeshall, both of whom describe
the discovery of the actual tomb at Glastonbury c.1191, although
the locus of the tomb in *Mort Artu* is the "Noire Chapele" (place
unspecified) rather than the abbey of Glastonbury.[23] In all three
accounts, the tomb is recognized by an inscription, which for
Ralph and Gerald is located on a lead cross on the tomb and refers
to Avalon.

The *Mort Artu* account differs from these not only by the
omission of reference to Avalon or Glastonbury, but also by
associating the tomb of Arthur in position, splendor, and
identifying inscription, with that of Lucan le Bouteillier, whom
Arthur had killed by crushing him with an embrace.[24] Girflet
finds both tombs in the Noire Chapele:

...il trova devant l'autel deus tombes moult beles et moult
riches, mes l'une estoit assez plus bele et plus riche que
l'autre. Desus la meins bele avoit letres qui disoient: CI GIST
LUCANS LI BOUTEILLIERS QUE LI ROIS ARTUS
ESTEINST DESOUZ LUI. Desus la tombe qui tant estoit
merveilleuse et riche avoit letres qui disoient: CI GIST LI
ROIS ARTUS QUI PAR SA VALEUR MIST EN SA
SUBJECTION .XII. ROIAUMES.

[Before the altar he found two rich and beautiful tombs, but one of them was far richer and more beautiful than the other. On the less beautiful one there was an inscription saying: "HERE LIES LUCAN THE BUTLER, WHOM KING ARTHUR CRUSHED TO DEATH." On the very splendid and rich tomb there was written: "HERE LIES KING ARTHUR, WHO THROUGH HIS VALOR CONQUERED TWELVE KINGDOMS."][25]

This account, like those of Gerald and Ralph, presents no hint that Arthur will return, and it has been suggested that the Plantagenets had political reasons for wishing to suppress the legendary return of Arthur; at the same time, Glastonbury stood to gain, by analogy with centers of pilgrimage dedicated to the cult of a saint.[26] Gerald, Ralph, and *Mort Artu* present an account of Arthur's death that stands in sharp contrast to the majority of twelfth-century versions, whether romance or chronicle: William of Malmesbury, Geoffrey of Monmouth, Wace, Langtoft, and Laȝamon all, to a greater or lesser degree, include the return, as do many of the later chronicles; the *Stanzaic Morte Arthur*, based on the *Mort Artu*, stands out similarly in the English tradition as omitting Arthur's return, but the *Alliterative Morte Arthure* and Malory's version combine the dicovery of the tomb with hope of the return in the wording of the inscription they both cite, "Hic jacet Arthurus, rex quondam rexque futurus."[27] In an examination of pictorial representations of Arthur's death, the most interesting question becomes whether the illustrations reflect the fact that the story had more than one ending, and to what extent the ending of *Mort Artu* is reflected in turn in the other illustrated versions of Arthur's death.

The Manuscripts: Cycles and Scenes

I begin by considering the manuscript tradition of *Mort Artu*. The chronology of the manuscripts has not been established with certainty. The composition of the text is not dated and most of the manuscripts also lack firm dates. Frappier suggests an approximate date of 1230 for the composition of the text, based on a rough sequence in which *Mort Artu* follows the *Lancelot* proper (c.1215-20) and *Queste* (c.1225); none of the extant MSS have been put earlier than the second quarter of the century, nor have they have ever been subjected to close scrutiny on palaeographical and codicological grounds. It remains to be seen whether Frappier's somewhat vague dating of the text is valid.[28]

Whether a sequence of illustrations was planned from the beginning is also unclear. The earliest manuscripts tend, as do those of the French prose *Queste del Saint Graal*, to contain a single miniature or historiated initial at the opening, but the "break points," even in these early manuscripts, are often marked with a champie or pen-flourished initials at the places in the text where later books have a historiated initial or miniature; and the earliest illustrated prose *Estoire*, which can be dated c.1220, includes a developed sequence of narrative images.[29] It is possible, then, that an early, fully illustrated *Mort Artu*, is lost. But manuscripts that are unillustrated or contain a single illustration continue to be produced throughout the period.

The earliest surviving MSS with a cycle of images date roughly from the middle of the thirteenth century, when a short cycle of some 22 illustrations is devised; this cycle also continues to be copied, with a few variations, until the end of the period. (What I imply with the term "cycle" is a sequence of illustrations whose subjects and whose textual locations were relatively firmly fixed.) The third development is the emergence of a long cycle of miniatures: an expanded version of the short cycle, which is sporadic both in date (1274, c.1290-1300, c.1315-25, and 1470) and in numbers of illustrations, ranging from 30 to 47. The unillustrated and sparsely illustrated books, and those with the short picture-cycle, are widespread in their distribution. The long cycle manuscripts, however, group into two major regions, with some probably produced at the same center: the region of northeastern Artois (Arras, St. Omer, Thérouanne) and western Flanders (Douai) on the one hand, and central France, in the orbit of Jacques d'Armagnac, duc de Nemours, great-grandson of Jean de Berry, for whom B.N. fr. 112 and B.N. fr. 113-116 were made, on the other.[30]

The events that surround Arthur's death in the *Mort Artu* for which images were developed are the following (listed here in the order in which they occur in the narrative): Arthur's death

anticipated in his dream of the dead Gauvain warning him that
he will die if he fights Mordret; Arthur's final battle with
Mordret in which each mortally wounds the other; Girflet
handing back Arthur's sword Excalibur to the lake, where it is
received by an outstretched hand; Arthur weeping; Arthur and
Morgan setting sail in a boat, watched by Girflet from the shore;
Arthur's tomb. I now analyze their distribution and emphasis
within the corpus of the 25 MSS that contain a sequence of
illustrations and the nine that have only one, and trace the ways
in which these scenes reappear in other versions of the story. The
distribution of scenes within manuscripts is presented in
Appendix 3.

The first point to emphasize is that the majority of the
manuscripts of *Mort Artu* (31 of the 52) omit scenes of Arthur's
death altogether.   Either no illustration of the death or any
other episode was preferred (15 MSS), or a single illustration
showing an episode from another part of the story (five of the
MSS with one illustration only), or a narrative sequence of images
that excludes any pictorial reference to Arthur's death (11 MSS,
including two where the relevant text passages are missing). Of
those that do include illustration of Arthur's death, there are
variations in how many and which episodes are selected, and in
how the same episode is treated in the different manuscripts for
which it was selected.

As described above, the final episodes of Arthur's death are
presented twice in the text of *Mort Artu*, once in the opening
paragraph and again toward the end. The emphasis is not quite
the same each time: at the beginning, King Henry wants to hears
about "la fin de ceus dont il avoit fet devant mention et conment
cil morurent..." ["the rest of the lives of those he (Map) had
previously mentioned (i.e. in the *Queste*, the previous branch of
the cycle), and the deaths of those whose prowess he had related
in his book."]. Map gives the title *La Mort le roi Artu* to the work
he has written

> por ce que en la fin est escrit conment li rois Artus fu navrez en
> la bataille de Salebieres et conment il se parti de Girflet qui
> si longuement li fist compaignie que apres lui ne fu nus hom qui
> le veïst vivant.

[because the end of it relates how King Arthur was wounded at the battle of Salisbury and left Girflet, who had long been his companion, and how no one ever again saw him alive.]

This paragraph, then, taken on its own, could reasonably be supposed to present a number of possible choices of subject which would be appropriate for an opening miniature. By the end, on the other hand, it becomes clear that there was a deeper level of meaning in the opening words "ne fu nus hom qui le veïst vivant" as Girflet discovers, by finding his tomb, that Arthur had actually died.[31]

The Tomb

There is not a single representation showing the discovery of Arthur's tomb by Girflet in the context of its occurrence in the narrative sequence (at the end, rather than at the beginning), even though the tomb is described as "merveilleuse et riche" and has the identifying inscription quoted above. The avoidance of the subject would already seem to suggest a reluctance, on the part of the patrons of manuscripts, and perhaps their manufacturers as well, to accept the death of Arthur as final. The contrast with the death of Judas Maccabeus and its illustrations in the late thirteenth-century Princeton MS of Gautier de Belleperche's version of *La Chevalerie de Judas Machabé*, Garrett 125 (Fig. 5), and in the B.N. MS of Pierre du Riés' version, B.N. fr. 15104 (Fig. 4), is striking: in both, the final illustration is that of mourners at the tomb of Judas, which in B.N. fr. 15104 is shown as an enormous tomb chest draped completely with a patterned cover.[32] The description of it by Pierre du Riés is summary, but Gautier de Belleperche's version is extremely detailed and includes mention of the statue of Simon Magus as Moses that stood on it, and which, as an air-based automaton, spoke the words commemorating Judas which normally would be those of an inscription incised on the tomb itself. The illustration, as Robert McGrath has noted, could be based only on a close reading of the text.[33]

Such attention to the text's description of the tomb of Arthur is not reflected in the two illustrations that do treat the subject.

Both of them place their image of it at the beginning of the text; in Paris, B.N. fr. 25520 (Fig. 3) it is part of a composite miniature in which the final battle of Arthur and Mordret is also shown, while in Paris, B.N. fr. 12580 (Fig. 2), the death alone is represented. In both manuscripts, the opening miniature is the only one in the book. Paris, B.N. fr. 25520 (Fig. 3) may date as early as the second quarter of the thirteenth century; the rubbed condition of the miniature makes an attribution difficult.[34] The painter of B.N. fr. 12580 is a lesser light among the group of painters associated with Folda's Hospitaller Master, whose roots are in the Paris-made *censier* of Sainte-Geneviève, Paris, Archives Nationales, Pièce S 1626, made in 1276.[35] Comparison with death scenes among the *oeuvre* of the shop makes clear that what is shown here is not simply Arthur on his deathbed, although his pose is similar to those of Fulk, Amaury, or Baldwin in two MSS of the *History of Outremer* from the same workshop.[36] The recumbent Arthur lies with hands crossed and head resting on a cushion on a three-arched stone tomb, with four chanting clerics, a cross, and candles behind the king. It is the stone arches that make this look like the actual tomb rather than simply a bier such as would figure in a funeral scene, of which there are many examples in the work of this painter and his shop.   The stone-work base, with its shrine-like arches, suggests that the recumbent figure of the king is more likely to be the sculpted (and painted) effigy which by the 1280s had become an expected component in fashionable royal tomb design in France and England.[37]

The stone arches of the tomb in B.N. fr. 12580 (Fig. 2) lead one to press the analogy with royal tomb design still further, and wonder whether, in addition, there is a deliberate association here with ideas not only about contemporary royal burial practices, but also about the canonization of defunct kings. King Louis IX died in 1270, and this book was made in Paris some time in the period after his death and in all probability before his 1297 canonization. The tomb shown here is quite different from the plain marble tombs that occur most frequently in the illustrations of Vulgate Cycle MSS of the thirteenth and fourteenth centuries, and which would have also suited the text's neutral description of Arthur's tomb, needing only the addition of the inscription.[38] The notion of canonization was already present, implicitly, in Gerald of Wales' account of Arthur's translation at Glastonbury,[39] but here the impending contemporary canonization would add another level of meaning to an image commissioned by a Parisian patron, especially if he or she were themselves members of the royal family.[40] Arthur's "return" would be equated with his eternal presence in the ranks of sainthood, and intermediary, like Charlemagne, between great rulers of France in history and legend and the present and future of the Capetian dynasty. Even if the arches are accidental, and the scene is meant, after all, to show Arthur on his deathbed (a common enough subject in the historical MSS made in the same workshop), the image would still present an emphasis that depends not on a close reading of the text, but rather on the particular cultural milieu in which it arose.

For an English patron, the associations with royal burial and canonization would not have been so very different, with the rebuilding of Westminster Abbey and the shrine of St. Edward providing the major focus of artistic activity from the second quarter of the thirteenth century.[41] Heraldic evidence in B.N. fr. 25520 (Fig. 3) suggests that the book was in all likelihood made for an English patron as one of the protagonists in the combat scene that accompanies Arthur's death bears the arms of England on crest and shield (the shield clearly shows two leopards, but I assume a third, obscured by the arm that couches the lance). Presumably this knight is Arthur. The shield of the other protagonist, Mordret, is too rubbed to be readily identified; the crest is a pair of wings. The death scene is similar to the one in B.N. fr. 12580 but shows Arthur recumbent, draped except for his crowned head, with a cloth that reaches the ground, with two candles in front and a candle and a cross behind. Clearly the scene is that of the king himself on his death-bed and not an effigy. Did the artist (or his manager) simply read the first paragraph of the text and select from a standard stock of death-bed scenes? Two figures stand behind the dead king; their treatment suggests that the image depends on a more careful reading of the text and that its components were deliberately chosen. The accompanying figures are not tonsured clerics singing the Office of the Dead, as in B.N. fr. 12580; although the paint layer is missing, both have substantial heads of hair. They are likely to Girflet (grieving, with clasped hands and bowed head) and the hermit who shows him Arthur's tomb. Why, then is not the tomb show, either pain, as the text describes it, or with an effigy, as in B.N. fr. 12580? Could it be that by choosing the death-bed image, an English patron, probably someone with royal connections, was consciously rejecting both the possibility of Arthur's eventual return and also that of his apotheosis?

The Warning

Another image that makes use of the motif of Arthur lying in bed illustrates his dream of Gauvain's warning that he will die if he enters combat with Mordret. There are seven sexamples in the illustrative tradition. The text describes this occurrence taking place in a forest while Arthur and his men are encamped prior to the battle. Arthur is therefore often shown lying in bed in a tent (Yale 229, fol. 350; Paris, Arsenal 3482, fol. 638v [Fig. 6]; B.N. fr. 116, fol. 734); but the tent is sometimes omitted (Rylands fr. 1, fol. 255; Rawl. D. 899 [Fig. 1]). Gauvain appears, according to the text, with a group of paupers; the number of figures included with Arthur is irregular.

As a literary and visual topos, the image of the dream has a long history, within which two particular associations are of interest here. One is with the other great ruler, Charlemagne, whose call by St. James to fight the Saracens in Spain occurs in a dream and is the main focus of illustration of the Pseudo-Turpin account of Charlemagne's Spanish campaigns. There, of course, it is Roland who will die, not Charlemagne, and Roland's death is not the point of the vision, nor even mentioned in it. The Charlemagne image is based on a standard episode in saints' lives and is particularly close to the image of Christ appearing to St. Martin in the *Life of St. Martin*, and there are Old Testament parallels in eleventh-century Bibles and Gospels. More interesting here are models like Christ appearing to St. Ambrose to announce his death on the altar of Sant'Ambrogio, Milan, or an angel appearing to St. Millán to announce his death on the ivory casket of San Millán de la Cogolla.[43] None of these examples, however, is sufficiently close visually to be the undisputed source for the Arthurian image, particularly for those images that include the tent, although the literary sources in saints' lives again inform the *Mort Artu* text and the inclusion of the illustration accentuates that association, if only in general terms.

Arthur's Battle Against Mordret

The final combat between Arthur and Mordret, of which two different versions occur in Rawl. D.899 and B.N. fr. 25520, is by far the most popular image of Arthur's death in the manuscript tradition as a whole. It is shown in 14 *Mort Artu* MSS, in Wace's *Brut*, and in the chronicles and treatises. Several of the *Mort Artu* MSS devote more than one image to the battle: four are grouped together in B.N. fr. 344 (Fig. 7), four separate images are included, on sequential pages, in Yale 229 (Fig. 8), and there are two images in Geneva, Bodmer 147, one at the opening of the text (Fig. 9) and the other toward the end; B.N. fr. 112, where *Mort Artu* is part of a special compilation of the text commissioned by Jacques d'Armagnac in 1470, has two miniatures showing the combat. The use of the device of repetition as a means of emphasizing the subject is an interesting feature of B.N. fr. 344, Yale 229, Geneva, Bodmer 147 and B.N. fr. 112, but in other respects their cycles are not particularly close; B.N. fr. 344 and Bodmer 147 have short cycles, while B.N. fr. 112 is closer to the long cycle, but they have fewer illustrations than Yale 229, which is the longest of the long cycle MSS.

In Rawl. D. 899 (Fig. 1), Arthur is shown to the left of the combat, presumably watching and about to enter it, although he lacks a helm. This version may result from a compression of the battle scene with another episode that shows Arthur and his men riding through a forest on their way to fight Mordret (Oxford, Rawl. Q.b.6, fol. 399v; Yale 229, fol. 350; Paris, Arsenal 3482, fol. 638v [Fig. 6]).

The treatment of the battle in these copies of *Mort Artu* is often somewhat bland and generalized: it is not always clear, in a general melée, or even in single combat, which figure is Arthur, as crowns and shields are frequently omitted, in single scenes as well as in multiple representations. Arthur wearing the arms of England, as in B.N. fr. 25520 (Fig. 2), is rare, and there is only one representation of him bearing the arms of the Virgin Mary, as described in Geoffrey of Monmouth and illustrated in Langtoft's chronicle, of the mid-fourteenth century.[44] By the late fourteenth century, Arthur's arms are well known as *az 3 crowns or* (with the crown increasing to 15 in the rolls of arms), but these arms become standard only gradually. The three crowns emerge in the late thirteenth century in the region of eastern Artois or western Flanders, in the Arras- or Douai-based workshop that made B.N. fr. 770 and Oxford, Bod. Digby 223 in the 1280s-90s, then in the workshop of Add. 10292-4, Royal 14.E.iii and Amsterdam / Rylands fr. 1 / Douce 215 in the period 1315-30, although both groups of MSS show Arthur with the "wrong" tinctures: pink or *az* for the field, but white rather than *or* for the crowns (Fig. 12), or *or 3 crowns sa* in the Hague *Spiegel historiael* of Jacob van Maerlant, KA XX.[45]

In the later *Mort Artu* MSS, as opposed to the chronicles, interest in the final combat declines somewhat, to the point where, in the fifteenth century, the subject occurs only in two books, B.N. fr. 111 and B.N. fr. 112.[46] It is as if the chronicles and treatises had by then taken over the role of projectors of Arthur's image that once was the domain of the romance tradition, and in so doing polarized it to emphasize its negative aspects, the ultimate destruction of the kingdom, and by implication, through the lack of another scene to present a more positive ending, Arthur's resulting death. This emphasis seems to begin in the fourteenth century, and the Hague image is a particularly interesting instance because of its unusual emphasis on the ignominy of Arthur's death, showing his wounded body taken away in a cart after the battle. Even in the Egerton MS of Wace's *Brut*, made after 1338, which devotes 17 of its 118 illustrations to Arthur's reign, and whose text normally ends with Wace explaining that legends about Arthur's return exist, but about which he himself will not take a position, has the combat between Arthur and Mordred as its final illustration.[47] To focus on Arthur's death in battle and the resulting destruction of the kingdom fits the aims of Boccaccio's and Laurent de Premierfait's moralizing purpose, as that of the *Trésor des histoires* in which Arthur's final combat also occurs, and may be anticipated in the chronicles, although it is also notable that Arthur's return plays a part, on occasion, in the texts of the chronicles, and that more neutral scenes of Arthur and his knights sitting at the Round Table sometimes provide an alternative illustration for Laurent de Premierfait's text.[48]

The Sword and the Lake, and Avalon

What, then, of the sword and the lake, and Arthur's departure to Avalon (or, more properly, in *Mort Artu* to an unnamed location)? The manuscripts are enlightening about who it was that considered this part of the story interesting enough to demand illustration. These episodes do not appear with illustrations in the chronicle traditions, so far as I have been able to determine; their absence suggests that the psychological complexity which this part of the story presents, and which its illustrations underline, was not felt to be appropriate to the aims of the chronicle, even if the text contained hints of Arthur's return. By the same token, the subtleties of the royal burial associations that emerged in a few of the *Mort Artu* MSS similarly play no part in the chronicles or treatises.

Although the text of *Mort Artu* disclaims the possibility of Arthur's ultimate return, the events that lead up to his departure with Morgan are accorded a significant place in the narrative and make an important contribution to the complexity of Arthur's psyche and to the pathos of his end. Only three *Mort Artu* manuscripts reflect this in their illustrations, Yale 229, B.L. Add. 10294, and B.N. fr. 112. They are among the most fully illustrated *Mort Artu* MSS in general, and, as discussed above, the Yale MS and B.N. fr. 112 also have multiple scenes of Arthur and Mordret's battle.[49] The Yale MS has three scenes of the final episodes, the first a two-register miniature, fol. 359 (Fig. 10), showing, at the top, Arthur in a chapel with Lucan le Bouteillier and Girflet, and, below, Girflet throwing Excalibur into the lake, where it is received by an outstretched hand in the water; on fol. 359v (Fig. 11) Arthur and his horse are invited by Morgan and her ladies aboard her ship. Add. 10294 has one scene, on fol. 94 (Fig. 12), the only one to show Arthur weeping, in a seated pose, with head on hand, while Girflet throws back Excalibur to the lake, where it is received, as in Yale 229, by an outstretched hand.[50] In

B.N. fr. 112, Girflet stands on the shore of the lake holding the sword and Arthur himself is excluded.

A particularly striking connection between Yale 229 and Add. 10294 is that both come from the same region. The provenance of neither is absolutely certain, as the MSS themselves contain no written evidence, but both can be attributed for stylistic reasons to workshops making books for patrons who lived or were associated with northeastern Artois, specifically St. Omer and Thérouanne; western Flanders (Ghent); and southwest Hainaut (Cambrai). Yale 229 is by two painters, one of whom made a book of hours of the use of Thérouanne, Marseille 111, and the other of whom illustrated the so-called Psalter of Gui de Dampierre, count of Flanders, Brussels, B.R. 10607, attributed to the patronage of Gui on the basis of the heraldic shields on its borders, although close examination of the MS shows that the shields have been overpainted at least once, and I do not think there can be a conclusive interpretation in the absence of a technical analysis.[51] I have suggested that the shield *Flanders a bend gu* in the margins of Yale 229 might indicate the patronage of Guillaume de Termonde, son of Gui de Dampierre and noted in other contexts as a patron of contemporary literature, but the attribution must remain tentative in the absence of confirmation from documents, and because of the inconspicuous location of the shield, tucked away in a border rather than prominent on an opening page.[52] None of the books related to Yale 229 is securely dated, and the omission of St. Louis (canonized in 1297) from the calendars and litanies of the devotional books provides the main chronological anchor in the period, if one that is of doubtful value.[53]

Add. 10294 is one of three Vulgate Cycle MSS produced in the same shop, and that shop may be, a generation later, the one that made B.N. fr. 95/ Yale 229. The other two sets associated closely with Add. 10292-4, are Amsterdam, Bibl.Hermetica/ Manchester Rylands fr. 1/ Oxford, Bod. Douce 215, and London, B.L. Royal 14.E.iii.[54] The Amsterdam/Rylands/Douce MS is less fully illustrated than Add. 10294, and, although there are gaps in the text, it is possible that no scene of Arthur's death was included originally. Royal 14.E.iii on the other hand presents a pattern, for the parts of the text that it preserves, that is extremely close to that of Add. 10294; the whole of the last part of the text is missing, and it is very likely that this section was also densely illustrated. Add. 10294 is part of the three-volume set, Add. 10292-4, edited by Sommer, and dated in or after 1316 by the inclusion of that date on the incised tomb shown in the miniature on fol. 55v of Add. 10292.[55] Other illuminations made by the same painter as the chief artist of Add. 10292-4 include the frontispiece to the psalter, St. Omer 270, added in 1323 by Guillaume de Sainte-Aldegonde to commemorate his presentation of the book, a psalter of the use of Tournai (Flanders) to the chartreuse of Longuenesse, near St. Omer (diocese of Thérouanne, and county of Artois).[56] Other books illustrated by the three painters whose distinct styles appear in Add. 10292-4, Amsterdam/Rylands/Douce, and Royal 14.E.iii, include other books written in French, Dutch (among which is the much-mentioned *Spiegel historiael*, The Hague KA XX),[57] and books in Latin made for patrons in St. Omer, Ghent, Cambrai, and points farther east.

The third manuscript that includes the Girflet-Excalibur episode is B.N. fr. 112, made in 1470 for Jacques d'Armagnac, duc de Nemours, and written by Micheau Gonnot, who completed the writing on 4 July of that year.[58] The text of this is a special version that draws on the Vulgate Cycle and other texts, and also includes material unknown elsewhere, as Pickford and others have shown, and it is thought that the scribe Micheau Gonnot was also the compiler.[59] Jacques d'Armagnac's collection of Arthurian manuscripts included the Vulgate Cycle sets B.N. fr. 117-20, which he inherited from his grandfather Jean de Berry, and whose paintings he had altered c.1470, and B.N. fr. 113-6, which was his own commission.[60] Jean de Berry's book had none of the scenes that are under discussion here; B.N. fr. 116 includes only Arthur's dream of Gauvain's warning, while B.N. fr. 112 has Girflet returning the sword to the lake.[61] Jacques d'Armagnac's books, together with the unstudied volume B.N. fr. 111, are the most important of the fifteenth-century *Mort Artu* MSS in general; B.N. fr. 116 has the short cycle of 23 miniatures, while the other two MSS show the influence of the long cycle, although their cycles are shorter than those in Yale 229 and Add. 10294, as B.N. fr. 111 has 28 miniatures and B.N. fr. 112 has 30. Further study is required to determine the extent to which, overall, the miniatures in B.N. fr. 111 and 112 depend on the earlier Artesian-Flemish books, Yale 229 and Add. 10294. Jacques d'Armagnac's painters are not directly associated with Artois or Flanders, and regional factors would not explain the iconographical links between B.N. fr. 112 and Add. 10294 and Yale 229.

The density of illustration in these books in general shows a greater-than-usual interest in the subject matter of the text as a whole, and in addition, Yale 229, Add. 10294, and B.N. fr. 112 are distinct from the rest of the tradition in including the most detailed treatment of the complexity of Arthur's death. Whether one can go so far as to say that the patrons of these three books were more interested than others in Arthur's return may be pressing the evidence too far, particularly as it is the Add. 10292-4 workshop that also produced the miniature that most emphazises the ignominious aspects of Arthur's end. At the same time, it is in Hainaut, which borders on Flanders and Artois, that the fifteenth-century chronicle B.R. 9423 preserves, again, an exceptionally full sequence of Arthurian miniatures, even if it is a sequence in which aspects of Arthur's death do not play an important role.[62] Political tensions between the counts and countesses of Artois and Flanders and the French crown were important issues in the thirteenth and fourteenth centuries, while Hainaut occupied the border position of being a political fief of the Empire but owed ecclesiastical allegiance to the Archbishop of Reims; and the major cities, Arras, Douai, Tournai, Cambrai and Mons were linked by important rivers and road systems, which meant they belonged to the same commercial and cultural network. It was a milieu in which, by the late thirteenth century, bourgeois patronage had begun to play a role in the collecting of Arthurian manuscripts, as the will of Jean Cole of Tournai attests in 1303.[63]

It is in fact to this region, centered on the River Scheldt, that most of the surviving *Mort Artu* and other Vulgate Cycle MSS can be attributed. Did Arthur have a particular appeal as a legendary hero because this was a region in which the reality of kingship left much to be desired? Trade and dynastic links with England would surely have helped to encourage the positive reception of the Matter of Britain in Artois and Flanders, while the *Chroniques du Hainaut* even claim Arthur as legendary ruler of Hainaut.[64] Jacques d'Armagnac, although his lands were in La Marche in central France rather than in Artois, Flanders, or Hainaut, is a specific case of an adversary of the king with a distinct interest in Arthur. His antagonistic position in relation to the crown culminated in his execution by Louis XI for treason in 1477, whereupon his books were seized by the king. A common link, then, between the three manuscripts that include the Girflet-Excalibur-Avalon scenes is an adversarial standpoint *vis à vis* the French crown.

The only other place, to my knowledge, where Arthur's departure to Avalon in Morgan's ship occurs, is in the Italian *Tavola Ritonda* compilation in Florence, Bibl. Naz. Cod. Pal. 556, written in 1446, and attributed to Venice.[65] It shows Girflet on horseback watching Arthur sail away, alone, while an outstretched hand brandishes Excalibur; Sir Ivain lies dead on the ground beside Girflet. It is interesting to speculate about whether this image, and the rest of the cycle in this MS, might be in any way dependent on models from the region that produced Yale 229 and Add. 10294, or might depend on the special version B.N. fr. 112. François Avril has shown that a painter from the Add. 10294 workshop was active in Italy in the early fourteenth century, although at Naples rather than Venice; it is not impossible that the Venetian draughtsman had access to a model from the Artois/Flanders region.[66] In other respects, however, the pictures in the Florence MS seem to depend directly on a reading of the text of that MS; the Girflet/Excalibur scene includes the dead Ivain whose presence at the lakeside occurs only in that text. Another instance of the originality of both text and picture is that of the death of Guenevere. This is the only manuscript, and the only text, to portray Guenevere dying in the arms of Lancelot.[67]

The textual accounts of Arthur's death, in their romance and chronicle versions, bear witness to shifts in emphasis and meaning between the twelfth and fifteenth centuries, governed by a complex network of factors in which political aims played a significant role. Many of the same factors, particularly the political sympathies of the patrons, seem also to have created a parallel network of links among the illustrations. While the Florence MS may, after all, be exceptional for manifesting a direct dependence of picture on text, the treatment of Arthur's death in French-speaking lands shows that the illustrations may present a variety of perspective on the text's narrative. Their range is from relative disregard, in the unillustrated copies, to the alteration or even distortion of its meaning, in the illustrated copies where the pictures provide an overlay or gloss created not only from the repertoire of visual sources which the artists had available, but also, to some degree, from the variant interpretations of other textual versions, and often reflect contemporary regional or personal concerns as well. Perhaps this analysis of what seems to be on the one hand an overt interest in Arthur and his knights among the aadversaries of the crown in France, and on the other hand, in Paris, a subversion of the story to Capetian goals, may help to explain one of the puzzles of the Arthurian manuscript tradition in Britain, namely its relative absence. Was there a deliberate suppression? It is hoped that future study of the illustrative cycles in these manuscripts, their pictures and their patrons, will elucidate the question further.

NOTES

1.   For the Latin sources the best survey is still E. K. Chambers, *Arthur of Britain*, (London: Sidgwick and Jackson, 1927), reprinted 1966; see also *Arthurian Literature in the Middle Ages*, ed. Roger Sherman Loomis (Oxford: Clarendon Press, 1959), and *The Romance of Arthur*, eds. James J. Wilhelm and Laila Zamuelis Gross (New York: Garland, 1984), and *The Romance of Arthur II*, ed. James J. Wilhelm (New York: Garland, 1986).

2.   For a preliminary study of the iconography of the French prose *Mort Artu* see my doctoral thesis, "The Illustration of the French Prose Lancelot in Belgium, Flanders and Paris, 1250-1340" (University of London, 1970/71). For the fifteenth-century MSS, I draw, with kind permission, on the work of Susan Blackman, who is preparing a Ph.D. dissertation at the University of Pittsburgh on the Arthurian MSS of Jacques d'Armagnac.

3.   See the chapters by Richard M. Loomis in Wilhelm and Gross, *The Romance of Arthur*; and John J. Parry and Robert A. Caldwell in R. S. Loomis, *Arthurian Literature*; for the manuscript tradition see Chambers, p. 30. For the historical context in general, see Antonia Gransden, *Historical Writing in England c. 550-c. 1307*, (London: Routledge and Kegan Paul, 1974). One should be wary, though, of

judging popularity only on the basis of surviving MSS, as it is also possible that much-used books fell to pieces and were discarded.

4. There are some 300 extant manuscripts of the Latin, to say nothing of the French translations: for the former, see André de Mandach, *Naissance et développement de la Chanson de Geste en Europe*: I, *La Geste de Charlemagne et de Roland*, (Genève/Paris: Droz, 1961), Appendix G. By contrast, the *Chanson de Roland*, in French assonanced laisses, enjoys an extremely limited manuscript tradition and is most frequently edited from Oxford, Bod. Digby 23, the only manuscript of its version.

5. To my knowledge, no thorough investigation has been made; in addition to the giant episode in Douai 880, fol. 66v, reproduced in Roger Sherman Loomis and Laura Hibbard Loomis, *Arthurian Legends in Medieval Art* (New York: Modern Language Association of America, 1938), Fig. 340, see London, B.L. Royal 13 A.iii (early 14th c.), which has marginal drawings of towns and shields, but no Arthurian illumination, and Cotton Claudius B.vii, a miscellany which includes Book vii of Geoffrey's *Historia*, the *Prophetia Merlini*, with a mid-thirteenth-century miniature showing Merlin and Vortigern (reproduced in Loomis, *Arthurian Legends*, Fig. 384).

6. They are the Hague MS of Jacob van Maerlant's *Spiegel Historiael*, c.1330, and the Lambeth MS of the *St. Alban's Chronicle*, c.1470. Jacob van Maerlant's *Spiegel Historiael*, The Hague, K.B. KA XX, fol. 163v includes a scene showing the final battle between Arthur and Mordred, with Arthur ignominiously carried away in a cart (reproduced in Loomis, *Arthurian Legends*, Fig. 342). Jacob van Maerlant's text is based on Vincent of Beauvais' Latin *Speculum historiale*, composed for St. Louis, where Arthur is discussed in Book 21, chapter 56, and Book 22, chapter 74, ending with Arthur wounded in the battle with Mordret, his journey with Morgan to an island, and Vincent's report that there is uncertainty about whether he died or lived after that. Vincent manuscripts, if illustrated at all, include one historiated initial for each Book. There is no complete study of the corpus of Vincent illustration; among the earliest illustrated MSS are Boulogne 130 and Boulogne 131, the latter one of two surviving volumes written in 1297 for Eustache Gomer de Lille, abbot of St. Bertin at St. Omer; Boulogne 130 is a two-volume direct copy of Boulogne 131, but neither illustrate the Arthurian section. See Stones (1970/71), pp. 448-49, and *The Minnesota Vincent of Beauvais Manuscript and Cistercian Thirteenth-Century Book Decoration* (Minneapolis: The

James Ford Bell Lectures, 1977), pp. 7, 22. The most extensive illustrative treatment of Arthur in the chronicle tradition occurs not in England but on the Continent, in Hainaut, in the Brussels manuscript of Jean Wauquelin's *Chroniques de Hainaut*. Jean Wauquelin translated and copied this French version of the *Annales Hannoniae* by Jacques de Guise in Mons between 1448 and 1453 for Philip the Good, Duke of Burgundy, and the three volumes now in Brussels were illustrated in the 1460s by a number of illuminators, including Guillaume Wielant or Vrelant (volume 2) and Loyset Liedet (volume 3), both of whom were paid for their work in 1468. B.R. 9242-4 contains seven Arthurian scenes but avoids Arthur's death. See Loomis, *Arthurian Legends*, pp. 126-27, figs. 343-48; *La Librairie de Philippe le Bon, Catalogue*, eds. Georges Dogaer and Marguerite Debae (Brussels: Bibliothèque Royale, 1967), nos. 188-89; Pierre Cockshaw, *Les Miniatures des chroniques de Hainaut, 15e siècle* (Mons: Hainaut-Tourisme, 1979), pl. 104-17. The only other chronicle that illustrates a scene from Arthur's end is the *St. Alban's Chronicle*, Lambeth Palace 6, written in English by a Flemish scribe and illuminated by a Fleming c. 1470; there are nine Arthurian scenes including, at fol. 66v, the battle between Arthur and Mordred. Still to be thoroughly investigated is the role of Arthur in such late medieval compilations as the *Trésor des histoires* and Boccaccio's *De casibus virorum illustrium* in Laurent de Premierfait's 1409 translation, made for Jean de Berry; some examples that include Arthur's final combat are given in Millard Meiss, *French Painting in the Time of Jean de Berry, I, The Late Fourteenth Century and the Patronage of the Duke* (London: Phaidon, 1967); in his *The Boucicaut Master* (London: Phaidon, 1968), especially pp. 108-13, Fig. 298, and *The Limburgs and Their Contemporaries*, 2 vols. (New York: George Braziller, 1974); and in E.G. Gardner, *Arthurian Legend in Italian Literature* (London: J.M. Dent and Sons, 1930), frontispiece; see Appendix 3 below. These compilations, like that of Vincent of Beauvais, tend to include one illustration, if that, for the Arthur section, and some MSS prefer a scene of Arthur and his knights seated at the Round Table, for which see the Laurent de Premierfait MSS Geneva, Bibl. Pub. et Univ. 190, fol. 139, Paris, Arsenal 5193, fol. 349v (Meiss, 1974, p. 283), and London, B.L. Add. 35321 (Gardner, facing p. 234). The English chronicles tend to show, if anything, Arthur's coronation.

7.   Laȝamon's *Brut*, composed between 1189 and 1204, is the earliest Arthurian legend written in English; it exists in two mid- or late thirteenth-century manuscripts, London, B.L. Cotton Caligula A.ix

and Cotton Otho C.xiii. See Laȝamon, *Brut*, eds. G.L. Brook and R.F. Leslie, Early English Text Society, Original Series 250, 277 (London: Oxford University Press, 1963, 1978). The *Stanzaic Morte Arthure*, composed in the late fourteenth century, exists in one late fifteenth-century manuscript, London, B.L.Harley 2252. I quote this text and the *Alliterative Morte Arthure* from *King Arthur's Death*, ed. Larry D. Benson (New York: Bobbs-Merrill, 1974). The *Alliterative Morte Arthure*, composed c.1400, survives in Lincoln Cathedral Library MS 19, a miscellany written c.1440 by the Yorkshire scribe Robert Thornton. See *The Thornton Manuscript (Lincoln Cathedral MS 91)*, Introduction by D.S. Brewer and A.E. Owen (London: Scolar Press, 1975, rev.1977). The manuscript of Malory's *Morte Darthur* now in the British Library, was discovered in 1934 at Winchester College as MS 13; see *The Winchester Malory: A Facsimile*, ed. N.R. Ker, Early English Text Society, Supplementary Series 4 (London: Oxford University Press, 1976). Caxton's version, printed at Westminster in 1485, is based on another manuscript, now lost. Surviving copies of Caxton's printing are in the Pierpont Morgan Library, New York, see *Le morte d'Arthur, printed by William Caxton 1485, reproduced in facsimile from the copy in the Pierpont Morgan Library*, ed. Paul Needham (London: Scolar Press, 1976); Manchester, The John Rylands University Library; and there was once a single leaf at Lincoln Cathedral Library, which is now lost. I am grateful to Jeanne Krochalis for her help with the English MSS and text versions.

8.   For Wynkyn de Worde's editions of 1498, preserved in the the John Rylands University Library, Manchester, and 1529, see Loomis, *Arthurian Legends*, p. 143, and Edward Hodnett, *English Woodcuts 1480-1535* (London: Oxford University Press, 1973). The series includes four scenes of battle, of which Hodnett nos. 1274 and 1287 include a crowned figure and might therefore show, in generalized terms, Arthur's combat with Mordred.

9.   This Italian compilation is Florence, B.Naz.Pal. 556, illustrated with over 200 line drawings. See Gardner (16 plates) and Loomis, *Arthurian Legends*, p. 121, figs. 337-39. The MS is not in B. Degenhart and A. Schmitt, *Corpus der italienischen Zeichnungen 1300-1450*, 2 parts in 4 vols. (Berlin: Mann, 1968, 1980), and a complete description of it was not available to me. For Wace's text, see *Le Roman de Brut*, ed. Ivor Arnold, 2 vols. (Paris: SATF, 1938). Arnold lists 23 MSS and fragments and notes the presence of a miniature showing five standing kings in Montpellier Fac. Méd. 251, fol. 207v. Does it include Arthur? The famous and

copiously illustrated mid-fourteenth-century manuscript in the British Library, Egerton 3028, contains an abridged version of Wace's text and is not included in Arnold's list. This remarkable book, whose text ends with the beginning of the Hundred Years' War in 1338, includes 118 illustrations which are listed in the *Catalogue of Additions to the Manuscripts 1916-1920* (London: British Museum, 1933), pp. 338-42. It has 17 scenes in the Arthur section—more than any of the chronicles—starting with Arthur's coronation (fol. 37) and ending with Arthur's battle with Mordred (fol. 53). Wace's unabridged version includes the Breton hope of Arthur's return. I lack information on whether or not this also features in the Egerton text.

10.   References given here are to Jean Frappier, *La Mort le Roi Artu, Roman du XIIIe siècle* (Paris: Droz, 1964). Translations are from *The Death of Arthur*, trans. James Cable (Harmondsworth: Penguin, 1971). The attribution to Walter Map, court satirist to Henry II and author of *De nugis curialium*, occurs in the opening sentence (Frappier, p. 1). It has never been taken seriously since the supposed date of composition of the *Mort Artu*, c.1220 (arrived at without substantial reasoning), would preclude Map's actual authorship, as well as the patronage of Henry, who died in 1189. But Henry and Eleanor were the patrons of Gerald of Wales and of Wace, both of whom treat Arthur, although with different endings to the story. Wace's *Brut*, completed in 1155 and dedicated to Eleanor (Chambers, pp. 101-05), has Arthur's possible return, while Gerald describes the discovery of Arthur's tomb at Glastonbury, thus precluding any hope of Arthur's return (Chambers, pp. 112-14). Gerald is ambiguous about whether the discovery occurred in Henry's reign or after his death in 1189, and indeed the *De principis instructione* which describes the discovery, was probably composed between 1193 and 1199. Nevertheless, the possibility that Walter Map (d. c. 1208–1210) had also written a text about Arthur for Henry can not be dismissed out of hand, although no twelfth-century MSS of the French prose *Mort Artu* survive, nor is there an extant Latin version by Map. A hint that there might have been a Latin version is perhaps provided by the opening illustration in B.N. fr. 342 (fol. 150), which shows Map writing at King Henry's command, and where the words that we read in the book Map writes are not those of the French text, but are in Latin: "Hic incipit de mortuo Artus regis et sociorum suorum" (reproduced in Loomis, *Arthurian Legends*, Fig. 215). A version that includes Arthur's death and tomb would be appropriate for the

may have excavated that tomb, or who is likely to have known that such an excavation was planned.

11. See note 2, above.

12. See Appendix 1 for my list of manuscripts, based on Brian Woledge, *Répertoire des romans et contes en prose française antérieurs à 1500* (Geneva: Droz, 1954, repr. 1975), *Supplément 1954-1973* (Geneva: Droz, 1975); Alexandre Micha, "Les manuscrits du *Merlin* en prose de Robert de Boron," in *Romania* 79 (1958), 78-94, and "Les manuscrits du *Lancelot* en prose," *Romania* 81 (1960), 45-187, 84 (1963) 28-60, 478-99; Stones (1970/1), and Jean-Paul Ponceau, *Etude de la tradition manuscrite de l'Estoire del Saint Graal, Roman du XIIIe siècle* (Thèse en vue du Doctorat de Troisième Cycle, Université de Paris IV-Sorbonne), 1983, rev. 1986. Appendix 2 shows the chronological and geographical distribution in relation to density of illustration.

13. See note 9 above. No illustrated manuscripts survive from Spain or Catalonia; the *Tristan*, B.N. fr. 750, signed by Pierre de Tiergeville in 1278 and attributed to Spain in Loomis, *Arthurian Legends*, pp. 91-92, has recently been reattributed to Italy or the Holy Land; see François Avril and Marie-Thérèse Gousset, with Claudia Rabel, *Manuscrits enluminés d'origine italienne, 2, XIIIe siècle* (Paris: Bibliothèque Nationale, 1984), no. 194. I thank François Avril, Marie-Thérèse Gousset, and Patricia Stirnemann for their generous assistance at the Bibliothèque Nationale.

14. Meiss (1968, p. 47) notes that the illustrative tradition begins with the MSS of Laurent de Premierfait's translation, second version, made in 1409. For the text see *Laurent de Premierfait's "Des Cas des nobles hommes et femmes,"* ed. and trans. P.M. Gathercole (Chapel Hill: University of North Carolina Press, 1968). See also note 6 above.

15. Loomis, *Arthurian Legends*. Most subsequently discovered Arthurian material illustrates scenes from Tristan or Iwain. Interesting in this connection is the description of walls painted with Arthurian subjects that surround the wounded Arthur in Guillem Torella's *La Faula*, discussed in Loomis, *Arthurian Legends*, p. 24.

16. This is not the place to launch into polemic about the lack of methodological models for the study of illustrated non-liturgical manuscripts in Latin or the vernacular. Hugo Buchthal, *Historia troiana, Studies in the History of Medieval Secular Illustration* (London: The Warburg Institute, and Leiden: E.J. Brill, 1971), and Sandra L. Hindman, *Christine de Pizan's "Epistre d'Othéa,"*

Painting and Politics at the Court of Charles VI (Toronto: Pontifical Institute of Medieval Studies, 1986), are examples of studies where the relatively small number of surviving manuscripts (less than 20), and the relatively small number of illustrations in each, makes a comparative examination or diachronic approach possible. But the more popular stories, those of Alexander, Arthur, and the *Roman de la Rose* exist in hundreds of illustrated copies, and each manuscript may contain hundreds of illustrations; for texts like these, the sheer volume of illustration has impeded thorough investigation. For Arthur see Loomis, *Arthurian Legends*; Stones 1970/71; and "single-case" studies, such as Emmanuèle Baumgartner, "La couronne et le cercle: Arthur et la Table Ronde dans les manucrits du Lancelot-Graal," in *Texte et Image, Actes du Colloque international de Chantilly, 1982* (Paris: Les Belles Lettres, 1984), pp. 191-200. For an ahistorical or synchronic treatment of some illustrations in *Roman de la Rose* manuscripts see John V. Fleming, *The Roman de la Rose, A Study in Allegory and Iconography* (Princeton: Princeton University Press, 1969). The semiotic approach is represented by Pickering and Schapiro, see note 50 below.

17. For Paris see Robert Branner, "Manuscript Makers in Mid-Thirteenth Century Paris," *Art Bulletin* 48 (1966), 65-67; Françoise Baron, "Enlumineurs, peintres et sculpteurs parisiens," in *Bulletin archéologique* n.s. IV (1968), 37-121; Robert Branner, *Manuscript Painting in Paris during the Reign of Saint Louis* (Berkeley and Los Angeles: University of California Press, 1977), pp. 1-21. In the thirteenth-century accounts of the count and countess of Flanders, there is evidence that the various skills involved in the making of books were paid for separately, perhaps with the implication that the work was done by the craftsmen at the castle, as still occurred with Jean de Berry and his illuminators, the Limburg brothers among others. Relevant documents are listed (but not transcribed) in Robert-Henri Bautier and Jacqueline Sornay, *Les sources de l'histoire économique et sociale du moyen âge*, II, *Les Etats de la maison de Bourgogne*, 1, *Archives des principautés territoriales*, ii, *Les principautés du Nord* (Paris: CNRS, 1986). For Jean de Berry's practice of retaining painters in his household as "valets de chambre" see Meiss, 1967, pp. 43-5, and 1968 and 1974 passim.

18. For a review of the situation affecting the illustration of vernacular texts in thirteenth-century France see my "Indications écrites et modèles picturaux, guides aux peintres de manuscrits enluminés aux environs de 1300," forthcoming in *Artistes, artisans et*

production artistique au moyen âge, actes du colloque international 2-6 mai, 1983, II, ed. Xavier Barral I Altet (Paris: Picard, 1988). The use of notes and sketches is not confined to vernacular or secular texts, but two situations are particularly noteworthy. 1) The use of notes and sketches as intermediaries is especially common at the beginning of an iconographical tradition. This seems to be the case with the *Roman de la Rose* Vatican Urb. lat. 376 of c.1285-1300 (see Stones, 1970/71, pp. 277, 279, 303), and the Jacobus de Voragine *Legenda Aurea* San Marino, Huntington Library H 3027 of about the same date. François Avril notes the same phenomenon much earlier in the B.N. Virgil MS of c.1200, B.N. lat. 7936; see his "Un manuscrit d'auteurs classiques et ses illustrations," in *The Year 1200, A Symposium* (New York: The Metropolitan Museum of Art, 1975), pp. 261-71. Robert Branner, *Manuscript Painting,* p. 21, n. 66) cites references to illustrated Aristotle MSS with notes and/or sketches, and Elizabeth Peterson tells me that the Aristotle MS in Erfurt can be added to his list. 2) The other situation is among manuscripts that were mass-produced, as in the Paris workshops of the early fourteenth century that made such MSS as the *Roman de la Rose* B.N. fr. 802, the Saints' Lives B.N. fr. 241 and Munich, clm 10177, and many others (see Stones 1970/71, p. 303). The *Histoire ancienne* at Princeton, MS Garrett 125, is another book with marginal notes that has gone unnoticed, and I thank Jean Preston for drawing it to my attention. For some examples of notes and sketches as intermediaries in biblical illustration see J.J.G. Alexander in Barral I Altet, cited above.

19. See Stones 1970/71 and below.
20. Frappier, p. 1.
21. Frappier, p. 251, quoted below.
22. The account given by E. Jane Burns in the entry on the Vulgate Cycle in *The Arthurian Encyclopedia,* ed. Norris J.Lacy et al., (New York: Garland, 1986), p. 613, is misleading in this respect.
23. For Ralph see Chambers, p. 268; Gransden, pp. 322-23. The chronicle covers the years 1066-1224, but the date of the compilation is uncertain, as is its attribution to a single author. For Gerald see Gransden, pp. 242-46; the discovery of Arthur's tomb is recounted in *De principis instrucione,* begun c.1193; see Chambers, p. 269. For uncertainties about the date of the excavation and the question of whether Henry II had an interest in it, see note 10 above.
24. Frappier, pp. 246-47.

25. Frappier, p. 251. The translation is drawn from *The Death of King Arthur*, trans. James Cable (Harmondsworth: Penguin, 1982), p. 225.
26. Chambers, p. 123.
27. William of Malmesbury, c.1125, provides the first written testimony that legends existed about Arthur's return; see Chambers, pp. 17, 250. Geoffrey of Monmouth perpetuates the myth, see Chambers, pp. 39, 256. Wace's version, in his *Roman de Brut*, is more explicit, relating the Breton view that Arthur will return (Chambers, p. 104). Peter Langtoft's account is similar (*The Chronicle of Pierre de Langtoft*, ed. Thomas Wright, [London: Longmans, Green, 1866–88], vol. 2, p. 224). Laȝamon's *Brut* presents an account that is also similar (Chambers, p. 106), as are the numerous other Latin accounts of the twelfth century drawn together by Chambers; see also Vincent of Beauvais' treatment of the subject mentioned in note 6 above. It would be interesting to see the extent to which the other chronicles—by Maerlant, Wauquelin, and the St. Alban's chronicler—are as explicit as Vincent of Beauvais. The *Stanzaic Morte Arthur* progresses from Sir Bedivere witnessing Arthur's departure to Aveloun with Morgan, to his discovery of his tomb "that was new dight / And covered it was with marble gray, / And with riche lettres rayled aright..." (Benson, p. 99), although the words of the inscription are not given in the text. For Arthur's burial at Glastonbury in the *Alliterative Morte Arthure* and the inscription see Benson, p. 238; for Malory see *The Works of Sir Thomas Malory*, ed. Eugène Vinaver (Oxford: Clarendon Press, 1973), III, pp. 1242 and 1655.
28. Frappier, p. viii. What is needed is a thorough paleographical analysis, demonstrating how these MSS relate to dated books; MSS that seem to be particularly early are Chantilly 476(644), Copenhagen Thott 1087, B.L. Royal 19.C.xiii, Paris, B.N. fr. 25520, and Modena E 39.
29. Do the use and placement of large minor initials at "break points" mean that placement sequences had been already thought out in the very earliest manuscripts, even though they more often than not lack historiation? Or are they simply by-products of a chapter-division invented to facilitate reading, and which are then co-opted for illustration? Often they start with the formula "Or dist li contes...," which includes the letter "O," the most convenient letter of the alphabet for inserting historiation in an initial. But they do not simply break up the texts into units of equal length; they are sometimes very closely spaced, on the same or adjacent pages. This raises the issue of the extent to which they function to

emphasize the particular episodes they introduce, rather than others.   My working chart shows that the placing of the large pen-flourished or foliate initials corresponds closely to that of the historiated initials or miniatures in manuscripts containing the short cycle of 22 miniatures. The only discussion of the question is in C.E. Pickford, *L'Evolution du roman arthurien en prose* (Paris: A.G. Nizet, 1959), pp. 154-75, where the issue is touched upon in relation to compositional procedures in B.N. fr. 112.

30.   The most detailed study is Pickford.

31.   Frappier, p. 1; Cable, p. 23.

32.   B.N. fr. 15104 has a reference to Guillaume de Flandre in the text and is thought to have been the presentation copy of Guillaume de Termonde, son of Gui de Dampierre, count of Flanders; see J.R. Smeets, *La chevalerie de Judas Machabé* (Assen: Van Gorcum, 1955).   It was illuminated by a painter from a workshop based in Hainaut or Flanders and making books for patrons associated with Cambrai, Mons, Tournai, and St. Omer (see Stones, 1970/71, ch.III, with previous literature, and my forthcoming study on this workshop).   Princeton, Garrett 125, which also contains texts by Chrétien de Troyes, was connected with the Boisrouvray Psalter (use of Amiens) by Robert L. McGrath, "A Newly Discovered Illustrated Manuscript of Chrétien de Troyes' *Yvain* and *Lancelot* in the Princeton University Library," *Speculum* 38 (1963), 583-94; also by the same painter are the Vulgate Cycle B.N. fr. 12573 and part of a psalter-hours of Amiens in the Philadelphia Free Library, Widener 9.   For the Maccabees component see Robert L. McGrath, "The Romance of the Macabees in Medieval Art and Literature" (diss. Ph.D., Princeton, 1963), and J.R. Smeets, *Le Fragment de la Chevalerie de Judas Machabé de Gautier de Belleperche contenu dans le ms. Garrett 125 de la Princeton University Library* (Leiden: The Hakuchi Press, 1985).

33.   McGrath, "The Romance," pp. 266-67.

34.   It was probably made in Northern France or Flanders rather than England, although for and English patron, as the arms of England are used for Arthur, on which see below.   Avril and Stirnemann did not include it among the English MSS in Paris, see François Avril and Patricia Danz Stirnemann, *Manuscrits enluminés d'origine insulaire, VIIe-XXe siècle* (Paris: Bibliothèque Nationale, 1987. Woledge ascribes it to the thirteenth century. See note 28 above, where I recognize the need for more work on the "early" MSS.

35.   See Jaroslav Folda, *Crusader Manuscript Illumination at Saint-Jean d'Acre, 1275-1291* (Princeton: Princeton University Press, 1976); for

the *censier* see figs. 33-36. The workshop also illustrated the Vulgate Cycle MSS Tours 951 (in collaboration with an Italian painter, Folda pp. 122-23). It contains *Estoire, Merlin,* and the catchword for *Lancelot,* and is illustrated with historiated initials. I attribute the *Lancelot* Vatican Reg.lat. 1489 to this workshop, as well as the *Queste* and *Mort Artu* B.N. fr. 12580 (Stones, 1970/71, ch.II). The three are similar in dimensions and page layout and might possibly have constituted parts of the same set, were it not for the fact that the Vatican and B.N. MSS each contain two miniatures only, while the Tours MS has a cycle of historiated initials, in which the Italian painter also participated.

36.   Paris, B.N. fr. 9084, fols. 197, 290v, 249v, and Florence, Laur. Plut. LXI.10, fols. 126v, 246 (Folda, figs. 109, 114, 136, 151, 160).

37.   For an account of French royal funeral practices and tombs to the end of the thirteenth century see Alain Erlande-Brandenburg, *Le Roi est mort: Etude sur les funérailles, le sépulture et les tombeaux des rois de France jusqu'à la fin du XIIIe siècle,* Bibliothèque de la société française d'archéologie 7 (Geneva, 1975), and, for the later period, Elizabeth A.R. Brown, "The Ceremonial of Royal Succession in Capetian France, The Funeral of Philip V," *Speculum* 55 (1980), 266-93. For England see Lawrence Stone, *Sculpture in Britain in the Middle Ages* (Harmondsworth: Penguin,

38.   See Loomis, *Arthurian Legends,* figs. 248, 250, 252, 274, for other representations of tombs in Vulgate Cycle MSS. The famous example with the date of 1316, showing tombs commissioned by Duchess Flegetine, in Add. 10292, fol. 55v (Loomis, Fig. 248), is exceptional in showing both an engraved image and an inscription; the same episode is shown in Royal 14.E.iii, but without the date, and the scene is omitted in the third MS illustrated by the same painter, Amsterdam/Rylands Fr.1/Douce 215. See Alison Stones, "Another Short Note on Rylands French 1," in Neil Stratford, ed., *Romanesque and Gothic: Essays for George Zarnecki* (Bury St. Edmunds: Boydell and Brewer, 1987), p. 188, n. 15. In the thirteenth and early fourteenth century, tombs in Vulgate Cycle MSS tend to be shown as if made of plain marble, shaped like coffins, and unadorned either with inscriptions or images. Paul Binski has suggested to me the interesting idea that these unadorned tombs might have provided the model for Edward I's plain marble tomb, which would be an interesting corollary to these examples where it is life that influences art. At the same time it is worth noting that Edward had Arthur's tomb opened in 1278 and the remains of Arthur and Guenevere moved before the high altar of Glastonbury.

(Chambers, p. 125.) They seemed to have been reburied in the same tomb (made c. 1189) which Leland saw in 1534 and 1539, and described as being of black marble, with two lions at each end and an image of the king at the foot; it also had epitaphs with the name of Abbot Henry (1189–1193); Chambers, p. 125.

39. Chambers, p. 269, and above.
40. The evidence for connecting Arthurian MSS with the patronage of the French royal family is entirely circumstantial. It is possible that Rennes 255 was a royal commission, but only because it comes from the same workshop as devotional books that clearly were (Stones, 1977). More is known about the vernacular books owned by the counts of Flanders and Hainaut, although it is hard to match up the surviving books with the documents. For collectors of later Arthurian MSS see Pickford, pp. 252-90. Another book that is probably of Parisian manufacture (although it has no demonstrably royal connection) is Oxford, Rawl. D. 899 (Fig. 1]. It is included as French in Otto Pächt and J.J.G. Alexander, *Illuminated Manuscripts in the Bodleian Library, Oxford*, 1: *German, Dutch, Flemish, French and Spanish Schools*, (Oxford: Clarendon Press, 1966), no. 559, and dated s.xiii ex.   A mid-thirteenth century date may be more likely
41. See, most recently, the catalogue *The Age of Chivalry, Art in Plantagenet England, 1200-1400*, eds. Jonathan Alexander and Paul Binski (London: Weidenfeld and Nicholson, 1987).
42. For texts that include the arms of England, particularly as borne by Tristan, as flattery, see Gerald R. Brault, *Early Blazon* (Oxford: Clarendon Press, 1972), pp. 19-23. The only illustrated *Mort Artu* MSS that were made in England are B.N. fr. 123, made in all probability for Blanche of Artois and Edmund Crouchback, Earl of Lancaster, whose marriage took place in 1275 and whose arms appear in the backgrounds of the initials; (see Avril and Stirnemann, no. 152); and B.L. Royal 20.C.vi, attributed to a London workshop c.1280 by Adelaide Bennett, "A Late Thirteenth-Century Psalter-Hours from London," in *England in the Thirteenth Century, Proceedings of the 1984 Harlaxton Symposium* (Grantham: Harlaxton, 1985), pp. 15-30, esp. p. 26. I am grateful to Adelaide Bennett for helpful discussion of the English MSS.
43. For references see Alison Stones, "Four Illustrated *Jacobus* Manuscripts," in *The Vanishing Past, Studies of Medieval Art, Liturgy, and Metrology presented to Christopher Hohler*, eds. Alan Borg and Andrew Martindale, B.A.R. International Series 111 (Oxford, 1981), p. 207, n. 14.

44. B.L. Royal 20.A.ii, fol. 3v (Loomis, *Arthurian Legends*, Fig. 386); see note 6 above.
45. For B.N. fr. 770 and Oxford, Bod. Digby 223 see Stones 1970/71, pp. 340-42, and Brault, p. 44 for B.N. fr. 770. Jean-Bernard de Vaivre wonders whether the crowns in B.N. fr. 770 might not be later additions, but the existence of another book from the same workshop with the same feature suggests that they are indeed contemporary, and of interest in Arras or Douai, where the books were probably made. See Jean-Bernard de Vaivre, "Les trois couronnes des hérauts," in *Archives héraldiques suisses* 86 (1972), 30-35, esp. n. 26. For later Arthurian heraldry in the Rolls of Arms see Michel Pastoureau, *Armorial des chevaliers de la table ronde* (Paris: Le Léopard d'or, 1983). For the workshop of Add. 10292-4, Royal 14.E.iii, Amsterdam/Rylands/Douce and The Hague KA XX, see Stones 1987, with previous bibliography, and note 6 above.
46. For B.N. fr. 112 see note 58 below; B.N. fr. 111 is unpublished apart from its mention in Paulin Paris, *Les Manuscrits françois de la bibliothèque du roi*, 7 vols. (Paris: Techener, 1836-48), I, p. 151; Woledge, p. 74; and Micha (1960), pp. 150-51. It contains a substantial cycle of miniatures and a shield of ownership that is so far unidentified.
47. See note 9 above.
48. See note 14 above. Arthur and his knights at the Round Table is the subject in the Laurent de Premierfait MS, B.L. Add. 35321, reproduced in Gardner, facing p. 234. How Arthur is otherwise treated in the illustrations of Laurent's *Trésor des histoires* and similar texts would be a fruitful topic for further investigation. Mary Robertson kindly informs me that Arthur does not appear in the Huntington MS of Lydgate's *Fall of Princes*, HM 268.
49. See Appendix 3. For a description of the Yale MS and list of subjects, see Barbara A. Shailor, *Catalogue of Medieval and Renaissance Manuscripts in the Beinecke Rare Book and Manuscript Library, Yale University*, I: *MSS 1-250*, (Binghamton, N.Y.: Medieval and Renaissance Texts and Studies, 1984), no. 229.
50. Reproduced in Loomis, *Arthurian Legends*, Fig. 249. The visual topos is more akin to Pickering's David/Walter von der Vogelweide lamenting figure than to Christ weeping over Jerusalem (Luke 19:41-44), which would involve a standing figure but which must be the model for the literary topos. For the question of the extent to which transference of visual motif also implies transference of meaning see F.P. Pickering, *Literatur und darstellende Kunst im Mittelalter* (Berlin: Erich Schmidt, 1966),

English trans. by the author, 1970; and Meyer Schapiro, *Words and Pictures: On the Literal and the Symbolic in the Illustration of a Text* (The Hague: Mouton, 1973). These works also informed my discussion of Arthur's tomb, above. For further examples of the transfer of imagery from sacred to profane contexts and vice-versa see my "Sacred and Profane Art: Secular and Liturgical Book-Illumination in the Thirteenth Century" in *The Epic in Medieval Society: Aesthetic and Moral Values*, ed. Harald Scholler (Tübingen: Max Niemeyer, 1977), pp. 100-12. For the textual sources of the sword motif see Joël H. Grisward, "Le Motif de l'épée jetée au lac: la mort d'Arthur et la mort de Batradz," in *Romania* 90 (1969), 289-340, 473-514.

51. The currently accepted view is based on L.Stijns, "Het Psalter van Gwijde van Dampierre," in *De Vlaamse Gids* (1953), 85-94, who dates the book between 1266 and 1275; these dates are actually quite reasonable, particularly c.1275, although the condition of the shields presents insoluble problems. There is still a great deal to do to sort out stylistically the products of the shop that made B.N. fr. 95/Yale 229 and B.R. 10607.

52. Alison Stones, "Secular Manuscript Illumination in France," in *Medieval Manuscripts and Textual Criticism*, ed. Christopher Kleinhenz (Chapel Hill: University of North Carolina Press, 1976), pp. 83-102, esp. p. 87. I do say there that the owner "may perhaps be traced"—not to disclaim the tentative nature of the suggestion! Guillaume de Termonde is otherwise known as the patron of Pierre du Riés' *Judas Machabé*; see Smeets, *La Chevalerie*, and above for the tomb of Judas Maccabeus.

53. The basic reference books are by Victor Leroquais: *Les Bréviaires manuscrits des bibliothèques publiques de France* (Paris: Protat, 1934); *Les Livres d'heures manuscrits de la Bibliothèque nationale* (Paris: Protat, 1927); *Les Pontificaux manuscrits des bibliothèques publiques de France* (Paris: Protat, 1937); *Les Psautiers manuscrits des bibliothèqes publiques de France* (Paris: Protat, 1940-41); *Les Sacramentaires et les missels manuscrits des bibliothèques publiques de France* (Paris: Protat, 1924). What is not clear is the extent to which the canonization of St. Louis was observed among lay circles in the provinces, particularly in Artois, Flanders, and Hainaut, and how quickly it entered books made for private devotion in that region.

54. Loomis, *Arthurian Legends*, pp. 97-98. For the workshop see Stones, 1970/71, ch.VI, and 1987.

55. *The Vulgate Version of the Arthurian Romances, edited from Manuscripts in the British Museum,* ed. H. Oskar Sommer, 8 vols. (Washington, D.C.: The Carnegie Institution, 1908-16). Reproduced in Loomis, *Arthurian Legends,* Fig. 248.

56. Reproduced in Leroquais, 1940-41, p. 203, pl. 111, and Stones, 1987.

57. See note 6 above.

58. Paulin Paris, I, p. 151, was the first to observe that the inscription which now reads "Micheau Gantelet, prêtre, Tournai" contains two alterations, "Gantelet" and "Tournai"; for the identification of Gonnot's hand in other manuscripts see Pickford, pp. 19-24.

59. Pickford, pp. 19-24.

60. Pickford, with extensive bibliography; see particularly A. Thomas, "Jacques d'Armagnac, Bibliophile: notes et documents complémentaires," in *Journal des Savants* (1906), 633-44.

61. See Appendix 3.

62. See note 6 above.

63. See A. de la Grange, "Choix de testaments tournaisiens," in *Annales de la société historique de Tournai* 2 (1897) 38, cited in Stones, 1987, pp. 190, 192.

64. For Arthur's ownership of Hainaut see Loomis, *Arthurian Legends,* p. 126.

65. Gardner, p. 153, gives its text as a variant, deriving from the same source as the *Tavola Ritonda.* For reproductions see the pages facing pp. 26, 112, 122, 174, 178, 180, 190, 208, 268, 272, 286; Loomis, *Arthurian Legends,* p. 121, figs. 337-39.

66. François Avril, "Un atelier 'picard' à la Cour des Angevins de Naples," in *"Nobile claret opus," Festgabe für Frau Prof. Dr. Ellen Judith Beer zum 60. Geburtstag, Zeitschrift für Schweizerische Archäologie und Kunstgeschichte* 43 (1986) 76-85. A Brunetto Latini *Trésor* from the workshop of Add. 10292-4 and its group that was written before 1327 when it was already in the possession of Henry of Ventimiglia, is Vatican Reg. lat. 1320, on which see Stones, 1987, p. 189.

67. Gardner, facing p. 268.

APPENDICES:
AN ICONOGRAPHIC SURVEY OF
MANUSCRIPTS ILLUSTRATING
ARTHUR'S DEATH

Appendix 1: Working List of Mort Artu MSS

Based on Frappier (1964), Micha (1958, 1960, 1964), Woledge (reprinted 1975; Supplément, 1975), Stones (1970/71, 1977, 1987), Ponceau (1983, rev. 1986), and updated where possible (see note 12 above). There are 52 surviving MSS, of which 18 are unillustrated (this total includes 3 MSS on which I lack information (Geissen, Geneva 105, Mulhouse) and 1 whose opening page is missing (Lyon) and which may have been illustrated originally), which leaves 34 with one or more illustrations: 9 with a single illustration and 25 with a cycle of pictures. I include the entire list here although not all the MSS illustrate Arthur's death. Also included are textual contents and approximate date and provenance if known or attributable; MSS on the list are illustrated unless otherwise stated; they are listed in alphabetical order of place of preservation, with special versions of the text at the end.

Amsterdam, Bibl. Hermetica (ex Phillipps 1045/7 [erased] and 3630 i and ii)/Oxford, Bod. Douce 215/Manchester, The John Rylands University Library, French 1, Complete Vulgate Cycle, c.1315-25, northern Artois (St.Omer or Thérouanne) or western Flanders (Ghent)

Berkeley, University of California, UCB 73 (ex Phillipps 4377; Sotheby's 30.xi.65, lot 12), Queste, Mort Artu, mid 13th c., France or Flanders, one historiated initial for the opening of Queste; Mort Artu has pen-flourished initials only

Bonn, University Library 526, Complete Vulgate Cycle, written in Amiens in 1286, school of Thérouanne or Cambrai

Brussels, B.R. 9627-8, Queste, Mort Artu, c. 1260-70, Paris (?)

Chantilly, Musée Condé 476(644), Estoire, Queste, Mort Artu, second quarter 13th c., France, pen-flourished initials only

Chantilly, Musée Condé 649(1111), *Mort Artu*, c. 1288, Italy, Genoa or Modena

Copenhagen, Thott 1087, *Mort Artu*, second quarter 13th c.?, France, pen-flourished initials only

Geneva, Bodmer 105 (ex coll. Dr. Lucien Graux), *Lancelot, Queste, Mort Artu*, 15th c., France, illustrations in *Lancelot*; *Queste* and *Mort Artu* unillustrated?

Geneva, Bodmer 147 (ex Phillipps 1046, Sotheby's 1.vii.46, lot 8), *Estoire, Merlin, Queste, Mort Artu*, c.1300, eastern or southern France?

Giessen, Univ. 93, 94, fragments of *Lancelot, Queste, Mort Artu*, 15th c., France? unillustrated?

London, B.L. Royal 14 E.iii, *Estoire, Queste, Mort Artu*, c.1315-25, northern Artois or western Flanders

London, B.L. Royal 19 C.xiii, *Lancelot, Queste, Mort Artu*, France or Flanders, second quarter 13th c., one historiated initial for the opening of *Lancelot*; *Queste* and *Mort Artu* unillustrated

London, B.L. Royal 20 C.vi, *Agravain, Queste, Mort Artu*, c.1270-80, England, one miniature for the opening of each branch

London, B.L. Add. 10292-4, Complete Vulgate Cycle, in or after 1316, northern Artois or western Flanders

London, B.L. Add. 17443, *Queste, Mort Artu*, third quarter 13th c., northern France or Flanders, one miniature for the opening of each branch

Lyon, Pal. des Arts 77, *Agravain, Queste, Mort Artu*, third quarter 13th c., northern France or Flanders, miniature at the beginning of *Queste* cut out, opening of *Mort Artu* missing; pen-flourished initials

Mulhouse, Dr. Longuet Library, 2 ff. of *Mort Artu*, France? unillustrated?

New York, Columbia University Library, Western MSS 24 (ex H.L. Goodhart; ex R.S. Loomis), *Mort Artu*, 14th c., France, unillustrated

New York, Morgan M 807, *Agravain, Mort Artu*, (ex Yates Thompson LXXXVIII; ex Cortland Bishop 22) mid-15th c., France, one miniature in *Agravain*; *Mort Artu* unillustrated

Oxford, Bod. Digby 223, *Agravain, Queste, Mort Artu*, c.1280-1300 Arras or Douai

Oxford, Bod. Douce 189, *Mort Artu, Tristan,* late 13th c., Northern Italy, foliate and pen-flourished initials only

Oxford, Bod. Rawl. D.874, *Queste, Mort Artu,* late 14th c., Northern Italy, foliate and pen-flourished initials only

Oxford, Bod. Rawl. D.899, *Agravain, Queste, Mort Artu,* c. 1250, Paris(?), one miniature and one historiated initial at opening of *Mort Artu*

Oxford, Bod. Rawl. Q.b.6, *Lancelot, Queste, Mort Artu,* Paris(?), c. 1300-1310

Paris, Ars. 3347, *Lancelot, Queste, Mort Artu,* mid 13th c., Paris, one miniature for the opening of each branch

Paris, Ars. 3479-80, Complete Vulgate Cycle, c.1405, Paris, Master of Berry's *Cleres Femmes* and Master of the *Cité des Dames*

Paris, Ars. 3482, *Merlin, Agravain* (incomplete), *Queste, Mort Artu,* second quarter 14th c., Paris

Paris, B.N. fr. 95/New Haven, Yale University 229 (ex Phillipps 130, Sotheby's 1.vii.46, lot 6), Complete Vulgate Cycle (also includes *Sept Sages* and *Penitence Adam*), c.1290-1300, St.Omer or Thérouanne

Paris, B.N. fr. 98, Complete Vulgate Cycle, 15th c., Paris(?), three painted borders with shields, for the openings of *Estoire, Merlin, Lancelot; Queste* and *Mort Artu* have pen-flourished initials only

Paris, B.N. fr. 110, Complete Vulgate Cycle, c.1290-1300, Thérouanne or Cambrai

Paris, B.N. fr. 111, *Lancelot, Queste, Mort Artu,* mid 15th c., Paris(?)

Paris, B.N. fr. 113-6, Complete Vulgate Cycle, c.1470, made for Jacques d'Armagnac, central France

Paris, B.N. fr. 117-20, Complete Vulgate Cycle, c.1405, purchased by Jean de Berry in 1405, repainted c.1470 for Jacques d'Armagnac

Paris, B.N. fr. 122, *Lancelot (Charrete), Queste, Mort Artu,* 1344, Tournai, workshop of Pierart dou Thielt (cf. Paris, Ars. 5218, *Queste,* written, illuminated and bound in 1351 by Pierart dou Thielt)

Paris, B.N. fr. 123, *Lancelot (Charrete), Queste, Mort Artu,* c. 1275-80, England

Paris, B.N. fr. 339, *Lancelot* (incomplete), *Queste, Mort Artu*, c. 1250, Paris(?)

Paris, B.N. fr. 342, *Agravain, Queste, Mort Artu*, written in 1274, Arras or Douai

Paris, B.N. fr. 344, Complete Vulgate Cycle, c.1290-1310, Metz

Paris, B.N. fr. 751, *Lancelot* (incomplete), *Queste, Mort Artu*, mid 13th c.(?), northern France or Flanders, one miniature, at the opening of *Lancelot; Queste* and *Mort Artu* have only pen-flourished initials

Paris, B.N. fr. 1422-4, *Agravain, Queste, Mort Artu*, c. 1330-40, Flanders, Tournai

Paris, B.N. fr. 12573, *Agravain, Queste, Mort Artu*, c. 1280-1300, Arras or Amiens

Paris, B.N. fr. 12580, *Agravain, Queste, Mort Artu*, c. 1280, Paris, one miniature for the opening of each branch

Paris, B.N. fr. 24367, *Mort Artu*, mid 13th c., France or Flanders, unillustrated

Paris, B.N. fr. 25520, *Queste, Mort Artu*, second quarter 13th c., France or Flanders, one miniature at the opening of *Mort Artu*

Paris, B.N. n.a. fr. 1119, *Agravain, Queste, Mort Artu*, c. 1275-80, Paris, one rubbed miniature at the openings of *Agravain, Queste* and *Mort Artu*

Paris, B.N. n.a. fr. 4380, *Mort Artu*, mid 13th c., France or Flanders, unillustrated

Vatican, Vat. Pal. lat. 1967, *Mort Artu*, c.1275-80, Paris(?), one miniature for the opening of *Mort Artu*

Special versions:

Modena, B. Estense E 39, *Josephe-Merlin-Perceval-Mort Artu* cycle, second quarter 13th c., France(?)

Paris, B.N. fr. 343, Pseudo-Robert de Boron, abridged *Queste, Tristan, Mort Artu*, c.1385-90, Italy, Milan or Pavia, one illustration in *Mort Artu*

Paris, B.N. fr. 758, abridged *Tristan, Queste, Mort Artu*, c. 1300, Arras, one miniature at the opening of *Tristan; Queste* and *Mort Artu* have pen-flourished initials only

Paris, B.N. n.a. fr. 4166 (Didot MS), 1301, France or Flanders, same text as Modena E 39, unillustrated

Paris, B.N. fr. 112, 1470, commissioned by Jacques d'Armagnac, written by Micheau Gonnot, Central France

Appendix 2: *chronological list of* Mort Artu *MSS, with density of illustration* (Mort Artu *only), including the variant versions*

before 1250

Copenhagen, Thott 1087	France	0 illustration
B.L.Roy.19.C.xiii	France or Flanders	0 illustration
Chantilly 476(644)	France	0 illustration
Modena E 39	France or Flanders	2 historiated initials
B.N. fr. 25520	France or Flanders	1 miniature (2 columns)

c.1250

Oxford, Bod.Rawl.D.899	Paris ?	1 miniature (1 column), 1 historiated initial
Berkeley UCB 73	France or Flanders	0 illustration
B.N.fr.751	France or Flanders	0 illustration
B.N.fr.24367	France or Flanders	0 illustration
B.N.n.a.fr.4380	France or Flanders	0 illustration
Ars.3347	Paris	1 miniature (1 column)

c.1250-60

B.N.fr.339	Paris ?	16 historiated initials (some textual lacunae ?)

c.1260-70

B.R.9627-8	Paris ?	22 historiated initials

1274

B.N.fr.342	Arras or Douai	33 miniatures (2 or 1 column)
c.1270-80		
B.L.Roy.20.C.vi	England	1 miniature (1 column)
c.1275-80		
B.N.fr.12580	Paris	1 miniature (1 column)
B.N.n.a.fr.1119	Paris	1 miniature (1 column)
Vat.Pal.lat.1967	Paris	1 miniature (1 column)
B.N.fr.123	England	17 historiated initials
c.1275-1300		
Lyon 77	France or Flanders	0 illustration (textual lacunae)
Oxford, Bod.Douce 189	Northern Italy	0 illustrations
B.L.Add.17443	France or Flanders	1 miniature (1 column)
c.1280-1300		
Oxford, Bod.Digby 223	Arras or Douai	4 miniatures (1 column)
B.N.fr.12573	Arras or Amiens	28 miniatures (1 column)
1286		
Bonn 526	Amiens/Thérouanne/Cambrai	23 miniatures (1 column)
1288		
Chantilly 649(1111)	Italy, Genoa or Modena	5 historiated initials

c.1290-1300

B.N.fr.110	Thérouanne or Cambrai	4 miniatures (1 column) (many textual lacunae)
B.N.fr.95/Yale 229	St.Omer or Thérouanne	43 miniatures (1 column, often in 2 registers, or half a column) and historiated initials

c.1290-1310

B.N.fr.344	Metz	19 miniatures (clustered in 2 columns) and historiated initials

c.1300

B.N.fr.758	Arras	0 illustrations
Geneva, Bodmer 147	Eastern or Southern France ?	22 miniatures (1 column, some in 2 registers, or half a column) and historiated initials

1301

B.N.n.a.fr.4166	France or Flanders	0 illustration

c.1300-1310

Oxford, Bod.Rawl.Q.b.6	Paris ?	22 historiated initials

c.1316
B.L.Add.10292-4   St.Omer or Thérouanne   47 miniatures
                                                (1 column)
c.1315-25
B.L.Roy.14.E.iii   St.Omer or Thérouanne   22 miniatures
                                                (1 column)
                                                (many textual
                                                lacunae)
Amsterdam/Ryl./Douce 215   St-Omer or Thérouanne
                                                17 miniatures
                                                (1 column)
                                                (some textual
                                                lacunae)

c.1325-40
Ars.3482   Paris   22 miniatures
                                                (1 column)

c.1330-40
B.N.fr.1422-4   Tournai   22 historiated
                                                initials

1344
B.N.fr.122   Tournai   22 miniatures
                                                (1 or 2 columns)

c.1350
New York, Columbia 24 France   0 illustration

c.1375-1400
Oxford, Bod.Rawl.D.874 Northern Italy   0 illustration

c.1385-90
B.N.fr.343   Italy, Milan or Pavia   1 miniature (1
                                                column)

c.1405
Ars.3479-80   Paris   2 miniatures (1
                                                column)

c.1405/c.1470
B.N.fr.117-20	Paris/Central France	2 miniatures (1 column)

c.1450
New York M 807	Paris ?	0 illustration
B.N.fr.98	Paris ?	0 illustration
B.N.fr.111	Paris ?	28 miniatures (1 column)

c.1470
B.N.fr.113-6	Central France	24 miniatures (1 column)

1470
B.N.fr.112	Central France	31 miniatures (1 column)

15th c.
Geneva, Bodmer 105	France	0 illustration ?
Giessen Univ.93, 94	France ?	0 illustration ?

?
Mulhouse	France ?	0 illustration ?

Appendix 3: Arthur's Death and Departure

MSS are grouped according to their textual contents, and within texts in approximate chronological order of production.

Arthur's dream of Gauvain's warning that he will die if he fights Mordret
Mort Artu (Frappier p.225)

Oxford, Bod. Rawl. D. 899, c. 1250, Paris ?
fol. 206 two-register miniature in one text column (Fig. 1)
Top right: Gauvain appears to Arthur who lies in bed (cf. also Arthur's final battle with Mordret).

Yale 229, c. 1290-1300, St.Omer or Thérouanne
fol. 350 two-register miniature in one text column
Arthur sets out through a forest to fight Mordret; Arthur, in bed
in a tent sees Gauvain and a group of paupers in a dream

Ryl. fr. 1, c. 1315-25, St.Omer or Thérouanne
fol. 255 one-column miniature
Arthur, in bed in a forest, sees Gauvain and a group of paupers in a
dream

B.N. fr. 1424, c. 1330-40, Tournai
fol. 117v initial "O"
Arthur, in bed, sees Gauvain and the paupers in a dream

Ars. 3482, c. 1325-50, Paris
fol. 638v one-column miniature (Fig. 6)
Arthur and his men ride through a forest (to fight Mordret);
Arthur, in bed, sees Gauvain in a dream

B.N. fr. 111, c. 1450, Paris?
fol. 294v one-column miniature
Arthur in bed, guarded by a group of knights

B.N. fr.116, c. 1470, Central France
fol. 734 one-column miniature
Arthur in a tent, asleep in bed

Arthur's final battle with Mordret
Mort Artu (Frappier pp.231-245)

Paris, B.N. fr. 25520, second quarter 13th c.? France or Flanders
fol. 91 miniature in 2 text columns (very badly rubbed) (Fig. 3)
Left: mounted combat between 2 knights, left one with a shield *gu*
three lions passant guardant or and a helmet with a crest *a*
lion passant guardant, the right one with a rubbed shield
and a helmet with a crest of 2 wings. (cf. also Arthur's
death.)

Oxford, Bod. Rawl. D. 899, c. 1250, Paris?
fol. 206 two-register miniature in one text column (Fig. 1)
Lower register: Arthur about to enter the final combat? (cf.
   Oxford, Rawl. Q.b.6, fol. 399v).

Brussels, B.R. 9627-8, c. 1260-70? Paris?
fol. 143 initial "O"
Arthur, surrounded by dead bodies, kills Mordret

Paris, B.N. fr. 123, c. 1275-80, England
fol. 257v initial "O"
Final battle between Arthur and Mordret

Chantilly, Musée Condé 649 (1111), written in 1288, Italy, Genoa
   or Modena
fol. 1 initial "A" and border (very badly rubbed)
Initial shows an equestrian knight (Boort?); border includes
   foliage scrollwork forming two medallions containing two
   mounted knights confronting each other (Arthur and
   Mordret?)

Bonn 526, written in 1286 in Amiens, illumination by the school of
   Thérouanne or Cambrai
fol. 482v one-column miniature
combat between Arthur and Mordret

Yale 229, c. 1290-1300, St.Omer or Thérouanne
fols. 356, 356v, 357, 357v four miniatures, two in one text column,
   two in half a text column (Fig. 8)
Final combat between Arthur and Mordret and their armies

London, B.L. Add. 10294, c. 1316, St.Omer or Thérouanne
fol. 93 one-column miniature
Arthur and Mordret mortally wound each other

Geneva, Bodmer 147, c. 1300, Eastern or Southern France?
fol. 344 bottom part of opening miniature in one column (Fig. 9)
Generalized battle scene: final battle between Arthur and
   Mordret?

fol. 381 one-column miniature
Two groups of mounted knights face each other (including Arthur
   and Mordret?)

Paris, B.N. fr. 344, c. 1290-1300, Metz
fol. 544 a four-part miniature (Fig. 7) showing four different
   scenes of combat, in which the only distinguishable event is
   the death of King Yon, whose severed head is shown in the
   bottom right miniature. Possibly part of this may be
   intended to show the combat between Arthur and Mordret.

Oxford, Bod. Rawl. Q.b.6, c. 1300-1310, Paris?
fol. 399v Arthur leads his men on horseback into combat with
   Mordret, Mordret not shown, (cf. Rawl. D.899, fol. 260 and
   Yale 229, fol. 350)

Paris, B.N. fr. 111, mid 15th c. Paris?
fol. 296 one-column miniature
Arthur and his men in mounted combat against Mordret and his
   men.

Mort Artu in B.N. fr. 112 special version, 1470, made for Jacques
   d'Armagnac, Central France
fol. 226 one-column miniature
Mounted combat between Arthur and Mordret and their men
fol. 228v one-column miniature
Mounted combat in which Arthur spears Mordret with his lance

Mort Artu in the Pseudo-Robert de Boron version
Paris, B.N. fr. 343, c. 1385-90, Italy, Milan or Pavia
The only illustration in the *Mort Artu* section is a generalized
   scene of combat in which Arthur is in no way distinguished

Wace, *Le Roman de Brut* (abridged version, with an addition up
   to the beginning of the Hundred Years' War in 1338, text in
   Anglo-Norman)

London, B.L. Egerton 3028, second quarter or mid 14th c. (after
    1338), made in England
fol. 53 miniature in one text column
Arthur's final battle with Mordred

Chronicles
Jacob van Maerlant, *Spiegel historiael*, The Hague, K.B. K.A.
    XX, c. 1325-30, text in Dutch, made in Flanders: Ghent?
fol. 163v: miniature across three text columns
Arthur's final battle with Mordret: surrounded by mounted
    knights, Arthur (left) strikes Mordret (right) square down
    the spine with his sword; Mordret's sword strikes Arthur
    between his shield (*or 3 crowns sa*) and right arm; to the
    right Arthur, still crowned but lying beneath his shield, is
    borne away in a horse-drawn cart, followed by his men.

St. Albans Chronicle, London, Lambeth Palace Library 6, c. 1470,
text in English, illuminated by a Fleming
fol. 66v miniature in one text column
Arthur's final battle with Mordred: in front of a hillock, with
    their men grouped on either side, Arthur and Mordred in
    mounted combat confront each other with couched lances.

Boccaccio, *De casibus virorum illustrium*, French translation by
    Laurent de Premierfait, *Le cas des nobles hommes et femmes*
London, B.L. Royal 14.E.V, mid-fifteenth century, Paris?
Arthur and Mordret in single foot combat (Gardner frontispiece)

Trésor des histoires
Paris, Ars. 5077, c. 1415, style of the Boucicaut Master
fol. 298 Arthur (shield *az 3 crowns or*) and Mordret in single foot
    combat

Girflet throwing Excalibur back to the lake
Mort Artu (Frappier p.249)

Yale 229, c. 1290-1300, St.Omer or Thérouanne
fol. 359 two-register miniature in one text column (Fig. 10)

Arthur with Lucan le Bouteillier and Girflet in the Noire
Chapele (Frappier p. 246); Girflet throws Excalibur into the
lake where it is received by an outstretched hand

London, B.L. Add. 10294, c. 1316, St.Omer or Thérouanne
fol. 94 one-column miniature (Fig. 12)
Arthur deep in thought, seated, head on hand, while Girflet
throws Excalibur into the lake where it is received by an
outstretched hand.

Mort Artu special version B.N. fr. 112, 1470, made for Jacques
d'Armagnac, Central France
fol. 229v Girflet, standing at the edge of the lake, holds
Excalibur; a distant city (Salesbieres?) in the background.

Arthur sailing away to Avalon
Mort Artu (Frappier p.250)

Yale 229, c. 1290-1300, St.Omer or Thérouanne
fol. 359v one-column miniature (Fig. 11)
Morgan and her ladies in a boat invite Arthur on board

Mort Artu in the Italian adaptation based on *Tavola Ritonda*
Florence, B. Naz. Cod. Pal. 556, written in 1446, Italy, Venice?
Arthur setting sail in a boat, watched from the shore by Girflet
on horseback, with Sir Ivain lying dead on the ground beside
him (Gardner facing p. 272)

Arthur's Death
Mort Artu (Frappier pp.1, 251)

Paris, B.N. fr. 12580, c. 1275-80 Paris, Workshop of Folda's
Hospitaller Master
fol. 223v miniature in one text column (Fig. 2)
Crowned effigy of King Arthur on his death bed/tomb, with cross,
candles, and singing clerics.

Paris, B.N. fr. 25520, second quarter 13th c.? France or Flanders
fol. 91 miniature in 2 text columns (very badly rubbed) (Fig. 3)

Right: King Arthur, crowned, on his death bed, three candles in front, two figures standing behind, flanked by a candle and a cross.

MSS containing one or more images, with none of these scenes illustrated

Modena, B. Estense E 39, second quarter 13th c., France?

Paris, Ars. 3347, c. 1250, Paris

Paris, B.N. n.a. fr. 1119, c. 1275-80, Paris, Workshop of the Hospitaller Master

Paris, B.N. fr. 339, c. 1260-70? Paris?

Paris, B.N. fr. 342, written in 1274, Arras or Douai

London, B.L. Royal 20.C.vi, c. 1270-80, England

London, B.L. Add. 17443, c. 1275-1300 France or Flanders

Oxford, Bod. Digby 223, last quarter 13th c., Arras or Douai

Paris, B.N. fr. 12573, c. 1290-1300, Arras or Amiens

Paris, B.N. fr. 110, c. 1290-1300, Thérouanne or Cambrai, text of Arthur and Mordret's battle is missing; none of the other scenes above is illustrated

London, B.L. Royal 14.E.iii, St.Omer or Thérouanne, c. 1315-25, textual lacunae

Paris, B.N. fr. 122, 1344, Tournai

Paris, Ars. 3480, c. 1405, Meiss' Master of the Cité des Dames

Paris, B.N. fr. 120, c. 1410, repainted c. 1470 central France

[a]pres ce que meistre gautier
map ot traitie des auentures
del graal ainsi soustеanment
si com il samblort si fu auis
a roi henri son signor que
ce quil auott fatt ne deuott
pas consire. Se il ne racontoit
la fin de cels dont il auoit fait mention qment il
moururent dequil auoit les prouesses ramente
ues en son liure. Et pour ce qmenca il ceste derrie
ne partie. Et quant il lot mise ensamble il lapela
la mort le roi artul por ce que uers la fin est escrit
qment le rois artul fu naurez en la bataille de ca
lebieres et comment il separti de girflet qui tant

Fig. 4.1.   Oxford, Bodleian Library, Rawlinson D.899, fol. 206.
photo: Bodleian Library, reproduced by permission

ce tonces aueoir · Quant ilor aconte le
trespassemant de Galaad · et lamoer depec-
ceual · sienfuirent mout dolant acoer · mee
tontes uoies ce nre comforterent aumelz
qnil porent · Lors fist mettre iwif ar˚
enetant tontes les auentures du saint
Graal · que licompaignon delaqueste uoi
ent racontees enclaconrt · et quant ilor
ce fer · sidist · biauf seingneurs grandes
auentnos quans de noz compaignons uos
anons perdu enceste queste · et il wardee
maintenant · sitrouerent qnil leur enfail
loit · xxvii · parcontre · et de tou ceuf ni a
noit il · i · ceul qui ne fust morz pararmes
Lwis Artus auoit oi conforter que mil
res Gaui. enduoit ocis plusenrs · sietiss-
uenut deuant lin et lidist · Gami · ie uof re
quier sur le coremant que uof me feistes
quant ie uof fis chenalier premieremant
que uof me diez ce que ie uof demandere ·
Sire fer nulsire Gami · vof maues tant
coninre que ie ne leroie onnule manie

pres ce q mettre
Gautier map or
traire des auen
tures du saint
Graal · aes son
si canmant. si co
me ilh senbloit:
sifu aus anoi
[b]ann conseigneur que ce qnil auoit fer
ne deuoit pas souffire · et il ne racdroit

Fig. 4.3.   Paris, Bibliothèque Nationale, français 25520, fol. 91

photo: Bibliothèque Nationale, reproduced by permission

Fig. 4.4. Paris, Bibliothèque Nationale, français 15104, fol. 72
photo: Bibliothèque Nationale, reproduced by permission

Fig. 4.5.
Princeton University Library, Garrett 125, fol. 70v.
photo: Princeton University Library,
reproduced by permission

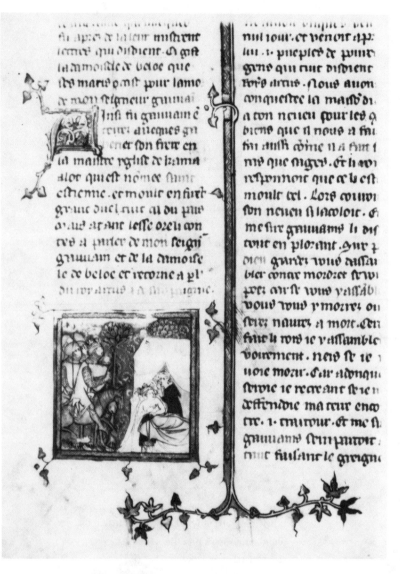

Fig. 4.6.   Paris, Bibliothèque de l'Arsenal, 3482, fol. 638v
photo: Colombe-Gérard, reproduced by permission of the
Bibliothèque de l'Arsenal

Fig. 4.7.   Paris, Bibliothèque Nationale, français 344, fol. 544

photo: Bibliothèque Nationale, reproduced by permission

Fig. 4.8. New Haven, Yale University, Beinecke Library, 229, fol. 357v

photo: author, reproduced by permission

Fig. 4.9. Geneva, Fondation Martin Bodmer, 147, fol. 344

photo: author, reproduced by permission

Fig. 4.10.   New Haven, Yale University, Beinecke Library, 229, fol. 359

photo: author, reproduced by pemission

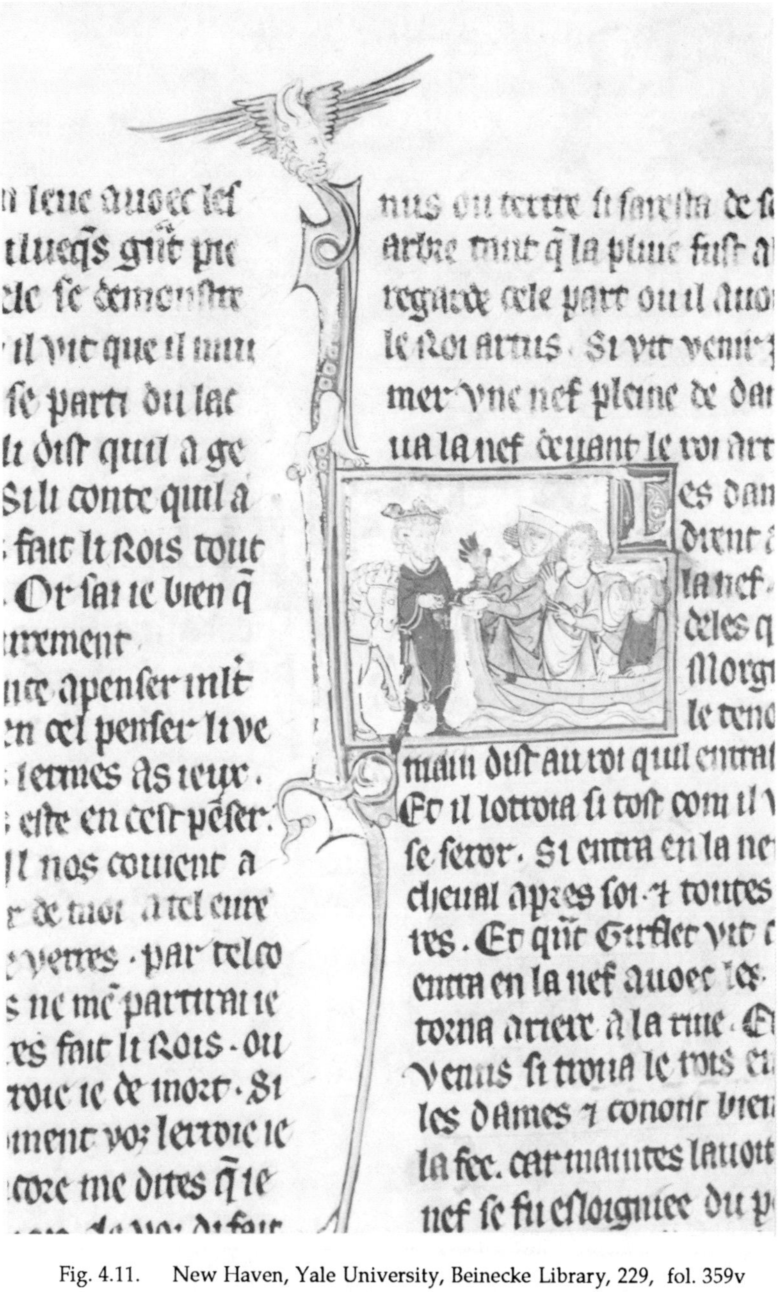

Fig. 4.11.   New Haven, Yale University, Beinecke Library, 229, fol. 359v

photo: author, reproduced by pemission

ra · car fans grit merueille ne fe
ra ele pas perdue · En si q̃ gyfles re
grardoit le main qui estoit hors du
lac qui print lespre le roy artu ·

vant gyfles voit que
faire li couient · si re
uient arriere la ou les
pre estoit · si la prent ꝫ la recome
ce a regarder ꝫ a plaindre mlt
durement ꝫ dist tot en plorant ·
ha · estre bone ꝫ lele plus que nu
le autre tant est griis damages

Sir Gawain and the Green Knight

Sir Gawain and the Green Knight: The Passing of Judgment

Marie Borroff

It is a commonplace of the criticism of *Sir Gawain and the Green Knight* that the drama acted out at the Green Chapel both ought and ought not to be read as a confessional scene. John Burrow, tracing out the analogy between what he calls the "pretend, secular confession" made by the hero and "a real, sacramental one," finds that the mock-confession "ends, as it should," with a mock-absolution:

> I halde þe polysed of þat ply3t [Bertilak says], and pured
> as clene
> As þou hade3 neuer forfeted sy þen þou wat3 fyrst borne.
> [2393-94]¹

[I hold you polished as a pearl, as pure and as bright
As you had lived free of fault since first you were born.]

Elsewhere in late fourteenth-century English poetry, some of the same words are spoken by another confessor the validity of whose role is subject to question:

> I yow assoile by myn heigh power,
> Yow that wol offre, as clene and eek as cleer
> As ye were born.²

Here, as always, similarity can instruct us about difference. The Green Knight's words, unlike those of Chaucer's Pardoner, are not, to use a modern term, to be taken as "performative." They do not purport to *bring about* the state of grace to which they refer.[3] Rather, they take the form of a lay judgment, a personal assessment based on observation and analysis of the facts. In the statement "I halde þe polysed of þat ply3t," *halde* means not "pronounce" but "consider."

The judgment passed by the Green Knight on Sir Gawain in these lines comes as a reassurance following upon the hero's first angry outburst. It is preceded by another judgment of a more comparative and conditional nature, based specifically on the fact that Gawain had not yielded to the sexual temptations of the lovely chatelaine:

> I sende hir to asay þe, and sothly me þynkkez
> On the fautlest freke þat euer on fote 3ede—
> . . . .
> Bot here yow lakked a lyttel, sir, and lewté yow wonted;
> Bot þat watz for no wylyde werke, ne wowyng nau þer,
> Bot for 3e lufed your lyf; þe lasse I yow blame.
>
> [2362-68]

> She made trial of a man most faultless by far
> Of all that ever walked over the wide earth;
> . . . .
> Yet you lacked, sir, a little in loyalty there,
> But the cause was not cunning, nor courtship either,
> But that you loved your own life; the less, then, to blame.

Here the element of subjectivity is again explicit: "sothly me þynkkez," " þe lasse I yow blame."

Non-sacramental and hence non-authorized though they may be, many if not most readers of the poem have nonetheless found the Green Knight's judgments satisfying. They are, indeed, the *only* considered judgments the poem provides. Sir Gawain's own anger and agonizings are exaggerated, and, to the degree that they are so, slightly comic. As for King Arthur, Queen Guenevere, and the lords and ladies of the court, they do not make any explicit judgments at all. They kiss and embrace their returned comrade, they laugh at his story, they comfort him, and they end by arbitrarily transforming a mark of blame into a badge of honor. It is to the words of the Green Knight that we must look if we seek a rationale for such leniency.

It is all very well to accept the Green Knight's judgments at the end of the poem, but for those of us who do so, a further, and formidable, question must be faced. Why should we accept his views? If he does not, like a real confessor, speak with institutional and hence putatively divine authority, what kind of authority does he represent? These questions are inseparable from the question of his identity, and by this we must understand his identity not only as the Green Knight, but as the exuberant host and huntsman of Fitt III, Lord Bertilak. Of the various and contradictory interpretations of the figure of the Green Knight that have been put forward in the criticism of the poem, I have found no one fully satisfying, and my own answer must itself be couched in paradoxical terms. The Green Knight/Bertilak figure is not, I take it, a spirit emanating from the cyclically renewed world of vegetative nature,[4] nor does he embody the word of God in its benevolent but severe aspect descending upon a profane feast,[5] nor is he a latter-day Hades, a lord of the land of the dead,[6] nor is he "a fiendish tempter," if not the Prince of Darkness himself,[7] nor, finally, is he a bluff but genial country gentleman masquerading, mummer fashion, as a kind of green-uniformed *miles gloriosus* who can be cut down and revived on-stage.[8] I suggest, more generally, that his affiliations are twofold. On the one hand, he belongs to the real world, as medieval human beings experienced it and as we experience it today. On the other hand, he represents an illusory perception, likewise universal, of that reality. Let me begin with the former.

It will be obvious that by "reality" as human beings experience it, I mean not a changeless realm of absolute values apprehended from the mortal perspective, but the mortal perspective itself: the mutable, transient condition of the embodied psyche.[9] "Life," so defined, is what Sir Gawain had loved and had not wished to lose. In passing judgment on him, the Green Knight accepts this high valuation. He also sees Gawain's fault as temporary, a departure from his true character limited to a particular time (*here*, in line 2366, must be taken to mean "at this point"), and as relative, a "lack" or failure to live up to an ideal, rather than a lecherous or vulgarly covetous deed. He would, we presume, agree with Sir Gawain's own excuse for not accepting the lady's glove: "Iche tolke mon do as he is tan" ["A man must keep within his compass"] (1811).

Throughout the poems of MS. Cotton Nero A. x., the poet sympathetically conceives of human experience, and hence of human action, as defined by circumstantial limitations. He also conceives of it as part of a natural continuum, as linked by kinship to the experience of other creatures who inhabit sentient bodies, whose behavior is constantly affected by the circumstances in which they find themselves, and who instinctively avoid pain and cling to life. Here is a poet who can take time out to imagine the queasiness of a whale after swallowing an indigestible human morsel—"heartburn," one of my students called it—and who can render the desperation of the wild animals about to be drowned in the Deluge with at least as memorable a poignancy as that of the human friends and lovers who share their fate:

> þe moste mountaynez on mor þenne watz no more dryȝe,
> And þeron flokked þe folke, for ferde of þe wrake.
> Syþen þe wylde of þe wode on þe water flette;
> Summe swymmed þeron þat saue hemself trawed,
> Summe styȝe to a stud and stared to þe heuen,
> Rwly wyth a loud rurd rored for drede.
>
> [*Purity*, 385-90]

[The greatest mountains on earth were then dry no longer, and the people crowded on to them, in terror of the vengeance. Then the wild creatures of the wood floated on the water. Some swam on it, thinking to save themselves; some climbed to a (high) place and stared toward heaven—roared pitifully for dread with a loud clamor.] [10]

When the narrator concludes his account by saying that "alle cryed for care to þe Kyng of heuen" (393), he makes no distinction, among the antecedents of *alle*, between "þe wylde" and "þe folke."

In *Sir Gawain and the Green Knight,* the affinities between human beings and other living creatures take on particular importance. They are emphasized by certain descriptive and verbal repetitions which I want now to discuss in detail.

To begin with, an embodied mortal creature is, by definition, made of vulnerable flesh and blood. The poem contains a series of references to bleeding which associate the Green Knight with Sir Gawain and, less conspicuously, associate both of them with the hunted deer. Phantasmal and faerie-like though he may seem in the first Fitt, the Green Knight does, it turns out, share with other living beings the ability to bleed when cut. After Gawain has beheaded him, the poet tells us, " þe blod brayd fro þe body, þat blykked on þe grene" ["The blood gushed from the body, bright on the green"] (429), and he later refers to the headless trunk as " þat vgly bodi þat bledde" (441). In the first hunting scene, the deer, thrown into panic by the surrounding beaters, hounds, and bowmen, are said to bray and bleed (1163), and the hounds are fed afterward with bread bathed in their blood (1361). Most significantly, there is a clear echo in the scene at the Green Chapel, after the *barbe* at the end of the Green Knight's ax-blade has sliced into the flesh of Sir Gawain's neck, of the wording of the earlier beheading scene. There, the blood of the Green Knight had *blykked,* or gleamed, on his green garments. Now, Sir Gawain sees his own blood *blenk,* or gleam, on the snow (2315). The two verbs are cognate. The poet, as is his wont, makes us experience the action from the point of view of its central figure, and we share his brief moment of relief and exultation:

Neuer syn þat he watz burne borne of his moder
Watz he neuer in þis worlde wyʒe half so bly þe

[2320-21].

[Not since he was a babe born of his mother
Was he once in this world one-half so blithe.]

To have been born of a mother is to be a mortal creature, and to see yourself bleed is to know you are still alive.

The poet further links the Green Knight, the hunted deer, and Sir Gawain as fleshly beings by means of a phrase evidently original with him, or at least found nowhere except in his works: *schire grece*, literally, "shining fat." The noun *grece* itself denotes the fatty flesh of human beings only in *Sir Gawain and the Green Knight*.[11] When Sir Gawain beheads the Green Knight in the court, the poet says that the ax "schrank þurȝ þe schyire grece [of the Green Knight's neck], and schade hit in twynne" ["cut the flesh cleanly and clove it in twain"] (425). At the end of his first day's hunting, Lord Bertilak, presenting Sir Gawain with his day's winnings, shows him the flesh of the deer, " þe schyree grece schorne vpon rybbes" ["the hewn ribs, heavy with fat"] (1378). At the Green Chapel, the wounding of Gawain's neck is described in a line which, like that about the blood gleaming on the snow, unmistakably echoes the earlier passage. The barb at the end of the blade, the poet says, "schrank to þe flesche þurȝ þe schyre grece" (2313).[12]

A less conspicuous but significant echo links Sir Gawain and the fox as creatures compelled by instinct to avoid a life-threatening blow. At the end of the fox-hunt, when the exhausted quarry emerges into view with the pack of hounds at his heels, Bertilak *castez*, or strikes, at him with his sword and, says the narrator, the fox "schunt for þe scharp, and schulde haf arered" (1902), that is, he flinched before the blade, and intended to have retreated. After Sir Gawain has flinched from the first stroke of the Green Knight's ax and been duly ridiculed, the words he speaks in his own defense include the same verb: "I schunt onez, / And so wyl I no more" (2280-81).

As for the boar, a retrospective link between that animal and the Green Knight, which is also a proleptic link with Sir Gawain, is implied by the hewing off of his head at the end of the second hunt and its presentation to Sir Gawain by Lord Bertilak—"a seasonable though somewhat tactless gift," as Burrow calls it.[13]

Warm-blooded creatures, human and non-human alike, are also vulnerable to cold, and this aspect of their kinship, too, is signified by the poem's descriptive content. When he sets forth in search of the Green Chapel at the beginning of November, Sir Gawain literally goes out into a cold world. The account of his travels from All Souls' Day to Christmas Eve, in lines 713 ff., falls into two parts. First, we are told of his many battles: not only against loathly and fierce, though otherwise unspecified, "foes," presumably human, but also against dragons, wolves, *wodwos*, bulls, bears, boars, and giants, all ticked off in a mere seven lines (715-17, 720-23). But these fade into the background of quest-romance convention as we learn that the winter weather was a worse hardship still (726), for the hero had to sleep in his iron mail on bare rocks, in falling sleet, with icicles hanging overhead. In the stanza that immediately follows, one of the poem's best-known details describes a company of Gawain's fellow-creatures, the wretched little birds on the bare twigs overhead " þat pitosly þer piped for pyne of þe colde" (747). At the beginning of Fitt IV, during the night preceding Gawain's fateful departure for the Green Chapel, the poet tells us how the wildest of winter storms kept him from sleeping, but, preoccupied though he is with the fate of his hero, his imagining of the scene outside the castle includes the pain inflicted by the driving snow on the creatures of the forest: "Þe snawe snitered ful snart, þat snayped þe wylde" ["Sleet showered aslant upon shivering beasts"] (2003).[14]

What is signified by descriptive details and verbal repetitions scattered throughout the poem is also signified, on a larger scale, by the hunting scenes considered in their entirety. So much critical acumen has been devoted to exploring the relations between these scenes, taken singly, and the bedroom scenes with which they are paired, that comparatively little has been said about their collective meaning and effect. In them, we see in vividly described action the overwhelming compulsion of vulnerable flesh and blood to save itself from death, as each of a series of three species of animal uses to the utmost the particular means of defense with which it is endowed by nature. The deer summon up all their speed; the boar charges out with all his strength; the fox uses all his tricks. Reading or hearing these scenes, we are made to share the point of view of the hunted creatures as much as that of the hunters, hearing with the deer the arrows whizzing under branches at every turn (1161), feeling with the boar the stinging showers of arrows that drive him out into the open (1454-61, 1564-66), seeing with the fox the three hounds, "all gray," who rush toward him out of the hunting-station at which he has unwittingly arrived (1712-14). As we follow the action in Sir Gawain's bedroom, seeing it build, on successive mornings, to his fateful acceptance of the green girdle, our attention is shifted periodically to the hunts in progress, where we witness, and much of the time experience vicariously, these desperate maneuvers on the part of living creatures who do not want to die. The proportionate extent of the shifts can easily be measured. Given a silent or oral reading rate of twenty lines per minute on the average, about forty minutes of "narrative time" elapse between Gawain's gleeful acceptance of Bertilak's invitation to stay and his promise to do whatever else he decrees (1079-82), and the moment of his acquiescence (1861). Of those forty minutes, the hunting scenes take up fourteen, or more than a third.

Insofar as the poet has made us sympathetic witnesses of the behavior of the animals in the hunting scenes, he has of course predisposed us to judge Gawain leniently when, bent on saving his own skin, he fails the Exchange of Winnings test. We ourselves thus become implicated in the action, or, to use a word of A. C. Spearing's, "entangled" in it [15]. But the sympathy we feel for our fellow-creatures in the poem does not, needless to say, include the Green Knight/Lord Bertilak figure. His flesh may have an outer layer of *schire grece*, he may bleed when his head is cut off, but for him the state of headlessness is strictly temporary—indeed scarcely an inconvenience. And except for the beheading stroke, he is never, until the spared Sir Gawain joyously confronts him at the Green Chapel, threatened with physical violence. On the contrary. In both his aspects, he is himself the hunter, the threatener, the inflicter of wounds, the dealer out of death and dismemberment. We can imagine him saying, to adapt the words Ted Hughes gives to his "Roosting Hawk," "My manners are cutting off heads."

Yet in the person of Lord Bertilak, he belongs as clearly to the real world as the Green Knight had belonged to the world of phantom and faerie. Though the castle in which he lives materializes suddenly, shimmering and shining like a mirage beyond the hoar oaks of the winter forest, nothing about it is incommensurate with Sir Gawain's previous experience except its superlative splendor: it is "a castel þe comlokest þat euer kny3t a3te" ["A castle as comely as a knight could own"] (767). (We have no reason to think that this judgment excludes Camelot; cf. the similar judgment that Bertilak's wife is lovelier than Guenevere [945].) Sir Gawain is impressed, but not shocked or daunted, by the lord's great size and fierce demeanor, and he immediately does what all of us do, consciously or unconsciously, when we encounter anyone for the first time in real life: he estimates his age, judging him to be "of hyghe eldee," that is, of mature years (844-45).[16] All in all, he thinks him well suited to be the head of an important estate, "to lede a lortschyp in lee of leudez ful gode" ["To be a master of men in a mighty keep"] (849). All this smacks as much of late fourteenth-century reality as of quest romance.

What is more surprising is the fact that Lord Bertilak's alter ego the Green Knight becomes assimilated, by the end of the poem, to the mortal realm. In the course of the fourth Fitt, he changes, and the change he undergoes is also a diminishment. It would perhaps be more accurate to say that a change comes about in the way Sir Gawain and we perceive him, but I see no need to choose between the two alternatives now, if ever. In any case, by becoming, or seeming to become, less than he was, he defines himself as part of a world in which we must expect the end to be heavier than, as well as different from, the beginning. You know the lines I am alluding to:

> Gawain watz glad to begynne þose gomnez in halle,
> Bot þaȝ þe ende be heuy haf ȝe no wonder;
> . . . .
> A ȝere ȝernes ful ȝerne, and ȝeldez neuer lyke,
> Þe forme to þe fynisment foldez ful selden. [495-99]

> [Gawain was glad to begin those games in hall,
> But if the end be harsher, hold it no wonder,
> . . . .
> A year passes apace, and proves ever new:
> First things and final conform but seldom.]

As seen by King Arthur and the court, and at the same time by the readers or auditors of the first section of the poem, the Green Knight is overwhelmingly splendid and strange, a domineering, enigmatic, uncanny figure, invulnerable to word and blow alike. In the course of the action at the Chapel, these qualities, without our being consciously aware of it, fade away. One might say that between his entrance in the first episode of the poem and his departure in the last, the Green Knight suffers a sea-change in reverse, becoming less rich and strange rather than more so. A close look at the descriptive style of the two passages will, I hope, confirm and clarify a shared perception of this difference.

I am aware that the entrance upon the scene of so in every way unprecedented a personage calls for a descriptive set piece— at least from this poet. We all know how brilliantly he rises to the occasion. Immediately after the Green Knight has been said to enter the court—" þer hales in at þe halle dor an aghlich mayster" ["There hurtles in at the hall-door an unknown rider"] (136)—the passage of time is suspended for eighty-five lines, whereupon the action resumes exactly where it had left off, with the line "Þis haþel heldez hym in and þe halle entres" ["This horseman hurtles in, and the hall enters"] (221). The result, measured again in terms of "narrative time," is that both audiences—the smaller audience within the poem and the larger audience outside of it—are made to stare fixedly at the Green Knight in admiration and amazement for over four minutes. This trick obviously cannot be played twice; the second entry of the Green Knight is not attended by another such description. But descriptive material in narrative works need not be confined to set pieces; it can be incorporated in varying amounts in the treatment of unfolding events. As he tells us of the confrontation at court, the poet dwells on the Green Knight's least mannerism and action in such loving detail, and in such a diversity of concrete and specific terms, that he continues throughout the scene to loom larger than life. Nowhere is this more apparent, or the effect of the technique more striking, than in the account of his behavior after his head has fallen to the floor and gone rolling around to be kicked by the spectators:

> He brayde his bulk aboute,
> Þat vgly bodi þat bledde;
> Moni on of hym had doute,
> Bi þat his resounz were redde.

For þe hede in his honde he haldez vp euen,
Toward þe derrest on þe dece he dressez þe face
And hit lyfte vp þe yȝe-lyddez and loked ful brode,
And meled þus much with his muthe, as ȝe may now here:
[440-47]

> [His bulk about he haled,
> That fearsome body that bled;
> There were many in the court that quailed
> Before all his say was said.

For the head in his hand he holds right up;
Toward the first on the dais directs he the face,
And it lifted up its lids, and looked with wide eyes,
And said as much with its mouth as now you may hear:]

It is true that in the Green Chapel episode, the poet compensates for the lack of a pictorial set piece by a brilliant display of auditory imagery. Before the Green Knight finally emerges into view, he makes a prolonged and unconscionable racket with his ax and whetstone, and this noise is described in terms of three onomatopoetic similes occupying a total of four long lines, as a result of which we hear it almost as clearly as Sir Gawain does himself:

Quat! hit clatered in þe clyff, as hit cleue schulde,
As one vpon a gryndelston hade grounden a sy þe.
What! hit wharred and whette, as water at a mulne;
What! hit rusched and ronge, raw þe to here.   [2201-04]

[Lord! it clattered in the cliff fit to cleave it in two,
As one upon a grindstone ground a great scythe!
Lord! it whirred like a mill-wheel whirling about!
Lord! it echoed loud and long, lamentable to hear!]

Nor are details of gesture and action, couched in concrete terms, entirely lacking in the narrative that follows. Once he appears, the Green Knight is said to be "gered as fyrst, / Boþe þe lyre and þe leggez, lokkez and berde" ["And in form as at first, . . . / His lordly face and his legs, his locks and his beard"] (2227-28). He sets the handle of his ax to the ground as he stalks along (2230) and uses it to vault over the stream (2231-32); he heaves it up for the first stroke "with alle þe bur in his body" ["With all the force in his frame"] (2261); before striking the second stroke, he glares as angrily as if he were mad (2289); before striking the third stroke he "frounsez bo þe lyppe and browe" ["scowls with both lip and brow"] (2306). But this is all, and all this, I submit, seems pretty thin beer when we compare its collective effect with that of the first episode.   Look at the last detail I quoted, "[he] frounsez bo þe lyppe and browe," in conjunction with a corresponding detail in the scene at court:

> Þe renk on his rouncé hym ruched in his sadel
> And runischly his rede yȝen he reled aboute,
> Bende his bresed broȝez, ɒlycande grene,
> Wayued his berde for to wayte quo-so wolde ryse.
>
> [303-06]
>
> [The stranger on his green steed stirred in the saddle,
> And roisterously his red eyes he rolled all about,
> Bent his bristling brows, that were bright green,
> Wagged his beard as he watched who would arise.]

Once the third and last blow has been struck, we are told that the Green Knight desisted, set the haft of his ax on the ground, and rested his arms on the head—a relaxed, placatory, and in every sense down-to-earth series of actions.   Immediately afterward, there occurs what Spearing calls an "almost vertiginous shift of perspective" (p. 189).   The shift is spatial, as Spearing says—we suddenly find ourselves looking at Sir Gawain through the eyes of the Green Knight rather than the reverse. And it is accompanied by a more radical shift in our "perspective" in the psychological sense.   For the first time, we are allowed to know *how* the Green Knight is seeing and what he is feeling, and this knowledge strips him once and for all of his aura of strangeness and menace.   Come to find out, he likes Sir Gawain very much, just as we do, and has evidently liked him very much all along.

As the Green Knight becomes both more like Sir Gawain and more like ourselves, he becomes less green. A simple corollary of this change is the virtual disappearance, from the descriptive and narrative passages of the final phase of the Chapel episode, of the word itself. It appears immediately after the Knight has struck the second blow, in line 2296, " Þen muryly eft con he mele, þe mon in þe grene" ["Then merrily does he mock him, the man all in green"] (I shall have something to say later about the wording of this line), and in the succinct account of the departure from the Chapel in lines 2475-78,

> Gawayn on blonk ful bene
> To þe kyngez burȝ buskez bolde,
> And þe knyȝt in þe enker-grene
> Whiderwarde-so-euer he wolde,

> [Gawain sets out anew;
> Toward the court his course is bent;
> And the knight all green in hue,
> Wheresoever he wished, he went.]

but not between the two.[17] In a passage of roughly equal length in Fitt I (containing 405 words versus the 385 of the other), from the moment when Sir Gawain approaches the Green Knight, gisarme in hand (line 375), until he and King Arthur laugh together after the Knight's departure (line 464), the word *green* occurs six times, that is, in about one line out of eight.[18]

The difference in effect between the two episodes is of course more than a matter of mere frequencies of words and details. As seen at court, the Green Knight is not only dressed in green, he *is* green, as are his ax and his horse:

> For vch mon had meruayle quat hit mene myȝt
> Þat a hapel and a horse myȝt such a hwe lach,
> As growe grene as þe gres and grener hit semed,
> þen grene aumayl on golde glowande bryȝter. [233-36]

> [For much did they marvel what it might mean
> That a horseman and a horse should have such a hue,

Grow green as the grass, and greener, it seemed,
Than green fused on gold more glorious by far.]

(Note the three occurrences of the word *green* in the last two lines.) Once his knightly credentials have been established, he is called "the Green Knight" (390, 417); in the final reference to him in the episode, the poet uses the adjective as a substantive, saying of King Arthur and Sir Gawain that "at þat grene þay laþe and grenne" (464). He is also called " þe kny3t [or gome] in þe grene" (377, 405), but these appellations, taken together with the others, give us little or no sense of disjunction between the apparel and the figure itself. Such a disjunction is, however, suggested in a number of ways, and ever more insistently, by the poet's treatment of the Green Knight in the Chapel episode. At the moment when he first greets Sir Gawain, after he has vaulted over the stream on his ax,[19] he is, to be sure, referred to as " þat grene gome" (2239). Thereafter he is called " þe gome in þe grene" twice (2227, 2259), and, immediately before the striking of the third blow, " þe mon in þe grene" (2295). (The presence of this most everyday of words in the line as originally composed is guaranteed by the alliteration on *m*.) The Green Knight himself, in this latter episode, seems to limit his own greenness to his attire. He tells Sir Gawain that he is giving him the fateful girdle as a memento because "hit is grene as my goune" (2396), not "as green as I am."

Once he has identified himself as Sir Gawain's host and the husband of the temptress of Fitt III, the Green Knight's physical presence seems to be superseded by that of Bertilak. The poet calls him þe lorde (2403) after he has invited Sir Gawain to return to Hautdesert, and the words in which Gawain finally addresses him indicate that he too now sees him in this embodiment, rather than his earlier one: "But one thing I would ask of you—be not displeased—since you are the lord of yonder land in which I have sojourned . . .How do you say your right name. . . ?" (2439-43).

When Bertilak explains what has set the sequence of events in motion, he tells Sir Gawain that Morgan le Fay had wanted to bereave the knights of the Round Table of their wits "with glopnyng of þat ilke gome þat gostlych speked / With his hede in his honde bifore þe hyȝe table" ["With awe of that elvish man that eerily spoke / With his head in his hand before the high table"] (2461-62), as though the Green Knight had been someone else entirely: a *gome*, that is, a human being, who spoke "uncannily" as he performed a magical feat, rather like a stage magician who has just succeeded in sawing the lady in half.

The demystifying of the Green Knight/Bertilak figure is most striking, of course, in the notorious transformation of the resident witch, "Morgan the Goddess," into Sir Gawain's aunt, the "old ancient lady" back home who would presumably now welcome a second visit from her wandering nephew. The "grieve-Guenevere-and-cause-her-to-die" project, whatever we may or may not wish to make of it, has evidently been abandoned.

It is not enough to say that by the end of the Chapel episode the Green Knight has simply turned into Lord Bertilak, for the Bertilak of that episode differs from the Bertilak of Fitts II and III in the same way that the Green Knight at the Chapel differs from the Green Knight at court. Limitations of space forbid my going into this at length, but let me point out that in the interior scenes at Hautdesert, we see the host continually laughing, leaping around, thinking up ideas for fun and games, talking and joking extravagantly, and generally behaving in wild and crazy fashion, to the point where either those around him or he himself, depending on how we want to interpret line 1087, can't imagine what he may do next. In the exterior scenes, as the leader of the hunts, he personifies to the fullest imaginable extent the joy of vigorous and masterful bodily activity, exultantly galloping from place to place, mounting and dismounting again, throughout the day of the deer-hunt; confidently striding into the running stream to confront the greatest of all wild boars; snatching the dead fox from the jaws of the hounds and waving it exuberantly in the air as he shouts to summon the rest of the huntsmen. Indeed, he might have been designed to personify the pronouncement of Gaston Phoebus in his late fourteenth-century treatise on hunting, that "hunters lyven in this world most joyfully of eny other men."[20] At the Chapel, once the Green Knight has set his ax down, leaned on it, and begun to assume his Lord Bertilak aspect, he remains immobile. In television parlance, he turns into a "talking head," saying his sensible say without a trace of the extravagance and irony that had characterized his language at Hautdesert.

At the beginning of this essay, I suggested that the *Gawain*-poet presents the Green Knight as, on the one hand, emanating from the real world, that is, the mutable and transitory world in which we live out our lives as human beings, and on the other hand, as representing an illusory view of that world. More specifically, our view of him as he first appears in the poem involves an admixture of illusion, as does that of the court. As the action plays itself out, our view of him becomes more realistic via a process of what I have called "diminishment" or "demystification." The two views correspond to an earlier and a later phase of human experience generally. John Ganim has said that the action of the poem is "a journey into age"[21], and this observation seems to me true in more ways than one. To make clear what I mean, let me derive from the story of Sir Gawain as I have analyzed it a more general, paradigmatic story, a story whose central figure is someone much like ourselves as we would like to see ourselves and to have others see us. In the first part of this story, someone older than we, having dominant or authoritative status, seems to us awesome, charged with a magical aura, invulnerable, larger than life.[22] Later, this same being comes to be seen as less awesome, less magical, no longer larger than life—in short, as more like us. This change in mode of perception is linked with a change in ourselves: we learn that we are not quite all we had hoped we would be and had believed we could be. In the *Gawain*-poet's version of the story, we are led, via a series of unpredictable, bewildering, and variously discomfiting situations, to what seems the very brink of death,[23] at which point we betray an ideal to which we had confidently dedicated ourselves. After all is over, we are judged benevolently, told that our trials are at an end, and assured that, even though our behavior did not measure up to an absolute standard of perfection, we have been found, not wanting, but acceptable, admirable, in fact. The name I give this paradigm is maturation, and maturation is what I see as the theme of *Sir Gawain and the Green Knight*. Thinking about it, I am reminded of a line from Wordsworth: the Green Knight and Lord Bertilak, as they merge into a single presence, simultaneously "fade into the light of common day." We have come through intact, we have done well, but neither we nor the world is as wonderful as we had thought.[24]

Having been so bold as to say these words, I want immediately to qualify them. The poem we call *Sir Gawain and the Green Knight* is neither a myth, nor a fairy tale, nor a paradigm of any kind; it is a fully realized narrative. It comes to us from the hand of a poet who was fascinated by the circumstantial and the contingent, by the exigencies of time and space. Sir Gawain is not a human being in the most general sense. He is a male human being, and he is, specifically, a knight, a knight not only of King Arthur's court but of a late medieval "present time" when professionalism—money paid for services rendered—was encroaching upon the older knightly ideals of feudal and Christian fidelity. The meaning of the pentangle is developed as an interlocking set of knightly virtues, put into practice in activities proper to a knight, both abroad, *in melly* (644), and in domestic settings, *in mote* (635). In his angry burst of self-denunciation after all has been revealed, Sir Gawain accuses himself of having forsaken his *kynde*, his nature, " þat is larges and lewté þat longez to kny3tez" ["largesse and loyalty belonging to knights"] (2380-81). A moment earlier, the Green Knight had said that "as perle bi þe quite pese is of prys more, / So is Gawayn, in god fayth, bi o þer gay kny3tez" ["As pearls to white peas, more precious and prized, / So is Gawain, in good faith, to other gay knights"] (2364-65). One reason that the Green Knight/Bertilak figure speaks with authority at the end of the poem is that he is a knight who is also a lord, the head of a knightly company. I have already quoted Gawain's judgment, on meeting him, that he was well suited "to lede a lortschyp in lee of leudez ful gode"(849). That is exactly what the members of Arthur's court, complaining of the king's foolishness in involving himself in a *cauelacioun* (683), had said Sir Gawain might have become if he had not committed himself to being beheaded:

A lowande leder of ledez in londe hym wel semez,
And so had better haf been þen britned to no3t,
Hadet wyth an aluish mon, for angardez pryde. [679-81]

[A great leader of lords he was likely to become,
And better so to have been than battered to bits
Beheaded by an elf-man, for empty pride!]

In terms of the legendary world of romance, Sir Gawain is the
nephew of the most glorious king in Christendom, and Bertilak is
nobody we have ever heard of. In terms of the poem's late
medieval present, Sir Gawain is a member of a household, and
Lord Bertilak is the head of one. When he assesses the actions of
the hero, we seem to see the institution of knighthood passing
judgment on one of its own.

Kent Hieatt has pointed out that the echo of the opening line
of *Sir Gawain* toward the end of the poem—"After þe segge and
þe asaute watz sesed at Troye"—occurs at line 2525. This number
seems clearly to allude, as he maintains, to the five fives of the
pentangle, and to correspond in its symmetry to the 1212 lines of
Pearl.[25] The reiterative long line is followed by an additional
five lines, the single bob-and-wheel sequence that closes the
poem. In the first two lines of the wheel, the poet says that
many such adventures have befallen in the past. In the third and
fourth lines, which are the last lines of all, he invokes the
divine judgment that follows life on earth, referring to Christ in
terms of his human suffering at the time of the Crucifixion:

Now þat bere þe croun of þorne,
He bryng vus to his blysse!

[May He that was crowned with thorn
Bring all men to His bliss!]

This concluding invocation stands outside the circle, implied by
reiteration, which encloses the dramatized narrative. That
narrative, as we know, is set in a Christian world, much of it at
two Christian courts. Even when Sir Gawain first sees the Green
Knight in what had seemed a chapel fit for a fiend's devotions,
he exclaims, reassuringly, "God þe mot loke!" ["God love
you. . . !"] (2239). I am certain that if we could ask the poet about
the state of Gawain's soul after his return, he would tell us,

perhaps somewhat bewildered by our inquiry, that of course he went to confession, told the whole story to a priest (as he had already told it to the entire court), and was absolved.[26] But the fact remains that he did not choose to say so. The poem as he wrote it ends with the non-sacramental, non-authorized judgment of a human being by a human being. In this respect, it anticipates, fleetingly yet clearly, the passing of judgment from the divine to the earthly realm which will so change the meaning of the Arthurian legends as they are handed down, from poet to poet, to our own day.

NOTES

1. *A Reading of "Sir Gawain and the Green Knight"* (London: Routledge & Kegan Paul, 1965), pp. 127-33. The references to "a pretend, secular confession" and "a real, sacramental one" occur on p. 133; the "absolution" is discussed on pp. 131-32. I quote here and elsewhere from Tolkien and Gordon's second edition of the poem, as revised by Norman Davis (Oxford: Oxford University Press, 1967). The translation cited is mine (New York: Norton, 1967).

2. *The Poetry of Geoffrey Chaucer*, ed. F. N. Robinson, 2nd ed. (Boston: Houghton Mifflin, 1957), p. 154.

3. Burrow observes that "the poet does not allow Ber[t]ilak to use the proper clerical term 'assoil'" (p. 132).

4. This view is best known as presented by John Speirs: "The Green Knight whose head is chopped off at his own request and who is yet as miraculously or magically alive as ever . . . can be no other than a recrudescence in poetry of the Green Man . . . . [The Green Man] is surely a descendant of the Vegetation or Nature god of almost universal and immemorial tradition . . . whose death and resurrection are the myth-and-ritual counterpart of the annual death and rebirth of nature . . . ." (*Medieval English Poetry: The Non-Chaucerian Tradition* [London: Faber and Faber, 1957], p. 219.)

5. Cf. Hans Schnyder, *"Sir Gawain and the Green Knight," An Essay in Interpretation* (Bern: Francke, 1961), p. 41: "In the context of our story the appearance of the Green Knight would consequently herald the manifestation of divine interference in the course of worldly events . . . . His behaviour is . . . that of a benevolent though severe father who deems it necessary to admonish unruly children."

6. "It is . . . clear that [the Green Knight] is not an ordinary executioner but a supernatural, an immortal one, in fact, the only deathless executioner known, namely Death itself. . . . The mysterious Green Knight is none other than the Lord of Hades, who comes to challenge to a beheading game the heroes sitting round the fire" (A. H. Krappe, "Who *Was* the Green Knight?," *Speculum* 13 [1938], 206-15; cf. 208, 215). Krappe views the Green Chapel as a version of the motif, common in Celtic legend, of "the fairy hill or elfin knoll, the abode of the dead ancestors" (p. 213).

7. Dale B. J. Randall, in "Was the Green Knight a Fiend?" (*Studies in Philology* 57 [1960], 479-91), argues that *Sir Gawain and the Green Knight* "achieved part of its impact on a medieval audience by means of its demonic overtones" (486). The Green Knight's appearance and behavior are "fiend-like" in a number of respects (479-85), and "the grim setting in which Gawain meets Bercilak," which he, like Krappe, associates with the fairy hill of Celtic legend, "may be regarded as hellish" (489). He does not, however, "insist that the Green Knight is *de facto* a fiend" (485); cf. the final paragraph of the essay, 491.

8. "The Green Knight, enacting the role of the Challenger, does so with all the gusto of an accomplished mummer. . . .Later, at the Green Chapel, . . . he drops on the instant his role of magic horror and becomes again the gallant, benevolent Bercilak, full of warm goodwill" (Laura Hibbard Loomis, "Gawain and the Green Knight," in *Critical Studies of "Sir Gawain and the Green Knight*," Donald R. Howard and Christian K. Zacher, eds. [South Bend: University of Notre Dame Press, 1968], pp. 19-20). Loomis' essay originally appeared in Roger Sherman Loomis, ed., *Arthurian Literature in the Middle Ages: A Collaborative History*, (Oxford: Oxford University Press, 1959).

9. A major rift divides those readers of *Sir Gawain and the Green Knight* who see the poet as sympathetic toward secular "reality," finding in human actions and institutions qualities of goodness and splendor commensurate with those of the divine realm, and those who see him as implicitly condemning human institutions and actions, however good or splendid they may seem, in terms of the eternal "reality" and absolute moral standards mediated on earth by the Catholic Church. The former view (with which I associate myself) has been definitively expressed by Derek Brewer, in "The *Gawain*-Poet: A General Appreciation of Four Poems" (*Essays in Criticism* 17 [1967], 130-42): "[The poet] admits that much of reality goes against the grain, but he is also passionately convinced of [its]

ultimate beauty and joy" (p. 131). For a clear and forceful statement of the latter view, see Derek W. Hughes, "The Problem of Reality in *Sir Gawain and the Green Knight*" (*University of Toronto Quarterly*, 40 [1971], 217-35). Hughes, having identified in the poem a "cluster" of four kinds of images of artifice, including "a translation of life into overtly fictional or theatrical terms so as to stress its distance from reality" (217), goes on to say that "all these ideas can also be found in other writings of the period, their normal function being to measure devotion to false, temporal good against the realities of eternity" (*ibid.*). Interpretations of the court at Camelot as innocent or culpable stem from an adherence to one or the other of these two views. To put it another way, critics such as Brewer assume that for the *Gawain*-poet, human and divine values, however greatly they may differ in degree, are the same in kind (in which case they are related metonymically, by underlying identity and contiguity); critics such as Hughes assume that human and divine values, however closely they may appear to resemble each other, are radically different (in which case, they are related metaphorically, by similarity and disjunction). See also note 12, below.

10. I quote from *The Poems of the Pearl Manuscript*, ed. Malcolm Andrew and Ronald Waldron (Berkeley and Los Angeles: University of California Press, 1982), p. 127. The translation is my own.

11. At least, without figurative allusion to pork. In the alliterative *Morte Arthure*, the giant killed by the king is said to be "greesse-growen as a galte" (1102), i.e. as a swine (*The Alliterative Morte Arthure: A Critical Edition*, ed. Valerie Krishna [New York: Burt Franklin, 1976]; I follow *MED*, s.v. *gres(e* n., in treating *greesse growen* as a compound. In *Destruction of Troy* 3838, Polidarius, one of the kings of Greece, is said to be "as a porke fate, / ffull grete in the grippe, all of grese hoge" (ed. George A. Panton and David Donaldson [EETS, 39, 56; 1869, 1894]).

12. Hughes, in "The Problem of Reality," notes "the strong awareness of the flesh of the deer and boar" in the first two hunting episodes (229). I agree, though, as I have already intimated, I do not follow Hughes in seeing a contrast between the world of the hunting scenes and the "artificial," game-oriented world of Arthur's court (cf. 219). For an eloquent statement of the opposing view, see A. C. Spearing, *The "Gawain"-Poet: A Critical Study* (Cambridge: Cambridge University Press, 1970), p. 181: "The Camelot of this poem is a young Camelot, a place of gaiety and elegance, where a

'fayre folk in her first age' (54) is ruled over by a 'childgered' king (86), who cannot bear to do any one thing for long . . . . It is a delightful place, an innocent version of the ideal aimed at by any of the great courts of Western Europe in the later Middle Ages."

13. *A Reading*, p. 94.

14. In view of this encompassing concern, I suggest that " þe naked" in line 2002 refers to the unclothed bodies of animals as well as the exposed flesh of human beings.

15. The *"Gawain" Poet*, p. 234.

16. The phrase is cited from the poem by *MED* , s.v. *heigh* adj. sense 6b, "full, complete, total," and translated "mature age."

17. My count is based on descriptive and narrative material only, including *inquits* interpolated in passages of dialogue: where the subject of these is the Green Knight, as in "quo þ þat o þer þenne" (2444), the poet might have used an appellation mentioning his color. The word *green* does occur twice in passages of dialogue between lines 2296 and 2478, once when the Green Knight says the girdle is as green as his gown (2396), once when he refers to " þe chaunce of þe grene chapel" (2399).

18. Here too the word *green* occurs twice in dialogue. It is used by the Knight both times in the phrase "the Green Chapel" (451, 454).

19. The poet does not say that the new ax the Green Knight wields at the Chapel is green. He describes it simply as "a felle weppen, / A denez ax nwe dy3t . . . / With a borelych bytte bende by þe halme" and a "lace þat lemed ful bry3t" (2222-26). The *grayn* of the original ax (Davis's gloss, "blade," seems preferable to *MED*'s "spike" [s.v. *grein* n. sense 1(c), "the edge of a horn, the spike of a gisarme"]) had been "al of grene stele and of golde hewen" (211).

20. I quote from the early fifteenth-century translation of Gaston's *Livre de Chasse* by Edward, Duke of York. See Douglas Gray, ed., *The Oxford Book of Late Medieval Verse and Prose*, (Oxford: Oxford University Press, 1985), pp. 145-46.

21. *Style and Consciousness in Middle English Narrative* (Princeton: Princeton University Press, 1983), p. 60.

22. As has often been noted, there are clear signs, especially in Fitt I, of a "generation gap" between the Green Knight and the court. Arthur and his knights and ladies are said to be "in their first age" (54), Arthur is described as *child-gered* (86), the Green Knight scornfully calls the knights of the Round Table "beardless children" (280), and so on. Beardedness, in fact, becomes recognizable in the poem as a motif, a sign of full physical maturity. The details of the description of the Green Knight include "a beard

include "a beard big as a bush" (182), and his beard is mentioned twice in the action that follows (306, 334); when Bertilak is introduced, the narrator devotes a full line to his "broad, bright" beard; and when the Green Knight reappears, he looks as he had looked at first, "flesh and legs, locks and beard" (2228). There are other, more subtle touches, as well; for example, the "bristly brows" of the Green Knight (305) are characteristic not of a youth but of an older person.

23.   If it is essential to the meaning of the poem that we should experience vicariously Gawain's surprise, bewilderment, discomfiture, and fear, and should thus find ourselves in accord with the lenient interpretation we see placed upon his lapse of loyalty at the end, then the Green Knight must be presented in such a way as to elicit these emotions with maximum force. I believe that the "overdetermined" character of his portrayal, its multiple symbolic suggestiveness, can best be understood in this light. Supporting evidence in the form of descriptive detail and wording can be, and has been, adduced for each of the identifications of the Green Knight which I listed on p. 107, above. He does seem to speak with a kind of supernatural severity, he does seem demonic, he does seem to embody the vitality of vegetative nature, he does seem to have the implacable and irresistible summoning power of death itself. He even seems, in retrospect, to be Lord Bertilak dressed up in mummer's costume, come to the court to entertain it with a terrifying feat of stage magic! Derek Brewer has said that the poet "presents his material entirely from Gawain's point of view" ("The *Gawain*-Poet," 137), and I take this to mean, among other things, that we cannot ask who the Green Knight, or Bertilak, "really is." Either of them is whatever Gawain thinks or feels him to be at a given point in the poem.

24.   In that it approvingly represents the progress of its youthful central figure, under the aegis of a man who is older but not yet elderly, toward a more mature and experienced view of life, *Sir Gawain and the Green Knight* is "Ricardian" in the sense established by John Burrow's well-known study, *Ricardian Poetry: Chaucer, Gower, Langland and the "Gawain" Poet* (New Haven: Yale University Press, 1971). Burrow argues that characters like Theseus, Harry Bailey, and Bertilak "embody an image of man which is not heroic, not romantic, and not at all 'monkish'. It is an image of 'high eld' which stands at the centre of Ricardian poetry, an ideal of 'mesure' which involves [a] sober acceptance of things as they are" (p. 126).

25.   "*Sir Gawain*: pentangle, *luf-lace*, numerical structure," in Alistair Fowler, ed., *Essays in Numerological Analysis*, (London: Routledge & Kegan Paul, 1970), pp. 122-23.

26.   I share the view finely and fully argued by P. J. C. Field, in "A Rereading of *Sir Gawain and the Green Knight*" (*Studies in Philology*, 68 [1971], 255-69), that the poet presents Gawain's act in withholding the green girdle from Bertilak as a venial rather than a mortal sin. "Gawain's lapse," Field concludes, "is real but minor: he has won but he has not triumphed. . . . And the court to which Gawain returns must be taken as giving the judgement of humanity" (269).

Leaving Morgan Aside:
Women, History, and Revisionism in
Sir Gawain and the Green Knight

Sheila Fisher

The anonymous author of *Sir Gawain and the Green Knight* knew how the story would end, both the story of Arthurian history and the story of his own romance. In the end is the beginning, because the end of Arthurian legend in the collapse of the Round Table accounts for the beginning of this poem, for its motivation, its selected and selective emphases, and its design. With a knowledge of the end, the romance focuses on the beginning and on one adventure of one young knight, for this is essentially a poem about beginnings: about the New Year and the first youth of King Arthur; about the young court's solidarity and the first assumption of the pentangle by Gawain.[1] Through its emphasis on beginnings, *Sir Gawain and the Green Knight*, as I will argue in this essay, tries to revise Arthurian history in order to make it come out right. The purpose of this revisionary agenda is nothing less than to demonstrate how the Round Table might have averted its own destruction by adhering to the expectations of masculine behavior inherent in Christian chivalry.

If the end is the beginning, it also serves as the means, the poem's directive for its revisionism. The poem alerts us to the connections between beginnings and ends through the cyclical emphases of its narrative and specifically through the articulations of historical betrayal and of the loss of a civilization that frame the romance: " þe segge and þe asaute watz sesed at Troye" ["Since the siege and the assault was ceased at Troy"] (lines 1 and 2525).[2] Projected onto the Arthurian past, these references to historical gain, loss, and betrayal forecast the Arthurian future. Given these narrative emphases, it is significant that, at the end of the poem, about a hundred lines from the closing reiteration of historical betrayal, we find Morgan le Fay, who is here not only named for the first (and last) time, but also designated as the generator of the romance, of the complex narrative of Gawain's testing. For Gawain's edification, Bertilak finally reveals Morgan's presence in the plot (and even then, once he has introduced her, it takes him ten lines [2446-55] to get to the point):

> Ho wayned me vpon þis wyse to your wynne halle
> For to assay þe surquidré, ȝif hit soth were
> Þat rennes of þ grete renoun of þe Rounde Table;
> Ho wayned me þis wonder your wyttez to reve,
> For to haf greued Gaynour and gart hir to dyȝe
> With glopnyng of þat ilke gome þat gostlych speked
> With his hede in his honde bifore þe hyȝe table.
>
> [2456-62]

> [She guided me in this guise to your glorious hall,
> To assay, if such it were, the surfeit of pride
> That is rumored of the retinue of the Round Table.
> She put this shape upon me to puzzle your wits,
> To afflict the fair queen, and frighten her to death
> With awe of that elvish man that eerily spoke
> With his head in his hand before the high table.]

Morgan's placement is not, as some critics have argued, a flaw in this carefully constructed narrative; it is neither an accident nor an authorial mistake.[3] The poem, as I will argue in this essay, deliberately leaves Morgan aside, positioning her at the end of the narrative when she is, in fact, its means: the agent of Gawain's testing.

   Sir Gawain and the Green Knight marginalizes Morgan le Fay because her marginalization is central to its own revision of Arthurian history. If, however, we take our cue from *Sir Gawain and the Green Knight* and reread the narrative backwards from the perspective of Morgan's agency, we can define the trajectory and the ideology of the poem's revisionism. Morgan and her marginalization are the means to the poem's end, because women are centrally implicated in the collapse of the Round Table and the end of the Arthurian Age. If women could be placed on the periphery, as Morgan is in this poem, then the Round Table might not have fallen. To deny the female would be to save the kingdom, and, in its revisionary agenda, that is precisely what *Sir Gawain and the Green Knight* attempts to do. In the name of a lost but presumably worthy cause, it attempts an uneasy, because necessarily incomplete, erasure of women from the poem. It should not be surprising, after all, that the poet who wrote a Christian dream-vision allegory to offer consolation for the death of a child could write what is, in essence, a political allegory of women's displacement to offer nostalgic consolation for the death of Britain's greatest king.

If Pearl has gone to a New Jerusalem far removed from the transience and decay associated with her death, Arthur and his court, in Fitt I of *Sir Gawain and the Green Knight*, have gone to an old Camelot far removed from the later struggles associated with its own decay and ultimate transience. As one strategy of its revisionism, the poem focuses on a conspicuously youthful court.

> With all þe wele of þe worlde þay woned þer samen,
> Þe most kyd kny3tez vnder Krystes seluen,
> And þe louelokkest ladies þat euer lif haden,
> And he þe comlokest kyng þat þe court haldes;
> For al watz þis fayre folk in hir first age,
>   on sille,
>   Þe hapnest vnder heuen,
>   Kyng hy3est mon of wylle;
>   Hit were now gret nye to neuen
>   So hardy a here on hille. [50-59]

> [In peerless pleasures passed they their days,
> The most noble knights known under Christ,
> And the loveliest ladies that lived on earth ever,
> And the comeliest king, that that court holds,
> For all this fair folk in their first age
>   were still,
>   Happiest of mortal kind,

King noblest famed of will;
You would now go far to find
So hardy a host on hill.]

Although some readers of the romance find Arthur and his retinue more youthful, more "childgered" (86), more "wylde" of "brayn" (89) than they ought to be, still, this is, as other readers have pointed out, a court in its first blush of youth, as green, one might say, as the giant who comes to test its pride.[4] As such, this court is conspicuously removed from later tensions and egoisms, from later intrigue and infighting.[5] It is thus, in the context of its own history, a prelapsarian court. And we see it, significantly enough, in the midst of its celebrations to inaugurate Christmas and the New Year: "Wyle Nw Зer watz so Зep þat hit watz nwe cummen" ["While the New Year was new, but yesternight come"] (60). The triple repetition of newness in this one line (that opens the stanza immediately following the long passage quoted above) emphasizes not only the birth of Christ and the rebirth of the year, but the poem's own revisionary regeneration of Arthurian legend.

This revisionary regeneration is a central strategy in the poem's characterization—in what is essentially its rewriting—of Gawain himself. According to one well-known branch of Arthurian legend, the king's nephew is something of a womanizer. Some critics, in fact, have suggested that *Sir Gawain and the Green Knight* actually plays with this aspect of its hero's reputation by making him confront it at Morgan's castle.[6] Another way of putting this would be to say that here the sins that Gawain has not yet committed come back to haunt him. In Fitt III, Gawain stands accused of being someone he knows nothing about, to the point that both he and the Lady will agree, with some justice, that he is not Gawain (1292-93).[7] For the poem does not want its audience to believe that this is the old Gawain either. Were the hero of this romance the womanizer of legend, the problem of the pentangle's appropriateness to him and the challenge in the bedroom would both be, quite obviously, somewhat beside the point, mysteries resolved for the audience by Gawain's reputation before Gawain ever mounts Gringolet or the Lady ever mounts her assault.

If the poem's revisionary agenda is evident in the initial description of Arthur's court, the portrait of Guenevere in Fitt I both emphasizes this agenda and indicates the ways in which the positionings of women are central to it. Indeed, one of the most conspicuous signals of the work's agenda is its rehabilitation of Guenevere. Guenevere and her betrayals of her king are, of course, notorious in the dissolution of the Round Table; she is most famous, in other words, for her association with the end. In *Sir Gawain and the Green Knight*, however, Guenevere is most prominent at the beginning. There are, in fact, few subsequent references to her in the poem: we are told that she sits near (the similarly rehabilitated) Gawain at the New Year's feast (109); Arthur bids her not to be bothered by the Green Knight's talking head (470-73); we later learn that she is not so beautiful as the Lady (945). The last reference to her in the poem is the most telling, for, as Bertilak informs Gawain, the third of Morgan's motives for sending him on his mission as the Green Knight was

> For to haf greued Gaynour and gart hir to dyȝe
> With glopnyng of þat ilke gome þat gostlych speked
> With his hede in his honde bifore þe hyȝe table.
> [2460-62]

> [To afflict the fair queen, and frighten her to death
> With awe of that elvish man that eerily spoke
> With his head in his hand before the high table.]

If Morgan had had her way, then, the beginning of the poem would be the end of the queen. Yet, by the time this plot against Guenevere has been revealed, it has been delayed so long, both within the narrative and within Bertilak's list of Morgan's motivations, that it seems somewhat beside the point. Had Morgan been successful, however, she might, some would argue, have done her half-brother something of a favor.

With the end of its story and of Arthurian history in view, the poem can figuratively if not literally accomplish Morgan's wishes. As she is portrayed in Fitt I, Guenevere, in one sense, could not be more dead than she already is. In her most detailed appearance in *Sir Gawain and the Green Knight*, she is utterly static. She does not speak (here or elsewhere in the poem). She simply sits and looks, and, perhaps more importantly, she is looked upon.

> Whene Guenore, ful gay, gray þed in þe myddes,
> Dressed on þe dere des, dubbed al aboute,
> Smal sendal bisides, a selure hir ouer
> Of tryed tolouse, of tars tapites innoghe,
> Þat were enbrawded and beten wyth þe best gemmes
> Þat my3t be preued of prys wyth penyes to bye,
>   in daye.
>   þe comlokest to discrye
>   þer glent with 3en gray,
>   A semloker þat euer he sy3e
>   Soth mo3t no man say.   [74-84]

> [Guenevere the goodly queen gay in the midst
> On a dais well-decked and duly arrayed
> With costly silk curtains, a canopy over,
> Of Toulouse and Turkestan tapestries rich,
> All broidered and bordered with the best gems
> Ever brought into Britain, with bright pennies
>   to pay.
>   Fair queen, without a flaw,
>   She glanced with eyes of gray.
>   A seemlier that once he saw,
>   In truth no man could say.]

As the syntactical circlings of this passage show, it is difficult to distinguish Guenevere and her worth from that of her splendid accoutrements. This is Guenevere fresh from the marriage settlement in which she, like most historical medieval women of her class, has been bought.[8] This is Guenevere set at the high table for all to admire, a token of Arthur's wealth, still the chaste queen who is the sign and symbol of the king to whom she refers. Her rehabilitation according to the revisionist directive of *Sir Gawain and the Green Knight* is inscribed in her stasis, in her function as the emblem of Arthur. Because she seems incapable of movement, she seems incapable of the specific movement that would lead her to a treacherous union with Lancelot.

Not moving or speaking, Guenevere is here marginalized to such an extent that she is buried in the plot of the poem.[9] For, if there is never just one margin, there is never just one way to be marginalized. Morgan le Fay is marginalized within the narrative by being placed at the end of the poem. But the poem marginalizes and thereby rehabilitates Guenevere by displaying her at the beginning of its own story, as a token of Arthur, and dissociating her from the end, where, as Morgan le Fay attempts to do in this romance, she will become the agent of his destruction. It is significant, however, that the initial description of Guenevere is placed as close to the opening mention of historical betrayal as Morgan's agency is placed to the closing repetition of "þe segge and þe asaute . . . at Troye." And it is significant, too, that when Guenevere *is* mentioned at the end of *Sir Gawain and the Green Knight*, a desire for her death as well as her own capacity for destruction are projected on to the single figure of Morgan le Fay.

Guenevere and Morgan may be marginalized in very different ways at the beginning and end of the poem, but there is always, of course, the Lady in the middle. In a romance that makes much of beginnings and ends because it is concerned with the end of beginnings, the Lady's placement squarely at the poem's center is significant for many reasons. If Morgan is the means to the end of trying young Gawain (and, by extension, the pride of the Round Table), then the Lady is a stand-in for Morgan, in the middle, literally and figuratively, as Morgan's intermediary, despite Bertilak's rather suspicious attempt in Fitt IV to claim her as *his* agent.[10] Bertilak tells Gawain:

Now know I wel þy cosses, and þy costes als,
And þe wowyng of my wyf; I wroȝt hit myseluen.
I sende hir to asay þe . . . . [2360-62]

[I know well the tale,
And the count of your kisses and your conduct too,
And the wooing of my wife—it was all my scheme!]

Although sex with her may temporarily seem an end in itself, it is, or would be, a means to the end of trying young Gawain. Moreover, it is no accident that one of the few references to Guenevere comes when Gawain sees the Lady for the first time:

> Ho watz þe fayrest in felle, of flesche and of lyre,
> And of compas and colour and costes, of alle o þer,
> And wener þen Wenore, as þe wyȝe þoȝt.
> He ches þurȝ þe chaunsel to cheryche þat hende.
> An o þer lady hir lad bi þe lyft honde,
> Þat watz alder þen ho, an auncian hit semed . . . .
>
> [943-48]
>
> [The fair hues of her flesh, her face and her hair
> And her body and her bearing were beyond praise,
> And excelled the queen herself, as Sir Gawain thought.
> He goes forth to greet her with gracious intent;
> Another lady led her by the left hand
> That was older than she—an ancient, it seemed. . . .]

This reference to Guenevere is not simply a conventional aesthetic observation.[11] As the construction of this passage shows, it serves to underline the Lady's placement between two marginalized females, Morgan and Guenevere, because she, the woman textually and sexually in the middle, is the common denominator between them.

If the Lady is the common denominator between these two female characters, what she denominates is, in essence, femaleness itself. Nor is this definition of the Lady so obvious, nor so reductive, as it would at first seem. And while it may seem strange to make much of Morgan's marginalization when the Lady is at the center of the poem, it is the nature of the femaleness ascribed to and designated by the Lady, and shared by both Guenevere and Morgan, that needs marginalizing if *Sir Gawain and the Green Knight* is to succeed in its Christian chivalric revision of Arthurian history. For, rather than contradicting the poem's agenda of leaving the female aside, the centrality of the Lady works to underline the poem's purpose. Situated as she is between Guenevere in Fitt I and Morgan in Fitt IV, the Lady is, as Gilbert and Gubar would define it, "framed" within the poem.[12] That is, she is both enclosed and "set up," as it were, in the poem's effort to contain and delimit her meaning. The Lady is contained and redefined in the text so that Gawain can be reintegrated, green girdle and all, into the reconstituted court at Camelot.

Indeed, containment, it seems, is the essence of the Lady who is always situated within and associated with enclosed and private spaces. We see the Lady first entering the closet in which she hears Mass on the first day of Gawain's stay in the castle: " Þe lorde loutes þerto, and þe lady als, / Into a cumly closet coyntly ho entrez" ["The lord attends alone: his fair lady sits / In a comely closet, secluded from sight"] (933-34). The poet's choice of the adverb "coyntly" to describe her entrance into the private space of the closet suggests to readers of Chaucer the famous pun on "queynte" as female genitalia, which marks the Wife of Bath's characterization of herself in her prologue.[13] Interestingly, Gawain repeats this adverb again at the beginning of his anti-feminist diatribe: " Þus hor knyȝt wyth hor kest han *koyntly* bigyled" ["They have trapped their true knight in their trammels so quaint"] (2412; emphasis mine). When the Lady emerges from the closet, with her retinue of ladies and with Morgan le Fay some eight lines later, one hardly needs to invoke Freud to catch the associations with female sexuality that the poem is making. And, of course, the Lady's most famous activities within private enclosed spaces occur not merely in Gawain's bedroom, but inside the curtains of Gawain's bed: "and ho stepped stilly and stel to his bedde, / Kest up þe cortyn and creped withinne" ["And she stepped stealthily,_and stole to his bed, / Cast aside the curtain and came within"] (1191-92).

The Lady, it might seem, can exercise considerable power even within such containment. But the containment of the Lady within the castle or the closet or the bedroom echoes her containment within the text, a containment that, while it places the Lady at the center, simultaneously underlines her marginalization. She is, as we will see, placed at the center in order to be displaced from it. And it is here that, in order to accomplish its revision of Arthurian legend, the poem takes as its model late medieval social and legal history. For, like her historical counterpart, the medieval noblewoman, the Lady is contained within the castle in order, finally, to be marginalized within aristocratic society.[14] She is so marginalized, in fact, that a poem that names everything, including Gawain's horse Gringolet, never names her. She has no ostensible existence outside the castle walls unless a man chooses to name her (Bertilak generally calls her "myn owen wyf" [2359] or "my wyf" [2361] as if to underline his ownership; Gawain mentions her as little as he can [2497]). She is simply the Lady. That is all there is to know and all we need to know.[15]

Contained as she is within the castle and the poem, the Lady and the femaleness she shares with Guenevere and Morgan become fundamentally associated with privateness. The Lady is associated with privateness because that is the realm she inhabits. But she is so thoroughly associated with privateness, that privateness itself becomes feminized in *Sir Gawain and the Green Knight*. Certainly, her privateness is linked to female sexuality, as the possible pun on "coyntly" suggests. The dangers associated with the Lady, the threat she poses to Gawain's life, may ultimately derive from this source and from the poem's inscription of the otherness of female sexuality according to the time-honored tradition of medieval misogyny.[16] But *Sir Gawain and the Green Knight* goes even farther, I believe, in order to suggest the political and social implications of the female's privateness and the fundamental disruptiveness attributed to the female and to the values associated with her in this poem. For it is through the redefinition of this privateness and of the emblematic girdle that the poem accomplishes its revision of Arthurian legend and provides a model of masculine behavior by which the Round Table might have been saved.

As the course of Arthurian history and of chivalric literature makes clear, trouble arises when the knight withdraws from public life to fulfill private desire, when the knight yields to private desire at the expense of public function. And Gawain, with his pentangle and armor locked away somewhere in one of this castle's many private rooms, is in such a precarious situation from the moment that he enters Morgan's castle in Fitt II. The plot of the romance has relegated him to privateness to test how he fares there, for the temptations posed by private desire are essentially the ones that Gawain must overcome both to save his life and to ensure the preservation and continuation of the Arthurian world.[17]

Gawain, in assuming the Green Knight's challenge at Camelot, has ceased to be a private individual. He has assumed the responsibility of acting as a token of Arthur's fame and reputation. In this capacity, he has no room for private desires, or at the very least, his private desires must be trained to the service of the public good. Indeed, when Gawain claims the test, he does so on the basis of relationship to Arthur, who is both his uncle and his king: "Bot for as much as ȝe ar myn em I am only to prayse, / No bounté bot your blod in my bodé knowe" ["That I have you for my uncle is my only praise; / My body, but for your blood, is barren of worth"] (356-57). There can be no more concise statement of the alignment of public and private in the worthy knight than Gawain articulates here. Arthur is in him; he stands for Arthur; and thus he publicizes his king and kingdom in the testings he undertakes. And this, then, is also the meaning of the pentangle, each of whose five interlocked points refers to the way the individual male's private virtues are inextricably interwoven with the public systems of belief, the ideologies, of Christianity and chivalry. The pentangle is a sign of the private male's conscription into the public order. The interconnectedness of these virtues underlines, then, the religious and political stability that would result from adherence to the values encoded in the pentangle.[18]

For Gawain to yield to the Lady would, in fact, involve more than yielding to the otherness of her sexuality. Implied in that yielding to otherness would be the Round Table knight's capitulation to privateness, to private desire, and to the feminization of the private that has been inscribed in this poem. But this romance's rehabilitated Gawain will not yield to mere sexual desire, despite his attraction to the Lady. Certainly, the confrontation at the Green Chapel preoccupies him, perhaps more than his agreement to exchange winnings with his host, and in its own terms, this preoccupation is understandable enough. At this point, however, the poem's revision of Gawain's often spotted past is especially telling. Unlike the Gawain of legend, and even more significantly, unlike Lancelot, this Gawain will not give in to the temptation of mere female flesh, even when, as we have been told, it is lovelier than Guenevere's. At this early stage of the Round Table's career, Gawain is a stronger knight than Lancelot will turn out to be. Gawain is too publically committed to take his private pleasure and to betray his vows to men, that is, to his king or to his unnamed host, until, indeed, he thinks that his life depends on it.[19]

And then Gawain fails and falls, but not so badly nor so far that the poem cannot reinstate him in its attempt to restore a prelapsarian Camelot. Gawain does not err because of desire for the Lady's body or because of the temptation of her or his sexuality. Rather, he falls because he yields to the desire to save his life, once he has learned of the magical properties inherent in the girdle:

> Þen kest þe kny3t, and hit come to his hert
> Hit were a juel for þe jopardé þat hym iugged were:
> When he acheued to þe chapel his chek for to fech,
> My3t he haf slypped to be vnslayn, þe sle3t were noble.
>
> [1855-58]

> [Then the man began to muse, and mainly he thought
> It was a pearl for his plight, the peril to come
> When he gains the Green Chapel to get his reward:
> Could he escape unscathed, the scheme were noble!]

This is, we might think, a natural enough desire, just as Gawain does at the moment and as Bertilak does later at the Green Chapel, when he judges Gawain:

> Bot here yow lakked a lyttel, sir, and lewté yow wonted;
> Bot þat watz for no wylyde werke, ne wowyng nau þer,
> Bot for 3e lufed your lyf; þe lasse I yow blame.
>
> [2366-68]

> [Yet you lacked, sir, a little in loyalty there,
> But the cause was not cunning, nor courtship either,
> But that you loved your own life; the less, then, to blame.]

But this yielding is particularly dangerous because the desire for life might well be the most natural and instinctive of all. As such, it is the private desire that includes all others within it. To yield to this desire might be only the beginning.

What is more, in political terms, to yield to this desire would spell the end of Arthur's kingdom, of its famous prowess, of its military strength. What would happen, after all, if members of the Round Table, individually and collectively, succumbed repeatedly to the desire to preserve their lives? Gawain may be over-reacting when he speaks later of his "cowarddyse and couetyse" (2374), but he is not entirely wrong. To assume the girdle, as the poem states, "for gode of hymseluen" (2031) is to think primarily of himself. It is to think not of the kingdom's reputation, of its security and solidarity, but of his private desire; it is, in essence, an act of cowardice in which Gawain also shows himself more greedy than he ought to be to save his own private neck.[20] In the feudal and chivalric world of this romance, a man's desire to save his life might be understandable, but wanting "lewté" is no minor political transgression.

The girdle initially signifies life, and specifically Gawain's desire to save his own. Because this private desire is linked in *Sir Gawain and the Green Knight* to the privateness that is the Lady, Gawain's action implicitly betrays the masculine codes of Christian chivalry affirmed as the central values of this poem. When Bertilak has revealed the shape of the testing to Gawain, Gawain's response shows his understanding of the political, ethical, and sexual consequences of his action. Flinging the girdle back at Bertilak, he admits that desire for his life caused him "to acorde me with couetyse, my kynde to forsake, / þat is larges and lewté þat longez to kny3tez" ["And coveting came after, contrary both / To largesse and loyalty belonging to knights"] (2379-80). His belief that he has betrayed his "kynde" cuts many ways; he has betrayed his nature, which is not only the virtues signified by the pentangle. It is also Arthur, and Arthur's blood, and the values of the Round Table's knighthood. In these terms, to betray his "kynde" is also to betray his masculinity, that is, his fundamental identity, for, in this poem, knighthood and masculinity are in the end the same thing. Without the synonymity of masculinity and knighthood, we are left in a romance world in which masculinity and masculine behavior become synonymous with courtliness, with love dalliance in the bedroom, with the world of ladies and Lancelot, with the world that is contained in Morgan's castle and contained by the narrative. And this is the world from which Gawain has just made a well-timed escape.

After the woman in the middle has compromised Gawain's manhood with her privateness, the poem provides for him, in Fitt IV, a father-confessor to conduct the process of marginalizing the woman and reintegrating Gawain into the court at Camelot. This father-confessor is none other than the Green Knight/Bertilak, whose words to Gawain should carry special weight because he has experienced the dangers of enclosure within the private world of women.[21] Bertilak, after all, can rapidly change color at Morgan's whim.

It is his father-confessor that Gawain has betrayed by failing to return the girdle in the exchange of winnings game. And it is from this father-confessor that Gawain receives an axiom that he should never forget and that will restore his knighthood and his masculinity. In two highly condensed and elliptical lines, Bertilak tells Gawain that "Trwe mon trwe restore, / Penne þar mon drede no wa þe" ["True men pay what they owe; / No danger then in sight"] (2354-55). One need not fear harm if the true man truly restores, that is, if he maintains the essential social contracts between men.[22] Then the true man will truly be a man, because he has not yielded to private and thus feminized desires. These lines might well serve as a motto for a poetic, political, and ethical program that would, in effect, save Arthur's kingdom. By following Bertilak's advice, Gawain in his completed confession and analysis of his motives is a redeemed man, here bought back from the woman with whom he has bargained for his life.[23]

But it is not that easy for Gawain, for the court of Arthur, or for the poem that knows the end of its own story and the end of the story of the Arthurian world. For if Arthur's blood is in Gawain, we learn, when we learn of Morgan's agency, that her blood is in him, too. Bertilak, the great revealer, finally reveals Morgan, at the end of the poem, but not until Gawain has shown himself ready for this revelation. By now, Gawain has sufficiently distanced himself from association with the Lady to guarantee his public reintegration into Arthur's court. By now, in an anti-feminist diatribe that has given many critics pause,[24] he has successfully completed this distancing by claiming that, since all great men fall to women's wiles, he might be excused for following suit:

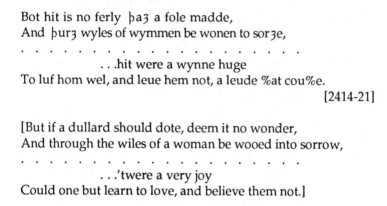

> Bot hit is no ferly þaȝ a fole madde,
> And þurȝ wyles of wymmen be wonen to sorȝe,
> · · · · · · · · · · · · · · · · · · ·
> · · ·hit were a wynne huge
> To luf hom wel, and leue hem not, a leude %at cou%e.
>
> [2414-21]

[But if a dullard should dote, deem it no wonder,
And through the wiles of a woman be wooed into sorrow,
· · · · · · · · · · · · · · · · · · ·
. . .'twere a very joy
Could one but learn to love, and believe them not.]

He can learn, then, that not only did Morgan concoct this adventure, but that she is also "Þyn aunt, Ar þurez half-suster" ["Your own aunt. . ., Arthur's half-sister"] (2464). Throughout the poem, the woman Morgan has been assigned to a privateness so complete that she cannot be admitted until this point, when Gawain has proven himself protected from the influence of her blood.   And yet, by Bertilak's admission, she is always simultaneously lurking at the fringes and inescapably at dead center, related to Arthur and to Gawain, just as her influence is at the narrative center of the romance. The poem forcefully leaves her aside because that is all it can do, but to do that, if it could be done, would be plenty.

And thus the fate of the green girdle, the love token that the Lady wove and wore and gave to Gawain as a sign not only of her, but of his life and his desire to save it. By the time Gawain rides back into Arthur's hall bedecked with the girdle, the Lady has vanished from the realm of its signification. She has been marginalized so that Gawain and the girdle can be publicized. Along the route of the girdle's redefinition and Gawain's return home, Bertilak has claimed that it is his, just as he claims to have pimped for his wife in order to test Gawain's virtue: "For hit is my wede þat þou werez, þat ilke wouen girdel" ["For that is my belt about you, that same braided girdle"] (2358). The girdle has gone from being a sign of Gawain's life and his desire to save it to a sign of his threatened death, his sin and his unkindness, his unnaturalness, all so that it can be, as Bertilak claims, a "pure token / Of þe chaunce of þe grene chapel at cheualrous knyghteȝ" ["token / How it chanced at the Green Chapel, to chivalrous knights"] (2398-99). The green girdle is a sign now not of the woman, but of the tested man, who has not been found so wanting after all.[25] The woman in the middle has effectively been displaced from the center, to become as marginalized as Guenevere and Morgan. And thus the token is pure, cleansed of female signification, and particularly of male alliance with the female at the expense of bonding with the male. "Trwe mon trwe restore."

But Gawain cannot accept the girdle back so easily. He himself must redefine it in order to associate it directly with his sins, and only marginally with the Lady. And yet the Lady is signified in the specific sin that Gawain links to the girdle: "Þe faut and þe fayntyse of þe flesche crabbed, / How tender hit is to entyse teches of fylþe" ["The faults and the frailty of the flesh perverse, / How its tenderness entices the foul taint of sin"] (2435-36). At this point, the Lady's marginalization and the placement of the female in the poem are complete. The Lady of the girdle is reduced to the corruption of the flesh, in an image that specifically evokes withered, old Morgan, the "auncian," as she has been described in Fitt II (947-69). The Lady, through this rapid deterioration, has been revised. Or perhaps we see here signs of the specific revision that this poem has worked on Morgan herself, because I, for one, find it difficult to understand how Arthur's half-sister could have become so old so soon, unless it were to link her with the corruption of the flesh, that, in this poem, becomes linked to the corruption that is women in the center of Arthur's court.[26]

The court, however, is ready to forgive and forget, just as, I would argue, the poem would like to forgive and forget, but primarily to forget as it nears the end of a revisionary agenda that it knows must fail. As a sign of its forgiveness, the court assumes the sign of Gawain's self-defined sin.

> Þe kyng comfortez the knyʒt, and alle þe court als
> Laʒen loude þerat, and lufly acorden
> Þat lordes and ladis þat longed to þe Table,
> Uche burne of þe bro þerhede, a bauderyk schulde haue . . .
> [2513-16]

[The king comforts the knight, and the court all together
Agree with gay laughter and gracious intent
That the lords and the ladies belonging to the Table,
Each brother of that band, a baldric should have. . . .]

In the process, the court collectively rehabilitates the girdle by making it a public sign of honor.[27] Interestingly enough, the rehabilitation of the girdle follows the same model as does the rehabilitation of Guenevere in Fitt I. Through this sign, the woman is safely placed within the court, safely placed specifically because she is removed from the dangerous realm of the private and the feminine and published as a token within a masculine world. If Guenevere in Fitt I is rehabilitated because she so surely refers to Arthur, then the publicized girdle is rehabilitated specifically because it now refers to the honor of Arthur's court.

The poem knows, however, that the end is not so easy and that its own means are insufficient to the end. The woman may have been marginalized by leaving Morgan aside, but the process of her marginalization involves her naming. In other words, it involves her publication, her removal from her own sphere of the private so that she can become the public sign of the male. But, as such, the woman as token becomes dangerously current within the court, just as the green girdle, redefined though it might be, is dangerously current in the closing scene at Camelot. For, among the male gazes directed at the static Guenevere in Fitt I is, we can assume, that of Lancelot (who is mentioned only once in the poem [553], included in the brotherhood of knights advising Gawain before his departure in Fitt II). And, unless Guenevere is blind as well as mute, she can, of course, look back.

In its marginalization of women, then, the poem provides a proleptic cure for Arthurian history. If Guenevere had been the static and silent queen, then the Round Table would not have fallen. If men could redefine and thereby control experience for other men, as Bertilak does for Gawain, and, indeed, as the poet does for his audience, then Morgan's power would be diffused. But the poem and its poet know better, because they know the story of Arthur and because women, in the legend and in life, cannot be effectively marginalized. The poem tries to suggest that the life-giving girdle and its giver are ultimately life-threatening. In the historical world of feudal chivalry, however, the bearers of death are not generally women. If our end comes from our beginning, we still know where that beginning starts. If women were legally and politically marginalized within feudal society, they were nonetheless central, biologically, economically, *and* politically, to its continuation. Guenevere's barrenness may thus discount her within this world. But Morgan is, as Bertilak admits, "þe goddes." Although Bertilak makes her magic secondary by attributing it to Merlin, that magic, as Morgan practices it, is powerful stuff. Bertilak may be bent out of shape by it, but he can still grow a new head. It is this regenerative capacity that enables the Green Knight to make his reappearance in Fitt IV.[28] His end, then, is only his beginning and the beginning of the narrative, thanks to Morgan le Fay.

It is no wonder then that the poem's erasure of women, of Guenevere, of the Lady, and of Morgan, is uneasy and incomplete. The odds of Arthurian legend and of human history are against it. Could the female be marginalized, then the Round Table would not have ended. But she cannot be, and it will. Nonetheless, the meaning of this end is not the end of the meaning, not of the "rex quondam rexque futurus" and not of his queen. And not, for that matter, of Morgan le Fay.

NOTES

1. See, for example, Larry D. Benson, *Art and Tradition in Sir Gawain and the Green Knight* (New Brunswick: Rutgers University Press, 1965), pp. 97-98; A. C. Spearing, *The Gawain-Poet: A Critical Study*

(Cambridge: Cambridge University Press, 1970), pp. 181 and 222; John Eadie, "Morgain la Fée and the Conclusion of *Sir Gawain and the Green Knight*," *Neophilologus* 52 (1968), 300-01; Robert W. Hanning, "Sir Gawain and the Red Herring: The Perils of Interpretation,"in Mary J. Carruthers and Elizabeth D. Kirk, eds., *Acts of Interpretation: The Text in its Contexts 700-1600: Essays on Medieval and Renaissance Literature in Honor of E. Talbot Donaldson* (Norman: Pilgrim Books, 1982), p. 11. In "Myth and Medieval Literature: *Sir Gawain and the Green Knight*," (*Speculum* 18 [1956], 172), Charles Moorman argues that the poem is "a highly compressed allegorical commentary on the entire Arthurian history" and that "the seeds of [its] tragedy were present even in the 'first age' of the youthful and joyous court at Christmas time." Moorman does not argue, as I do, that the poem valorizes the youthful court as part of its revisionist project. In a chapter on *Sir Gawain and the Green Knight* in her thesis, "Mordred's Hidden Presence: The Skeleton in the Arthurian Closet" (Ph.D., Yale, 1985), M. Victoria Guerin offers a thorough analysis of the ways in which the poem follows a revisionist program in its relation to the unnamed Mordred. I am grateful to Professor Guerin for sharing the manuscript of her chapter with me.

2   *Sir Gawain and the Green Knight*, ed. J. R. R. Tolkien and E. V. Gordon, 2nd ed. rev. Norman Davis (Oxford: Oxford University Press, 1967). All quotations of the poem are taken from this edition and are cited by line number. The translation cited is that of Marie Borroff (New York: Norton, 1967). On these lines, cf. Moorman, 164 and 171.

3   See Benson, for example, pp. 32-35. Morgan's traditional enmity toward the Round Table stands as the most frequent justification for her presence in the poem. Most book-length studies of the poem, however, give relatively little emphasis to Morgan's significance to the poem. The exception to the general neglect of Morgan occurs primarily in the articles published on her in the 1950's and 1960's: Denver Ewing Baughan: "The Role of Morgan la Faye in *Sir Gawain and the Green Knight*," *ELH* 17 (1950), 241-51; Albert B. Friedman, "Morgan la Faye in *Sir Gawain and the Green Knight*," *Speculum* 35 (1960), 260-74; Mother Angela Carson, O. S. U., "Morgain la Fée as the Principle of Unity in Gawain and the Green Knight," *MLQ* 23 (1962), 3-16; Douglas Moon, "The Role of Morgan la Faye in *Gawain and the Green Knight*," *NM* 67 (1966), 31-57. The most recent study of Morgan is Edith Whitehurst Williams' "Morgan la Fée as Trickster in *Sir Gawain and the Green*

Knight," *Folklore* 96 (1985), 38-56. To date, there has been no comprehensive feminist study of the placement of women in the poem.

4. In addition to the sources cited in footnote 1, see also Moorman, 167-72; Baughan, 244-47; and Friedman, 269.

5. Victoria Guerin's chapter on *Sir Gawain and the Green Knight* offers a comprehensive analysis of this issue in relation to the poem's themes and purposes.

6. For discussion of Gawain's traditional reputation as a "lady's man," see Friedman, 265; Benson, pp. 95 and 103; Spearing, pp. 198-99; W. R. J. Barron, *Trawthe and Treason: The Sin of Sir Gawain Reconsidered* (Manchester: Manchester University Press, 1980), p. 21. Guerin's chapter on *Sir Gawain and the Green Knight* offers a comprehensive discussion of this issue.

7. For a thorough and perceptive discussion of the fluctuation of Gawain's value and identity, see R. A. Shoaf's *The Poem as Green Girdle: "Commercium" in "Sir Gawain and the Green Knight"* (Gainesville: University Presses of Florida, 1984), especially the section, "What *Prys* Gawain?," pp. 34-36. Throughout my discussion of Gawain's activities in the bedroom and of the girdle's meaning, I am particularly indebted to Professor Shoaf's analysis as well as to the bibliography that he generously shared with me before his monograph appeared in print.

8. For a discussion of medieval women's legal, political, and marital rights, see Shulamith Shahar, *The Fourth Estate: A History of Women in the Middle Ages*, trans. Chaya Galai (New York: Methuen, 1983), pp. 11-21, and the chapter on aristocratic women, pp. 126-73.

9. In this essay, my thinking about the placement of women in narative has been influenced by Sandra M. Gilbert and Susan Gubar's chapter, "The Queen's Looking Glass," in *Madwoman in the Attic: The Woman Writer and the Nineteenth-Century Literary Imagination* (New Haven: Yale University Press, 1984), pp. 3-44, esp. pp. 20-27.

10. Benson, for example, writes that the Lady was "following Bertilak's orders," although he acknowledges Morgan as the source of Bertilak's activities (p. 55). Peter L. Rudnytsky takes the same approach to the Lady in "*Sir Gawain and the Green Knight*: Oedipal Temptation," *AI* 40 (1983), 377. Carson was the first to stress Morgan's responsibility for the plot *and* Bertilak's role as *her* agent (13).

11. Moorman, 167. Moorman's arguments resemble my own here, but he does not associate the Lady, Guenevere, and Morgan, as I believe the poem does, on the basis of the femaleness that they share.

12. I take this idea of "framing women in art" from Gilbert and Gubar, *Madwoman in the Attic*, pp. 13 and 42. My thinking about the significance of Guenevere's placement at Arthur's table was influenced by Susan Gubar's discussion of the dual meaning of Judy Chicago's *Dinner Party*: "But *The Dinner Party* plates also imply that women, who have served, have been served up and consumed." See "'The Blank Page' and the Issues of Female Creativity," reprinted in Elaine Showalter, ed., *The New Feminist Criticism: Essays on Women, Literature, and Theory*, (New York: Pantheon Books, 1985), p. 300 (originally printed in *Critical Inquiry* 8 [Winter 1981]). Hanning also notes that Guenevere in this scene is an "elegant courtly artifact" (11).

13. Speaking of her inexplicable love for Jankyn, the Wife of Bath says: "We wommen han, if that I shal nat lye, / In this matere a queynte fantasye," *The Riverside Chaucer*, ed. Larry D. Benson (Boston: Houghton Mifflin, 1987), III [D], 515-16. The pun on *queynte* as female genitalia occurs frequently enough in Chaucer that it does not seem too much to assume that its possibility would have been familiar to the *Gawain*-poet.

14. For a discussion of medieval women's marital position and rights, see Shahar, pp. 65-125. Throughout my analysis of women's placement within marital, political, and economic systems, I am indebted to Gayle Rubin's important feminist revision of Claude Lévi-Strauss' *The Elementary Structures of Kinship* in "The Traffic in Women: Notes on the 'Political Economy' of Sex," in Rayna R. Reiter, ed., *Toward an Anthropology of Women* (New York: Monthly Review Press, 1975), pp. 157-210.

15. For representative interpretations of the Lady as seductress, see Benson, pp. 38-40, and W. A. Davenport, *The Art of the Gawain-Poet* (London: Athlone Press, 1978), pp. 137, 167-68, and 187. Taking a much different approach, Victor Y. Haines, in *The Fortunate Fall of Sir Gawain: The Typology of Sir Gawain and the Green Knight* (Washington: University Press of America, 1982), argues that while the Lady seems to "corrupt" Gawain in a first reading of the poem, "in the redeemed history of [a] second reading, the lady is benevolent," because she wants to save Gawain's life (p. 145). According to Haines, the Lady operates as an emissary of Mary

(not of Morgan) because her love for Gawain is charitable, not concupiscent (pp. 131, 138-42, and 148).

16. Two important feminist contributions to the study of women's relationship to medieval literature include Joan M. Ferrante, *Woman as Image in Medieval Literature: From the Twelfth Century Through Dante* (New York: Columbia University Press, 1975), and E. Jane Burns' and Roberta L. Krueger's "Introduction" to *Courtly Ideology and Women's Place in Medieval French Literature, Romance Notes* 25 (Spring 1985), 205-19.

17. Cf. Shoaf's discussion, pp. 31-46. While Shoaf concludes, "Bertilak's Lady manipulates Gawain until he insists on private value exclusively" (p. 46), he studies Gawain's yielding to privacy in the context of medieval Christian sacramentality and not in the context of the inscription of the female in the narrative.

18. Spearing (pp. 175 and 196-98) and Burrow (pp. 50 and 105) offer representative interpretations of the criticism on the pentangle. In his monograph, Shoaf gives a new reading of the pentangle, which is based in medieval and postmodern sign theory and which gives full weight to the problematics of referentiality in the poem. See, especially, pp. 71-75.

19. Many of my ideas about the configurations of male homosociality in literary texts and the (dis)placement of women within these configurations are indebted to the introduction and first two chapters of Eve Kosofsky Sedgwick, *Between Men: English Literature and Male Homosocial Desire* (New York: Columbia University Press, 1985). While Sedgwick's book primarily discusses later literature, these opening sections are relevant to the study of medieval and early modern texts.

20. Critical disagreement about the poem is sharpest in the divergent interpretations of the seriousness of Gawain's sin. For three recent examples of this divergence of opinion, compare Thomas D. Hill, "Gawain's Jesting Lie: Towards an Interpretation of the Confessional Scene in *Sir Gawain and the Green Knight*," *Studia Neophilologia* 52 (1980), 279-86; Shoaf, pp. 15-30; and Williams, 51.

21. For representative interpretations of Bertilak's role in Fitt IV, see Moorman, 166; Burrow, pp. 137 and 169; Davenport, pp. 168-73; Spearing, pp. 31 and 221; and Barron, p. 132.

22. Cf. Shoaf, pp. 15-30.

23. See Shoaf's appendix (pp. 77-80) for an indication of the density of commercial images in this poem. For earlier discussions of the implications of the poem's commercial idiom, see Burrow, pp. 76-

77 and 88-89, and Paul B. Taylor, "Commerce and Comedy in *Sir Gawain and the Green Knight*," *PhilQ* 50 (1971), 1-15.

24. The conflicting reaction to Gawain's anti-feminist diatribe is one of the most interesting interludes in the history of the critical tradition on this poem.

25. Shoaf's monograph stands as the most comprehensive discussion of the complex significations of the girdle and of its thematic function within the poem.

26. Tolkien's footnote on Morgan's advanced age (p. 130) has been consistently accepted by most critics who have raised this issue. Others, like Benson (p. 32), associate Morgan's aging with the filth of the flesh whose presence within him Gawain must acknowledge as the wages of his sin. Carson argues, on the basis of the poem's sources, that Morgan and the Lady are one and the same because of the dual nature of Morgan. In Carson's reading, Bertilak is Uriens, and Morgan's traditional characterization becomes attributed to the two central women in the poem (5 and 13). While Carson's reading engages Morgan's centrality in the poem, it does not sufficiently engage the marginalization of Morgan that the poem accomplishes by substituting the Lady for her. Williams offers an analysis similar to Carson's, but bases her discussion on Jungian archetypes (41 and 49).

27. For a representative sampling of the disagreement over the poem's ending, see Moorman, 170; Burrow, pp. 158-59; Spearing, pp. 222 and 230; Benson, pp. 241-42; Edward Wilson, *The Gawain-Poet* (Leiden: Brill, 1976), pp. 130-31. Williams' discussion of the concluding presentation of the girdle comes close to my own, but she does not discuss the significance of the erasure of the Lady in the final scene (52).

28. See, for example, Benson, p. 94, and Hanning, pp. 6-7, on the meaning of the natural landscape. The complex meanings that circulate around the natural world in this poem align themselves in interesting ways with what Elaine Showalter has designated as "the wild zone" of female culture, that is, the private world of women's culture that men never see. See "Feminist Criticism in the Wilderness," in *The New Feminist Criticism*, p. 262 (originally published in *Critical Inquiry* 8 [1981]).

The "Syngne of Surfet" and the Surfeit of Signs in *Sir Gawain and the Green Knight*

R. A. Shoaf

In Memoriam
Judson Boyce Allen

Sir Gawain and the Green Knight contains many words and terms that ask for more than a narrowly secular reading of the poem to account for them. Examples that come readily to mind include "couetyse" (2374), "faut" (2435), "teches" (2436), "surquidré" (2457), and "surfet" (2433).[1] These and other words possess strong theological valence, and they are as important to interpreting the poem as are words that derive from courtly or heroic or other codes. As part of a book in progress, *"The Knot Why Every Tale is Told": Toward a Poetics of the Knot in Western Literature from the Classics to the Renaissance*, I am preparing a study of *Sir Gawain and the Green Knight* that focuses on the figure of the knot in the poem, its relation to the similar figure in Dante's *Commedia*, especially the *Paradiso*, and the importance of the figure to understanding the theological vocabulary of *Sir Gawain*. The following remarks derive from this study-in-progress, and although necessarily they must abbreviate many of my findings to date, they still provide a reliable sketch of several crucial elements in the figure of the knot in *Sir Gawain and the Green Knight*, especially the "syngne of surfet" and the surfeit of signs in the poem.[2]

Near the end of *Sir Gawain*, Gawain explains why he accepts the Green Knight's offer of the green girdle: not for its fabulous worth nor for its curious workmanship,

Bot in *syngne of my surfet* I schal se hit ofte,
When I ride in renoun, remorde to myseluen
Þe faut and þe fayntyse of þe flesche crabbed,
How tender hit is to entyse teches of fyl þe.

[2433-36; emphasis mine]

[But a sign of excess it shall seem oftentimes
When I ride in renown, and remember with shame
The faults and the frailty of the flesh perverse,
How its tenderness entices the foul taint of sin.]

Throughout the latter part of his adventure, of course, Gawain identifies his error by many names (most notably, perhaps, by the crucial pair of terms, "cowarddyse and couetyse"—2374), but "surfet" is, by no means, the least of these.[3] Echoing as it does "surquidré" ["pride"], which the Green Knight says he came to "assay" in Arthur's court (2457), and in many ways synonymous with *superbia*, "surfet" points to that excess traditionally known as pride; and here it is probably best taken to refer to an excess of self-reliance, a pride of mind: Gawain relies on his own "good" judgment in deciding to take the green girdle from Bertilak's Lady when, in fact, his judgment, far from good, is actually corrupt—and corrupt, moreover, in a particular way.

Gawain's judgment is corrupted not only by "surfet" but also by signs—to be precise, by the plethora of signs that confront him in his world and that by their very multiplicity vex and question any exclusivity in interpretation; the girdle, in this light, then, is not only, as Gawain says, a "sign of surfet," but also yet one more in the surfeit of signs that beset the Arthurian kingdom and that challenge its capacity to interpret them.

The most obvious instance of such a challenge involves the Green Knight himself—Arthur and his knights have not the foggiest notion what he means when he bursts into the castle at Christmas:

For vch mon had *meruayle* quat hit *mene* myȝt
Þat a haþel and a horse myȝt such a hwe lach
. . . .
Al *studied* þat þer stod, and stalked hym nerre

Wyth al þe *wonder* of þe worlde what he worch schulde.
For *fele* sellyez had þay sen, bot *such* neuer are;
For þi for *fantoum* and *fayry3e* þe folk þere hit *demed*.
[233-34; 237-40; emphasis mine]

For much did they marvel what it might mean
That a horseman and a horse should have such a hue

. . . .

All the onlookers eyed him, and edged nearer,
And awaited in wonder what he would do,
For many sights had they seen, but such a one never,
So that phantom and faerie the folk there deemed it.]

This passage is remarkable in many ways, not least among them
the number of words and phrases that relate to the process and
the difficulty of interpretation. But it is most important from the
present perspective for its indisputable insistence on the
incapacity of the courtiers, *despite* their extensive acquaintance
with wonders, to interpret the Green Knight; even after having
seen *many* wonders, even after *studying* the Green Knight, they
cannot interpret him—perhaps because they have seen *too* many
wonders, even perhaps a *surfeit* of wonders?

In light of such a passage, it is clearly more than just a
convenience to speak of a crisis of interpretation in *Sir Gawain*;
indeed, one can argue that the whole plot of the poem follows a
succession of such crises. But for present purposes, I would like to
narrow the focus to the emphasis on the role played in such crises
by the surfeit of signs. And at this point, it might be useful to
make a list of the principal signs in the poem—although this
list, long as it will be, is clearly far from exhaustive.

Such a list, arguably, should begin with the two most
portentous signs in the poem, at least after the Green Knight
himself—namely, the pentangle and the green girdle. The
pentangle is even introduced with a suggestion of the difficulty in
interpreting it:

And quy þe pentangel apendez to þat prynce noble
I am in tent yow to telle, *þof tary hyt me schulde*.
[623-24; emphasis mine]

[And why the pentangle is proper to the peerless prince
I intend now to tell, though detain me it must.]

If there were no difficulty, the poet would, of course, not protest
so much; but he does protest, especially the amount of time it will
take from his narrative, and this in itself is a sign of difficulty.
He then goes on to describe the, so to speak, genealogy of the
pentangle:

Hit is a *syngne* þat Salamon set sumquyle
In *bytoknyng* of traw þe, bi tytle þat hit habbez,
For hit is a *figure* . . . .
                    [625-27; emphasis mine]

[It is a sign by Solomon sagely devised
To be a token of truth, by its title of old,
For it is a figure . . . .]

Here we have three terms insisting on the hermeneutic process
which the pentangle necessitates, and the poet continues with
some thirty lines of interpretation in fulfillment of that process
and its expectation. And, as all modern students of the poem
know, countless lines and pages have been written, in just the past
forty years, in the effort to interpret, in turn, his interpretation.[4]
Clearly, it is not illegitimate here to speak of a *surfeit*.

It is also legitimate to speak of surfeit with regard to the
green girdle. For example, the green girdle is often mentioned in
the same breath with words for *sign* and *signifying*. As we have
seen, it is called a "syngne of surfet"; it is also called a "pure
token" (2398), a "token of vntraw þe" (2509); and, finally,
Gawain wears it "in *tokenyng* he watz tane in tech of a faute" [in
betokening of the blame he had borne for his fault] (2488;
emphasis mine). In effect, the green girdle precipitates a surfeit
of words for signifying. Then, in addition, of course, it itself
signifies: the trouble is, it signifies something different to
everyone who touches it. For Gawain, it signifies his "untruth";
for Arthur's courtiers, it signifies " þe bro þerhede" of the Table
(2515); for the Green Knight, it signifies "Pe chaunce of þe grene
chapel at cheualrous kny3tez" ["How it chanced at the Green

Chapel, to chivalrous knights"] (2399); for the Lady it signifies, as her gift to Gawain, her great affection toward him; for Gawain, again, finally, in the moment when he takes it from the Lady, it signifies no less than life itself. The green girdle, in effect, is the most *critical* sign in the poem; it always occasions the crisis of interpretation.

The poem is prolific with other signs, too. Take, for examples, the following two:

> Bot in his on honde he hade a holyn bobbe,
> Þat is grattest in grene when greuez ar bare,
> And an ax in his o þer, a hoge and vnmete,
> A spetos spar þe *to expoun in spelle*, quoso my3t.
> [206-09; emphasis mine]

> [But in his one hand he had a holly bob
> That is goodliest in green when groves are bare,
> And an ax in his other, a huge and immense,
> A wicked piece of work in words to expound.]

Crucially, the poet refers to the ax as an object "to expoun in spelle," as something, in other words, to be interpreted, as if, almost, the ax were a kind of text. Which, in an important sense, it is:

> And hit [the ax] watz don abof þe dece on doser to henge,
> Þer alle men for meruayl my3t on hit loke,
> And bi trwe *tytel* þerof to telle þe wonder.
> [478-80; emphasis mine]

> [And over the high dais it was hung on the wall
> That men in amazement might on it look,
> And tell in true terms the tale of the wonder.]

Not unlike a text or piece of writing, the ax signifies "bi trwe tytel" the "wonder" which men will tell of it.[5] And if the ax is thus a kind of text, it is reasonable in turn to suggest that the text is also a kind of ax, a mysterious weapon challenging the reader to a game in which he may lose his head. Be that as it may, the text is, in fact, a kind of ax in that it cuts between or severs conventional relations between signifiers and signifieds so as to expose and test those conventions in the eerie but brilliant light of its own fiction.[6] And our part is necessarily "to expoun [the ax/text] in spelle," even if we thus risk losing our heads.

Yet another sign in the poem is the "text" of knightly deeds:

And of alle cheualry to chose, þe chef þyng alosed
Is þe lel layk of luf, þe *lettrure* of armes;
For to telle of þis teuelyng of þis trwe kny3tez,
Hit is þe *tytelet token* and *tyxt* of her werkkez.
[1512-15; emphasis mine]

[And name what knight you will, they are noblest esteemed
For loyal faith in love, in life as in story;
For to tell the tribulations of these true hearts
Why, 'tis the very title and text of their deeds.]

Four words in this passage—*lettrure, tytelet token,* and *tyxt*— insist on textuality, writing, signifying, and interpreting.[7] This insistence is echoed and complicated by Gawain's response to the Lady at this point:

Bot to take þe toruayle to myself *to trwluf expoun,*
And *towche þe temez of tyxt and talez of armez*
To yow þat, I wot wel, weldez more sly3t
Of þat art, . . .
Hit were a folé felefolde . . . .
[1540-43, 45; emphasis mine]

[But to take to myself the task of telling of love,
And touch upon its texts, and treat of its themes
To one that, I know well, wields more power
In that art, . . .
It were folly . . . .]

Perhaps so, but such "felefolde folé," such manifold or multiple or plural folly is precisely what the critic must always confront, what he or she can never shy away from, at least without resigning the text to a certain darkness; and if Gawain retreats here, if he shuns the interpretive crisis, that just goes to prove the point, that he is not especially critical, that he suffers a certain naiveté, not unrelated I suspect to his "surquidré," that prevents him from really understanding, from fully interpreting the Lady's own text, the words with which she slowly but surely seduces him into trusting her.

And though I must resist the temptation to multiply interpretations here in what would amount to my own surfeit of signs, I would be remiss in my duty as precisely a critic if I did not observe that, just here, in these passages, this poem about a surfeit of signs is also about criticism: recall that the Greek word, *kritikós*, from which *criticism* derives, means "able to discern and decide," and the justice of this claim will be evident—the poem is also about criticism in that it is about that "distinguishing" or failure in "distinguishing" amidst the "folé felefolde" that is man's best and most characteristic response to the surfeit of signs in his world.[8]

Many other signs and terms related to or involved in signification could be added to the list—for example, "baldric," "blasoun," "cote-armure," "fourme," "ferly," "laykyng," "lote," "mervayle," "poynte," "songez," "tale," "ymage." But space does not permit even brief analyses of any of them. Hence, it will be more helpful to evaluate in detail the response of Arthur and his world to the surfeit of signs; this in turn may provide a context for our own response to the poem *Sir Gawain and the Green Knight*.

Confronted with a surfeit of signs, members of the Arthurian court often fail to be adequately critical in their interpretations of the signs. Arthur, and Gawain after him, for example, can only interpret the Green Knight's challenge as implying that he, Arthur or Gawain, is to strike the blow with the ax, whereas, in fact, the challenge is sufficiently ambiguous to leave open the possibility of Arthur or Gawain critically choosing the "holyn bobbe" as the weapon to use:

If any so hardy in þis hous holdez hymseluen,
Be so bolde in his blod, brayn in hys hede,
Þat dar stifly strike a strok for an o þer,
I schal gif hym of my gyft þys giserne ryche,

Þis ax, þat is heué innogh, to hondele as hym lykes,
And I schal bide þe fyrst bur as bare as I sitte.
If any freke be so felle to fonde þat I telle,
Lepe lyȝtly me to, and lach þis weppen,
I quit-clayme hit for euer, kepe hit as his auen,
And I schal stonde hym a strok, stif on þis flet.
[285-94]

[If any in this house such hardihood claims,
Be so bold in his blood, his brain so wild,
As stoutly to strike one stroke for another,
I shall give him as my gift this gisarme noble,
This ax, that is heavy enough, to handle as he likes,
And I shall bide the first blow, as bare as I sit.
If there be one so wilful my words to assay,
Let him leap hither lightly, lay hold of this weapon;
I quitclaim it forever, keep it as his own,
And I shall stand him a stroke, steady on this floor.]

To be sure, in the moment itself, under the extraordinary influence of the Green Knight's marvelous, eerie appearance, any person might, someone could object, be almost compelled to take the phrase "lach þis weppen" as referring to the ax; but, in fact, just such compulsion is what the critical temperament would try to avoid; the critical mind would see the ambiguity in "lach þis weppen" and would interpret that ambiguity in favor of the object in the Green Knight's other hand, the less lethal weapon, or the "holyn bobbe," with which a blow could be struck but a blow anyone would survive. As it is, Arthur not only chooses under compulsion but apparently, as he does so, takes the Green Knight for a fool—"And as þou foly hatz frayst, fynde þe behoues" ["Which whoso has sought, it suits that he find"] (324)—an interpretation whose error he will soon regret. Arthur and Gawain, in short, like the rest of the courtiers, haven't the critical temperament, at least not yet—neither can yet gloss the ax with the "holyn bobbe" and construe the two of them in terms of a different relationship. Hence, each fails to interpret the ambiguity, and Gawain as a consequence takes the lethal weapon, committing himself thus to a life-imperilling encounter a year hence.[9]

Such a reading of the challenge prepares a context within which to consider again the green girdle and the pentangle, arguably the two most critical signs in the poem, and the response of Arthur and his court to these signs. If we follow the poem's lead and think now of these signs as *knots* (see 662-65, 2376, and 2487-88), we can test the following formulation of my reading of the challenge: if Gawain fails to interpret the ambiguity in the Green Knight's challenge, it is because, on the one hand, the knot of the pentangle rigidifies his interpretive capacity and, on the other, the knot of the green girdle has not yet bound him in its liberating if also fearful indeterminacy.

The pentangle and the green girdle are compared each to a knot primarily for the ultimate purpose of the more clearly separating and distinguishing them from each other.[10] The pentangle is a knot that can hardly be untied, if at all (it is the "endeles knot"—630). The green girdle on the other hand forms a knot easy to untie ("þenne he kaȝt to þe knot, and þe kest lawsez" ["Then he grasps the green girdle and lets go the knot"]— 2376). Each of the knots, pentangle and green girdle, can be reckoned further, by extension, a figure for poetry—the pentangle as knot, a figure for abstruse and ornate and difficult poetry, to some extent defying interpretation; the green girdle as knot, a figure for a more open and free and possibly more humane poetry, easier to interpret.

Such an understanding of the knots finds important warrant in the example, almost certainly familiar to the *Gawain*-poet, of the famous "nodo" in Dante's *Purgatorio,* canto 24, the knot which Bonagiunta da Lucca says prevented him and Guittone and the Notary from writing in the "dolce stil nuovo" (*Purg.* 24. 55-62).[11] The "nodo" here figures a poetry and a style too complicated and abstruse to grant the spontaneity and liberality of the "dolce stil nuovo."

Both Dante and the *Gawain*-poet depend on a very ancient tradition in which the knot is frequently a figure connected in some way or another with textuality. For example, Horace writes in the *Ars Poetica:*

Neve minor neu sit quinto productior actu
fabula quae posci volt et spectata reponi.
nec deus intersit, nisi dignus vindice nodus
    inciderit.[12]

[Let no play be either shorter or longer than five acts, if when
once seen it hopes to be called for and brought back to the
stage. And let no god intervene, unless a knot come worthy of
such a deliverer.]

Again, moving forward in time, St. Augustine observes, of an
action recorded in Scripture, that

Cuius actionis figuratus quidam nodus nisi huius numeri
cognitione et consideratione non soluitur.[13]

[The knot, as it were, of this figurative action cannot be
untied without a knowledge and consideration of this
number.]

Next, Chaucer, a contemporary of the *Gawain*-poet, provides
important evidence. The Squire, whose narrative skill leaves
something to be desired, calls rather too much attention to
himself in the following passage:

The knotte why that every tale is toold,
If it be taried til that lust be coold
Of hem that han it after herkned yoore,
The savour passeth ever lenger the moore,
For fulsomnesse of his prolixitee,
And by the same resoun, thynketh me,
I sholde to the knotte condescende,
And maken of hir walkyng soone an ende.[14]

Here the knot has tied the narrator in knots, and we learn much
of Chaucer's attitude toward the Squire by ourselves untangling
this rhetoric.

Chaucer offers us another, even more important example,
which I must mention if only briefly. In Book 5 of *Troilus and*

Criseyde, the Narrator comments, in a famous passage, on Criseyde's resolve to return to Troy from the Greek camp:

> But God it wot, er fully monthes two,
> She was ful fer fro that entencioun!
> For bothe Troilus and Troie town
> Shal *knotteles* thoroughout hire herte slide;
> For she woi take a purpos for t'abide.
>   [*TC* 5. 766-70; emphasis mine]

Obviously this passage deserves an entire study to itself. Even so, we can pause here at least long enough to observe that the Narrator's comment suggests that Criseyde cannot hold, cannot bear, an intricate or complex meaning. As we learn elsewhere in the poem, she is like a text or indeed the parchment of a book which, however, cannot hold the imprint (so to speak) of Troilus' intense even fierce idealism.[15] Similarly, in her heart, the meaning in Troy and Troilus cannot form a knot, but like a straight limp rope must on the contrary simply slide through. Criseyde is too mutable for any knot to last in her.

Finally, a helpful example from Renaissance literature is found in Sir Thomas Chaloner's translation of Erasmus' *Encomium Moriae*:

> I perceive ye loke for an *Epiloge* or *knotte* of my tale, but than sure ye are verie fooles, if ye wene that I yet remember what I have spoken, after such a rablement of wordes powred foorth.[16]

Clearly, Chaloner's use of the word continues in the same tradition we have been observing in this brief, preliminary list. And many other examples from the Renaissance could be adduced—from Donne's "subtile knot, which makes us man" to Milton's description of the serpent, which "[i]nsinuating, wove with Gordian twine / His braided train."[17]

Although the figure of the knot enjoys such a long and intricate tradition, it is another example of "nodo" in Dante's *Commedia*, this one from the *Paradiso*, that most fully underwrites the significance of the knot in *Sir Gawain* and,

further, helps to explain why Gawain chose the ax rather than
the "holyn bobbe." This example is found in the ultimate canto of
Paradiso in Dante's description of his vision of "la luce etterna":

Nel suo profondo vidi che s'interna
legato con amore in un volume,
ciò che per l'universo si squaderna,
sustanze e accidenti e lor costume,
quasi conflati insieme, per tal modo
che ciò ch'i' dico è un semplice lume.
La forma universal di questo *nodo*
credo ch'i' vidi, perché più di largo,
dicendo questo, mi sento ch'i godo.
                    [*Para*. 33. 85-93; emphasis mine]

[In its profundity I saw—ingathered / and bound by love into
one single volume— / what, in the universe, seems separate,
scattered: / substances, accidents and dispositions / as if
conjoined—in such a way that what / I tell is only
rudimentary. / I think I saw the universal shape / which
that knot takes; for, speaking this, I feel / a joy that is more
ample (Mandelbaum, pp. 300-01).]

This knot is relevant to the knots in *Sir Gawain* primarily
because it also figures for Dante the "volume" which in turn
figures the inscribed plenitude of the divine. The knot, in short,
is a figure of the book, and as a figure of the book, it must have
attracted the *Gawain*-poet strongly. For in *Sir Gawain and the
Green Knight*, a "volume" figured as a "nodo" capacitates the
understanding of the knots of the pentangle and the green girdle
as each a "volume," or text or sign, which, as we have seen, must
be read and interpreted, each in its own special way.

Most particularly, we can see that the pentangle in this
figuration appears as a text similar (not, of course, identical) in
its mystery and profundity to the "volume" of God himself. This
is certainly consonant with the aura of mystery with which the
poet surrounds the pentangle, and once we have seen this we can
also see, immediately, why Gawain and indeed all of Arthur's
court are unable to live up to the ideals figured in the pentangle.

For no one, not even Gawain, can perfectly serve the ideals of the pentangle any more than he or any one else can perfectly interpret the meanings of the "volume" of God.

Both the pentangle and the "volume," in other words, as knots, are so intricate, so complex, so deeply intertwined, that they defy any merely human attempt at untying or interpretation—where untying or interpretation would imply human control of and power over the knots, pentangle and "volume." Moreover, to assume, even if unconsciously, that one can serve the one, the pentangle, or interpret the other, the "volume," is to commit the sin of pride. The most any one can do is to acknowledge without ever fully knowing the mystery in each. Doing so one can then affirm, with Dante, "più di largo / dicendo questo, mi sento ch'i' godo" ["more largely—with more largess— saying this, I feel that I rejoice"].

The largess of his rejoicing will increase—and just such largess, we should make a special point of noting, since the *Gawain*-poet clearly noted it, is what Gawain failed in when he tried to be fully and perfectly the knight of the pentangle:

"Corsed worth cowarddyse and couetyse bo þe!
In yow is vylany and vyse þat vertue disstryez."
Þenne he kaȝt to þe knot, and þe kest lawsez,
Brayde bro þely þe belt to þe burne seluen:
"Lo! þer þe falssyng, foule mot hit falle!
For care of þy knokke cowardyse me taȝt
To acorde me with couetyse, my kynde to forsake,
Þat is *larges* and lewté þat longez to knyȝtez."
　　　　　　　　[2374-81; emphasis mine]

["Accursed be a cowardly and covetous heart!
In you is villainy and vice, and virtue laid low!"
Then he grasps the green girdle and lets go the knot,
Hands it over in haste, and hotly he says:
"Behold there my falsehood, ill hap betide it!
Your cut taught me cowardice, care for my life,
And coveting came after, contrary both
To largesse and loyalty belonging to knights."]

He was simply not large enough for such largess. No man as man is.

The most man as man can be is humble, ready to acknowledge what he cannot know, as does Dante when he beholds the "nodo" of the "un volume." Any knot man as man ties he must be prepared, however much he dislikes it, to untie. And this precisely because he is bound in a volume, tied in a knot, more mysterious and more intricate than anything he will ever comprehend. And the texts of man, by the same token, howsoever bound or woven or knitted they be, he must be ready to untie or loosen, to analyze, as the contingency of human affairs demands. Man's knots and man's texts and the knottiness of his texts must resemble more the green girdle than the pentangle—otherwise, he risks idolatry and the consequent loss of his humanity.

The knots people tie in or with the green girdle are knots they can also untie when they have to, when it is called for. Unlike the knot of the pentangle, these knots are hardly geometrically pure, eternal, like numbers or Platonic forms. Quite the contrary, these knots are signs of the human and human signs: they will submit to analysis, and life will go on. Unlike such geometrically perfect knots as the pentangle, transcendental in the universality of their form, these knots, knots like the knot of the green girdle, are not the termination of signification. They are rather terms of signification, leading to more terms, more signification, the endless finitude of interpretation.[18]

In light of these comparisons, we can see that when Gawain accepts the ax to answer the Green Knight's challenge, he is indeed the knight of the pentangle, a servant of that knot, thinking to "live up" to it. Rigidly, even legalistically, he responds to the Green Knight, interpreting him as an agent of destruction, if not of malevolence, as a threat and therefore someone to hurt. Although deprecating himself relative to Arthur, his king (and his uncle), nevertheless he obviously assumes he has a duty as knight of the pentangle, and that duty obligates him, *knots* him, to the challenge—and ties him to it in a way that inhibits his seeing alternatives of interpretation. Like an exegete apparently privileged by the "volume" he glosses, Gawain interprets the situation before him according to the privileged code, unaware in effect of the plurality of codes at large in the world, such that by a different code he could have chosen the "holyn bobbe." The knight of the pentangle, in brief, is the knight of a knot that cannot be untied.

The knight of the green girdle, however, the knight Gawain has become by the end of his experience, is a knight of a different knot. At the end, he wears and presumably serves under a different kind of sign, one whose significance is not permanently knotted in one, final, exclusive shape. Although he still desires rigid, determinative interpretations,

> þis is þe token of vntraw þe þat I am tan inne,
> And I mot nedez hit were wyle I may last
> [2509-10]

[This is the badge of false faith that I was found in there,
And I must bear it on my body till I breathe my last]

he is also tolerant now of alternative, even radically different interpretations:

> and alle þe court als
> Laȝen loude þerat, and luflyly acorden
> Þat lordes and ladis þat longed to þe Table,
> Vche burne of þe bro þerhede, a bauderyk schulde haue,
> A bende abelef hym aboute of a bryȝt grene,
> And þat, for sake of þat segge, in swete to were.
> [2513-18]

> [and the court all together
> Agree with gay laughter and gracious intent
> That the lords and the ladies belonging to the Table,
> Each brother of that band, a baldric should have,
> A belt borne oblique, of a bright green,
> To be worn with one accord for that worthy's sake.]

His world is now a world that admits of indeterminacy and the concomitant pluralism of interpretation; even if he disagrees with the other courtiers, he does not, to judge from what the poem says, dispute or interrupt their accord. His desire for an absolute is no longer an absolute desire.[19] And so it is that two different, even competing interpretations of the green girdle exist side by side now in Arthur's court.

The surfeit of signs remains, then. Which, in fact, is what we would expect. But there is a difference. Plurality, whether we call it "folé felefolde" or the necessary condition of human liberty, distinguishes the Arthurian world now rather than the randomness and rigidity of the earlier time: the surfeit of signs is recognized as such.[20] The presence of plurality does not mean that things are any easier; in fact, just the contrary is probably true. The poem, after all, does end on a note of difference if not disharmony—the courtiers interpret the girdle one way, Gawain another. But the presence of plurality and of its unstable if flexible accord—visible in the ubiquitous baldric of the green girdle—does suggest that Arthur and his court are more aware now of what a sign is, how arbitrary its making, how important its knot.

NOTES

1. All quotations of the poem are taken from *Sir Gawain and the Green Knight*, ed. J.R.R. Tolkien and E.V. Gordon, 2nd ed. rev. Norman Davis (Oxford: Oxford University Press, 1967). The translation cited is that of Marie Borroff (New York: Norton, 1967).

2. My documentation also can only be suggestive, not exhaustive. A very useful bibliography on the *Gawain*-poet is now available: Robert J. Blanch, *"Sir Gawain and the Green Knight": A Reference Guide* (Troy: Whitston, 1983). Parts of the second half of this paper were read at the Fifth Annual Conference on Medieval and Renaissance Literature at The Citadel, March 15, 1985; I would like to take this opportunity to thank Professors David G. Allen, Robert J. Blanch, and Julian N. Wasserman for inviting me to participate in the Conference.

3. On the terms "cowarddyse and couetyse," see R. E. Kaske, *"Sir Gawain and the Green Knight,"* in George M. Masters, ed., *Medieval and Renaissance Studies*, Proceedings of the Southeastern Institute of Medieval and Renaissance Studies, Summer 1979 (Chapel Hill: University of North Carolina Press, 1984), pp. 24-44, esp. pp. 27-28.

4. Among the many studies, of special interest are Robert W. Ackerman, "Gawain's Shield: Penitential Doctrine in *Sir Gawain*

and the Green Knight," Anglia 76 (1958), 254-65; George
Engelhardt, "The Predicament of Gawain," *MLQ* 16 (1955), 218-25;
Richard H. Green, "Gawain's Shield and the Quest for Perfection,"
Journal of English Literary History (1962), 121-39; D. R. Howard,
"Structure and Symmetry in *Sir Gawain," Speculum* 39 (1964), 425-
33.

5.   The pentangle, also a kind of text, signifies "bi *tytle* þat it habbez"
(626; emphasis mine); and the "teuelyng of þis trwe kny3tez" (1514)
is "˟ þe *tytelet* token and tyxt of her werkkez'" (1515; emphasis
mine).

6.   For a discussion of cutting, severing, and severity in the signifying
process, see R. A. Shoaf, *Milton, Poet of Duality: A Study of
Semiosis in the Poetry and the Prose* (New Haven: Yale University
Press, 1985), p. 10-11, 60, 64.

7.   I have studied this passage and these words elsewhere, in *The
Poem as Green Girdle: "Commercium" in "Sir Gawain and the
Green Knight"* (Gainesville: University Presses of Florida, 1984), pp.
72-74.

8.   See, on this matter, the substantial and informative remarks of
Judson Boyce Allen, *The Ethical Poetic of the Later Middle Ages: A
Decorum of Convenient Distinction* (Toronto: University of
Toronto Press, 1982), esp. pp. 3-67.

9.   Robert J. Blanch and Julian N. Wasserman observe, in a paper
they delivered together at the Fifth Annual Conference on
Medieval and Renaissance Literature at The Citadel (March 15,
1985), that Gawain could have chosen the "holyn bobbe" rather
than the ax as his weapon. My own interpretation of this moment
derives from numerous conversations with the late Judson Boyce
Allen, who, developing remarks he had published on doubling in
the poem (in *The Friar as Critic: Literary Attitudes in the Later
Middle Ages* [Nashville: Vanderbilt University Press, 1971], pp. 144-
48), was moving toward an understanding of the "holyn bobbe" as a
gloss on the ax (Morgan le Fay, similarly, a gloss on Bertilak's Lady;
Hautdesert, a gloss on Camelot, etc.). I hope to continue Judson
Allen's investigations in my own study of the knot in *Sir Gawain and
the Green Knight,* paying particular attention to the *Gawain*-poet's
place in the ancient epistemological tradition of knowledge by
contraries—for preliminary bibliography on this tradition, see
Milton: Poet of Duality, p. 192, n. 9.

10.   See, further, Shoaf, *The Poem as Green Girdle,* pp. 74-75.

11.   The text and translation of Dante's *Commedia* cited here and
elsewhere is that of Allen Mandelbaum, in the Bantam Classic

edition, *Inferno* (New York, 1982), *Purgatorio* (New York, 1984), *Paradiso* (New York, 1986); the present passage is found in *Purgatorio*, pp. 222-23.

12.   Lines 189-92, ed. and trans. H. Rushton Fairclough, in the Loeb Classical Library (Cambridge: Harvard University Press, 1978), pp. 466-67.

13.   *De Doctrina Christiana* 2.16.25, ed. J. Martin, *Corpus Christianorum series latina* 32, p. 50; trans. D. W. Robertson, Jr., *On Christian Doctrine* (Indianopolis: Bobbs Merrill, 1958), p. 51.

14.   *Canterbury Tales* V (F) 401-08, cited from *The Riverside Chaucer*, gen. ed. Larry D. Benson, based on *The Works of Geoffrey Chaucer*, ed. by F. N. Robinson (Cambridge: Houghton Mifflin, 1987); all citations of Chaucer in this paper are from this edition.

15.   See R. A. Shoaf, *Dante, Chaucer, and the Currency of the Word: Money, Images, and Reference in Late Medieval Poetry* (Norman: Pilgrim Books, 1983), pp. 111-22.

16.   *The Praise of Folie* (London, 1549), Tiij (my emphasis); cited in Rosalie Colie, *Paradoxa Epidemica: The Renaissance Tradition of Paradox* (Princeton: Princeton University Press, 1966), p. 20.

17.   See "The Extasie," line 64, in *The Complete Poetry of John Donne*, ed. John T. Shawcross (New York: Anchor Books, 1967), p. 132; and *Paradise Lost* 4. 348-49, ed. Alastair Fowler (London: Longman, 1971), p. 216; and consult also Fowler's note to 4. 348: "St Augustine says that Satan chose the serpent for his instrument because it was 'a creature slippery, pliable, wreathed in *knots*, and fit for his work'" (my emphasis).

18.   For more on this issue, see R. A. Shoaf, "Chaucer and Medusa: *The Franklin's Tale*," *Chaucer Review* 21 (1986), 274-90.

19.   See, further, Shoaf, *The Poem as Green Girdle*, pp. 69-70.

20.   All the instances, e.g., of "token" and "tokenyng" occur in the second half of the poem, suggesting, especially in Gawain, a greater awareness of signs and signification *after* the experience of the Green Knight and his challenge.

Spenser's Arthur

The Passing of Arthur in Malory, Spenser, and Shakespeare: The Avoidance of Closure

A. Kent Hieatt

The primary reason that the Latinate words "empire," "power," "force," and "closure" are the ones which I must use for corresponding concepts below is that the Romans established by physical violence a political and cultural control over the lands from which these words of my language come. In an attenuated sense I am a victim (and a beneficiary) of political and cultural imperialism. A mass of signals from language and cultural artifacts in English-speaking regions bears witness to this arbitrary early act.

On Christmas Day 800, one region that had suffered from this Roman imperialism attained a symbolic revenge. The Frankish leader Charlemagne (later one of the Nine Worthies) was crowned emperor of the Western Roman Empire in Rome, by the Pope. Britain, however, the land in which my language was then developing, had no share in this compensatory gesture. On the contrary, later speakers of the Latinate language of the most important part of Charlemagne's former empire physically enforced their political and cultural rule on the land of my forebears, and imposed those Latinate words above, and many others, in forms close to my culturally compelled use of them today. If those French speakers had not physically dominated Britain, my, and your, entire linguistic culture would now be unimaginably different.

One motive for the above preamble is to excuse my intention to discuss the epic Arthur—the military conqueror—rather than the romance one who has standing in the remaining essays in this

volume. We do not like empire or *imperium*, power or an earlier
form of *pouvoir* from *posse*, force or late Latin *forcia*. Beyond the
obvious international kind, imperialism has become a social
metaphor for the subjection of the underprivileged: racial
minorities, women, and the so-called insane, for instance. In the
study of fiction, closure (from a Latin form *clausura*) may be
deemed an imperialism of the artificer - a violently reductive,
arbitrary imposition of finality upon a sequence of events whose
true *esse* is to continue. Perhaps our dislike of imperialism
accounts for present-day failure to attend to the heroic, power-
acquisitive Arthur, who has paramount standing in the body of
British documents concerned with Arthur up to fairly recent
times. One way of extenuating study of him is to foreground
oneself, and the writers of those British sources in which he
appears, as the victims of not one but at least two imperialisms
during the long period of history when Britain had some
pretensions to being a third-world area, and to show how two of
these writers sought fictional empire for Britain by postponing
closure of their fictions.

In the twelfth century, the British, having been mastered by
both Latin- and French-speaking political and cultural
hegemonists, concocted the beginnings of a revanchist *translatio
imperii*, or transfer of rule, to themselves. Unlike the Roman and
Carolingian variety, the physical force needed for this British
imperialistic purpose belongs to the realm of most Arthurian
specialists' interest, that of fiction. Geoffrey of Monmouth
related[1] that, unlike all other British rulers since the Roman
conquest of Britain by Julius Caesar, Arthur achieved his greatest
exploit by decisively destroying the entire force of the Roman
Lucius in France in the sixth century, long before Charlemagne.
Lucius having died in the climactic battle, Rome was at Arthur's
mercy. Arthur was nevertheless prevented from taking the city
and seizing the rule, because Mordred, left in charge in Britain,
had disloyally appropriated both the British kingdom and
Guenevere. Arthur was constrained to return home for the
familiar last battle and his own passing.

Epically and heroically, the situation remained much the
same in British accounts until the second half of the fifteenth
century, except that by then Lucius had become the Roman

emperor *in propria persona* and was dispatched by Arthur's own hand. In the intervening period, Wace, Laʒamon, and the alliterative *Morte Arthure* lengthened and heightened the story of what for them remained Arthur's chief exploit; emphasized the "Saracen," "paynim" character of Lucius' following (as in other chivalric fiction imitating the tales of Charlemagne's battles with the Moors); but continued to show this exploit aborted by domestic treason. Not so, however, in the late fifteenth-century account, attributed to Malory and printed in one version by Caxton in 1485 as *Le Morte Darthur*. Initiating the version most familiar to us, this text postpones closure to Book 21 by delaying Mordred's traitorous acts in Britain until Arthur's much later absence on other, familiar affairs. In Caxton's version, "the conquest that King Arthur had against Lucius the Emperor of Rome" is Book 5. In it, this only British representative of the Nine Worthies finally overtook the Frankish one.[2] His domestic affairs continuing in perfect order, Arthur followed up his victory over Lucius by a descent upon Rome, acceptance of the fealty of a decimated, terrified senate, and coronation as Roman emperor at the hands of the Pope, naturally at Christmas. By Geoffrey's former reckoning, this would probably have preceded Charlemagne's coronation by 258 years to the day.

My proposals in this article are twofold. It is familiar that, at the time of the initial publication of *The Faerie Queene*, Spenser let it be known that he entertained a plan to postpone closure of his narrative far beyond the evocation of Arthur's private virtues in a first set of twelve books, which were to be crowned by union with Gloriana. The first proposal, never before suggested, is that, under an impetus similar to the one I have cited for earlier compensatory imperialist gestures involving Arthur, Spenser's indicated plan to evoke in a second set of books the political virtues of Arthur would have been crowned with the conquest of Rome, as has never before been suggested. Obviously, one of Spenser's intentions in settling on this literal narrative of late antiquity would have been to realize allegorically the visionary option of contemporary English activist Protestantism to crush Roman Catholicism, establish a Universal Reformed Church, and end Spanish domination, particularly in Rome. My main evidence for this theory consists of a single, formerly uninterpreted line, whose meaning now seems indubitable. The theory entails some new conclusions about the nature of *The Faerie Queene* that we have.

My second proposal is less assured. In Shakespeare's late historical romance *Cymbeline*, the British king accepts Roman rule and the continuation of empire in spite of his followers' victory over the Roman general Lucius. He acknowledges, in fact, that he is a beneficiary, not a victim, of the Roman ascendancy. I believe that Shakespeare may have been reacting against Malory's fiction of Arthur and the Roman emperor Lucius and even against Spenser's supposed plan, suggested in the surviving *Faerie Queene* at a point where Spenser uniquely juxtaposes Arthur and his centuries-earlier predecessor Cymbeline, to the latter's disadvantage. The historical orientation of *Cymbeline* is anti-epical and anti-heroic, and reflects its time's pacific policy toward Spain and the forces of Catholicism.

The letter dated 23 January 1590 (N.S.)[3] from Spenser to Ralegh which is included in the first edition of *The Faerie Queene* speaks of the choice of Arthur as epic hero and of the total pattern within which he might be fictionally realized:

In which I haue followed all the antique Poets historicall, first Homere, who in the Persons of Agamemnon and Vlysses hath ensampled a good gouernour and a vertuous man, the one in his Ilias, the other in his Odysseis: then Virgil, whose like intention was to doe in the person of Aeneas: after him Ariosto comprised them both in his Orlando: and lately Tasso disseuered them again, and formed both parts in two persons, namely that part which they in Philosophy call Ethice, or vertues of a priuate man, coloured in his Rinaldo: The other named Politice in his Godfredo. By ensample of which excellente Poets, I labour to pourtraict in Arthure, before he was king, the image of a braue knight, perfected in the twelve priuate morall vertues, as Aristotle hath deuised, the which is the purpose of these first twelue bookes: which if I finde to be well accepted, I may be perhaps encoraged, to frame the other part of polliticke vertues in his person, after that hee came to be king.

It seems incredible that Spenser, competing with the two great Italian epics of his time, should not have taken the second half of this plan seriously, even if he needed to refer to it guardedly and hold some of its features in suspension pending short-term developments in politics and patronage. The Letter to Ralegh fails to correspond to certain details of the extant *Faerie Queene*, but we have seldom doubted that its main lines corresponded to his intentions in 1590. It is a shortcoming of our criticism not to take into account the imaginative relation which Spenser would have needed to keep in mind between Books I-III, published with this letter, and not only the next nine books but also the second set of books (no doubt twelve) which would finally have completed the story.

In the first twelve books, King Uther Pendragon's unknown son, a hero who proved himself as a private knight in company with others and who then contracted or was on the point of contracting a presumably marital relationship with Gloriana, would be a suitable romance-figure but does not stand up to the epic competition envisaged in this section of the letter. In general, the politic virtue of "a good gouernour" is not necessarily bellicose, but in an heroic poem the display of politic virtue typically culminates in the righting of what the values of some social unit identify as a wrong, by means of conquest of the center of wrongful power. In the *Orlando Furioso*, the initial siege, that of Paris by the unbelievers, fails, and the terminal, Christian siege of the unbelievers' center, Biserta, succeeds. (Much absurdity of a P.G. Wodehousian elegance accompanies these actions, but they are accomplished.) In the *Gerusalemme Liberata*, the unbelievers initially hold the Christian holy place; terminally the Christians capture it. What Spenser needed was the hero of an Arthuriad on the analogy of Agamemnon conqueror of Troy, Aeneas conqueror of Latium, Orlando mastermind of the conquest of the chief Muslim stronghold, and Godfrey of Bouillon conqueror of Jerusalem.

A difficulty in allowing for Spenser's imaginative grasp of his total story in relation to its first three books is, of course, that we have had only the vaguest idea of what kind of conquest Arthur would have achieved in XIII-XXIV of *The Faerie Queene* or in I-XII of an epic continuing the story. We do have at least one

sure reference in the existing *Faerie Queene* to an event belonging
to the time of the projected sequel. The actions analogous to the
traditional end of the Arthurian story in Avalon—Arthur's
death, and Gloriana's carrying his shield off to Faery Land
(I.vii.36)—are cited very briefly, without exclamatory force, as
though they formed part of a visualized, complete narrative
which needed only to be written down. Additionally, as John
Upton indicated[4] in 1758, the Knight of Holiness's sad, final
refusal to stay on with Una and her parents after he has killed
his dragon seems likewise to point forward to this sequel:

> For by the faith, which I to armes haue plight,
> I bounden am streight after this emprize,
> As that your daughter can ye well aduize,
> Back to return to that great Faerie Queen,
> And her to serue six yeares in warlike wize,
> Gainst that proud Paynim king, that workes her teene:
> Therefore I ought craue pardon, till I there haue beene.
>
> [I.xii.18]

Upton's claim in this case can scarcely be denied, because what
Redcrosse says his faith, plighted to arms, requires him to do for
six years after he has *returned* to Gloriana, seems transparently
to refer to a time *after* the annual feast of Gloriana, which was to
be described in Book XII. In XII, according to Spenser's letter, she
was to make the initial assignments of the adventures which are
retrospectively described in the existing *Faerie Queene* and in the
succeeding six books.

In general, we Spenserians have taken it as axiomatic that
Spenser broke the chain of inherited Arthurian material because
it was of little use to his moral, allegorical, modernly epideictic
enterprise. Working with Spenserian fictional events denuded of
geography and chronology, we tend to forget that Spenser
includes some definite signposts from the Arthurian tradition.
Arthur is the son of Uther, and Uther is battling the Saxons Octa
and Oza (III.iii.52), whose names belong to the sixth-century
happenings cited by Geoffrey and Tudor chroniclers. Arthur will
undergo death as in the tradition.

It is in fact generally acknowledged that Spenser must have had in mind some signal exploit for his hero between the time when Arthur's long search for Gloriana would be crowned by his union with her and the time of his death. It has usually been imagined as a struggle with the pagan Saxons or some unidentified paynim king without reference to Arthurian tradition. The Saxons, however, seem unsatisfactory candidates, although Arthur might have helped to fight them. A final victory over them was not available, because in *Faerie Queene* history they finally win out. Besides, Spenser clearly planned to leave the future struggle with the Saxons to Britomart and her spouse, the Arthur-surrogate *Art*-egal—equal to Arthur, and in fact his half-brother. Merlin's prophecy in III.iii.21-50 instructs us that the line of Artegal and Britomart is the historical one through which the struggle of Celtic Britain against the Saxons will continue until disaster in the time of Cadwallader, only to be righted when the Tudors, descendants of that line, return from the Welsh West to rule sempiternally. In this prophecy, enumerating each of the British kings following Artegal and Britomart, Arthur has no part. In the Book of Briton Moniments, concerned with British history up to Arthur, his traditional place is a hiatus, immediately after Uther (II.x.68). A few stanzas after Merlin's prophecy (III.iii.52), we learn that Uther has been fighting the Saxons; we know from this prophecy that Arthur's surrogate or double will continue this fight.

It is as though a more transcendent destiny were appointed for Arthur. The pattern here is built partly on that of the *Orlando* and the *Gerusalemme*. The heros Orlando and Godfrey have no future; their grand exploits are in the fictional present tense. Contrariwise, the main love-match in each poem—Rinaldo and Alcina, Ruggiero and Bradamante—teems with the prophesied future, up to the authorial present of the Ferrarese Este rulers, patrons of both Ariosto and Tasso. Just so, but more elaborately, the line of the lovers Artegal and Britomart will beget the prophesied Tudors of Spenser's present.

The notion that Arthur's exploit was to be built on a struggle with a paynim king rests on Spenser's appeal to his muse, before Redcrosse's battle with the dragon, to delay the true epic strain until it is time to sing of "Briton fields with Sarazin blood

bedyde,/ Twixt that great faery Queene and Paynim king..."
(I.xi. 7). This particular struggle, however, is more likely to
have been the one with the Saxons. They were traditionally the
ones who in Arthur's time were actually on British soil.[5] My
reasoning here (in anticipation of textual evidence in a moment)
is that, just as Arthur and Artegal cooperate as private gentlemen
in *Faerie Queene* V to fight severally two sets of enemies, so in
the sequel-epic they might have performed two parallel (but
ultimately not equally successful) politic roles as leaders against
the two enemies who are the main ones in British history as
recited in the Book of Briton Moniments and Merlin's prophecy.
Picts, Danes, and Normans are alluded to, but, from Julius
Caesar's time (II.x.47ff.) up to Arthur's, the British are mainly
embroiled with the Romans (x.62). Toward the end, these no
longer garrison Britain but they remain a danger until Arthur's
own day, when they vanish (see below). The Saxons first enter
Britain at the invitation of Arthur's uncle Vortiger (II.x.64ff.)
and then continually harry the British, finally dominating them
and driving out the line of Artegal at a much later date
(III.iii.41). Not only do the Romans and Saxons receive the most
attention as external enemies in Spenser's history, but also these
two sets of enemies are simultaneously threats to Britain only in
the time of Arthur, Artegal, and their contemporary relatives. In
that time, the Roman threat has not yet disappeared and the
Saxons have just arrived. According to Geoffrey of Monmouth,
Arthur battled both threats. In epic etiquette, however, Spenser
seems to have found it convenient to assign the ultimately fated
struggle on native soil to a double of Arthur created for this
purpose.

But what of the other half of the pattern, Arthur's exploit?
It is conceivable, of course, that Spenser would have cut a
fictional entity out of whole cloth, totally apart from Arthurian
tradition or actual history, because much else in *The Faerie
Queene* is like this. What I am proposing, however, is that this
fictional entity is traditional and Roman (associated with
paynims in one Arthurian traditional sense and in another,
Spenserian sense Roman Catholic, which in the *Faerie Queene*
system of values means "unbelieving" and is as bad as pagan).
Before finally coming to the textual evidence for this proposal, I

need to describe a prominent feature of Malory's story of Arthur's conquest of Rome. It is of nearly equal importance to all earlier tellers of the story from Geoffrey onward.

In Malory, ambassadors from Rome come to Arthur's court. They tell him that he is a rebel. He must (1) acknowledge the emperor Lucius as his lord and (2) pay tribute to the Empire, as his predecessors have done, according to the rules established first by Julius Caesar, conqueror of Britain.[6] After taking council, he replies in reverse order (1) that he owes no tribute and (2) that, instead of his being subject to Rome, Rome ought by right to be subject to him.[7] Further, unless this is acknowledged, he will forthwith subdue the Roman rebels. Subsequently, in a climactic victory on the way to Rome, he and his army kill Lucius, twenty allied monarchs, and sixty Roman senators. Arthur coffins them all suitably and tells three surviving senators to convey the bodies in procession to Rome and its authorities. He commands them to say that he will follow shortly, and "that I send them these dead bodies for the tribute that they have demanded. And if they be not content with these, I shall pay more at my coming, for other tribute owe I none, nor none other will I pay.... I command them upon pain of their heads never to demand tribute nor tax of me nor of my lands."[8] Thereafter he enters Rome and is crowned emperor, subjecting Rome to Britain and reversing the situation that had prevailed since Julius Caesar's conquest.

There is thus a set of compensatory, transparently symmetrical symbolic gestures in the story as Malory tells it (and as Geoffrey, Wace, Laʒamon, and the creator of the alliterative *Morte Arthure* tell it). Arthur reverses the relation of mastery and subjection between the Romans and the Britons, and in particular he pays the demanded tribute in a paradoxical way that ends it forever.

We now come to my piece of evidence. In *Faerie Queene* II.x, in the ruinous, ancient chamber of Memory in Alma's castle, Arthur is reading the Book of Briton Moniments, which ends with his present, i.e., with his presently reigning predecessor Uther. In listening to the authorial speaker's commentary on Arthur's reading (not to the text itself), we reach Julius Caesar's conquest of Britain in stanza 47-48, over five hundred years before Arthur in the chronology of Geoffrey and Tudor chronicles. Caesar conquers Britain only by the help of dissension in the then ruling family: "Nought else, but treason, from the first this land did foyle." In stanza 49 "*Caesar* got the victory," and:

> Thenceforth this land was tributarie made
> T'ambitious *Rome*, and did their rule obay,
> Till *Arthur* all that reckoning defrayd;
> Yet oft the Briton kings against them strongly swayd.

What does the transitive verb "defrayd" mean here? In all of Spenser's other uses of forms of "defray"[9] the meanings seem to be, either literally or figuratively, "to discharge (the expense or cost of anything) by payment: to pay, meet, settle" (*OED* "defray" 2). Perhaps the clearest parallel is in *Epithalamion* 315-18: "Now welcome night... / That long daies labour doest at last defray, / And all my cares, which cruell loue collected, / Hast sumd in one, and cancelled for aye."

The last four lines of this stanza mean, then, that, following Julius Caesar's conquest of the land, Britain was made tributary to Rome and obeyed its rule (was made to pay tribute to, and acceded to the rule of, Rome) until Arthur paid off or settled or cancelled (cf. *Epithalamion*) all that reckoning (a metaphor embodying both the tribute and the subjection, meaning that Arthur ended both). Nevertheless, British kings often fought powerfully, but unsuccessfully, against the Romans. All of these kings are previous to Arthur and his final defrayment; we hear no more of Roman rule or incursions after Arthur's time. Of these kings, Cymbeline, roughly five hundred years before Arthur, appears in the next stanza as the first unsuccessful swayer against Roman imperial power, a point to which we shall return.

It is seldom that a passage fits its possible source so precisely as does the clause, "Till *Arthur* all that reckoning defrayd." It matches the reversal, in Malory's and his predecessors' story, of a British subjection which dates back half a millennium to the time of Julius Caesar; but in particular Arthur's gruesome alteration of the coin of tribute, so as to cancel the equally long dishonor of tribute itself, is epitomized in a sinister financial metaphor—a quietus for an emperor and a quittance for rule—that could belong to Shakespeare nearly as easily as to Spenser.

It seems to me unavoidable that Spenser is here inserting into his fictional space the datum that his Arthur conquered Rome. Spenser does this just as clearly and coolly (as a matter already taken for granted and only needing to be written down) as he had already inserted the data that Arthur died and that Gloriana carried his shield off to Faery Land.[10]

We have never previously taken into our calculations this now apparently inescapable premise that the conquest of Rome inhabits the same fictional, imaginative space as all the other events cited or enacted in *Faerie Queene* I-III. We have never thought of it before. Given this new premise, it seems to me highly unlikely, once Spenser had certified this conquest, that he could have substituted some other, necessarily less important politic exploit for his Arthur in the continuation proposed in the Letter to Ralegh. It is difficult to imagine how the conqueror of Rome could have found a more important object of conquest, or even one for which he had time. It is similarly difficult to imagine a more attractive, if daunting, idea for the intending author of an English sixteenth-century epic. Given the relation to the realities of politics and patronage, such a work would have pointed to the Protestant destruction of contemporary Spanish-dominated, Roman Catholic power and the founding of a Universal Reformed Church. As such, it would have had great appeal to such earlier Protestant activists as Spenser's early patron Leicester and Sir Philip Sidney, with the latter's notions of a militant Protestant League of which Elizabeth would be the head. But the Protestant cleansing would have been performed allegorically. At the literal level the sequel would have built on a central British tradition of great antiquity, concerned with the most important British hero, leading a host in the cause of national honor and the right, to world-triumph over the greatest power ever known. As the Protestant, Reformationist epic of a crusade against Catholic unbelievers to liberate their power-center for the forces of purity, it would have challenged Tasso's great Catholic epic of the First Crusade and the liberation of Jerusalem from the unbelievers, and Ariosto's less seriously intended epic of the forces of Charlemagne who fight the unbelievers and finally capture their center.

To have formulated in an epic such a master-stroke of *translatio imperii* westward to Britain would have seemed a potent, ultimate gesture among the contending nationalistic mythologies of Renaissance Europe. It might have rejoiced many possible patrons, even though Spenser needed to be cautious of Elizabeth's distrust of actual foreign ventures. Other striking possibilities, depending on the execution, might have appealed to Spenser: the validation of a humanist culture of the north at least equal to the old one of the south; striking a blow for an independent literature in one of the less regarded modern languages against a universal *Latinitas* of which Virgil's epic was the exemplar; and even a meeting, across the gulf of oblivious time, of the Renaissance with the paradigmatic City of late classical antiquity, apparently irretrievably remote in Spenser's "Ruines of Rome."

In the extant *Faerie Queene*, the powers of both Catholicism and more general evil are frequently seen as paynims, Saracens, or loathsome giants. Spenser would have found Malory's account hospitable in this respect. The Emperor's guard consists of fifty fiend-begotten giants.[11] Other giants fight on his side. Spenser would have been grateful to know that Lucius is supported by many thousands of Spaniards. Lucius' respectable forces, whose faith is never specified, are increasingly sullied with guilt by association from the point where he stuffs a conquered castle with a garrison of "Saracens or Infidels." Gawaine does battle with Priamus, a good "saracen" who successfully requires to be christened in the true faith. Saracens finally seem inextricably confused with the rest of Lucius' forces.[12]

What can we deduce about the surviving *Faerie Queene* from the far-reaching proposal that in 1590 Spenser was thinking of a sequel in which Arthur becomes Emperor of Rome, and that in his own mind he had adjusted to this total plan the parts of *The Faerie Queene* which he had already composed? If the proposal is well accepted, it would be foolish to try to impose closure on such deductions at this point, but something may be said.

Regarding the somewhat old-fashioned question of Spenser's belief in the historicity of Arthur, we conclude hypothetically that he was willing to use a story which he himself regarded as mythical. None of the sixteenth-century chroniclers of Arthur accept the sixth-century conquest of Rome, and it is nearly impossible to believe that Spenser considered it historical, in the century of Justinian, the Lombard conquests, and St. Benedict. Likewise, it is unnecessary to posit that Spenser believed the English, or a Northern European coalition, could actually conquer Rome in his day (although he may have dreamed of it in 1590, eighteen months after the defeat of the Armada). In *Faerie Queene* V, for instance, he does his duty to his dead patron Leicester, who as Arthur is shown conquering an allegorically indicated Antwerp—something that Leicester never did. In competition with Tasso's actual, historical conquest of Jerusalem in the First Crusade, Spenser might be driven to allegory in depicting a conquest of Rome that ought to occur but was not likely to. On the other hand, he had many precedents for epic ahistoricity. Fictionally, Orlando and associated forces took Biserta; actually, Charlemagne's forces never reached even the continent of modern Bizerte, in Tunisia.

More importantly, Spenser in 1590 is likely to have thought of his projected first twelve books as in one way a sort of *Enfances Artus*, the doings of a hero in his youth before he came to the main part of his career, like the chansons de geste *Enfances Guillaume* or *Enfances Ogier*. What we think of as his only way of composing a heroic poem, with no localization of place or time in an often noted "never-never land" and with merely private chivalric adventures as in a romance, is likely to be off-center from his larger plan to "astound scared nations... with horrour sterne" (I.xi.6). Neither Ariosto nor Tasso particularize locale with local color, but Spenser would likely have had to follow them, and particularly Tasso, in accepting a geographical frame, in this case Britain, Rome, and intermediate places. Evoking a world-scale conquest, he would also have needed to follow Tasso in describing huge armies and the sage councils of leaders. The total, twenty-four-book conception, beginning with Holiness and its victory, seems, in fact, to be closer to Tasso's theocentric action in twelve books than the surviving *Faerie Queene* would lead us to think. There would at least have been localizations like the St. Albans of *The Ruines of Time* and the Rome of *Ruines of Rome*. Finally, the basic reason for the well-known dichotomy of Briton knights and Faery knights may lie in the needs of the sequel. In the existing *Faerie Queene*, the division is exploited with some elegance, but it seems to me difficult to understand why Spenser needed something so totally without literary precedent unless he intended to do more with it—perhaps to bring together the ideationally complementary realms of Britain and Fairy Land in some epic achievement. It might even be hazarded that the death of Arthur before that of Gloriana[13] (like Artegal's early death by treachery before Britomart's) would have related to some Mordred-figure's tearing apart this lofty unity, whose reachievement (in the end postponing closure) would be anticipated in the Tudors.

A more specific problem concerns *Faerie Queene* IV-VII. Did Spenser retreat from his plans for a sequel at some point after the 1590 Letter to Ralegh? The letter does not appear in the 1596 *Faerie Queene*, although it does in later editions. The allegorically rendered victories of Arthur over the Armada and the Spanish in Antwerp (and Artegal's victory in Ireland) in *Faerie Queene* V may have been Spenser's cobbled together substitute for a sequel which he had given up. These victories, however, do not follow the lines of some antique story like the conquest of Rome, and they are not politic: that is, they are the work of private gentlemen, not heroic leaders of armies.

What will most strongly suggest to many students that Spenser had given up his epic plan by 1596 concerns the character of IV, V in its earlier part, VI, and VII. The size and complexity of a Spenserian kaleidoscope which would relate their intricate symbolic systems of love and friendship, nature and nurture, and time and eternity to an epic scheme of conquest are hard to imagine. Also, many Spenserians are unable to see the poet emerging from VI's pastoral world of individual contentment and of skepticism about institutional accomplishment in order to orchestrate further warfare on the stage of history (although a praiseworthy Arthur and continued service to Gloriana are still in the picture). Yet the systems of I-III, published with the proposal of an epic scheme, are equally intricate, and the skepticism about worldly accomplishment in the *Complaints* of 1591 at least equals that of VI, published in 1596, and of VII, published posthumously.

Perhaps we cannot reach certainty here. In addition to Spenser's general protestations in *Amoretti* (1595) that he will continue with *The Faerie Queene*, there is the question of the Earl of Essex. After the death of Spenser's patron Leicester, the only possible candidate for future identification with Arthur in later parts of *The Faerie Queene* appears to be this man. He is unique in meeting all three qualifications of proximity to the Queen, high birth, and victories over England's enemies. In the first version of the Dedicatory Sonnets appended to the 1590 *Faerie Queene*, he is given pride of place, immediately after the necessarily first sonnet to the Lord High Chancellor.[14] The prefatory address of the sonnet to Essex is the most elaborate in the series. In the sonnet itself Spenser apologizes for not having honored Essex in the 1590 *Faerie Queene*, which is only lowly poetry compared with what will follow, and promises to make more famous memory of Essex's heroic parts when the poetry reaches a higher strain in the "last praises of this Faery Queene."[15]

Naturally this demonstrates nothing about Spenser's intentions after 1590, but ought to be compared with a passage about Essex in *Prothalamion* of 1596: Spenser praises Essex's recent victory (the capture of Cadiz) fulsomely, hopes that his prowess and victorious arms will free England from foreign harms and that "great *Elisaes* glorious name may ring / Through all the world, fil'd with thy wide Alarmes, / Which some braue muse may sing / To ages following. . ." (157-61). On the face of it, Spenser seems still to believe that his muse may have epic, worldwide plans up her sleeve.[16] We cannot be sure; Spenser himself may not have been. In three years he was dead. Essex paid for his funeral and was himself beheaded two years later.

Given our own attitudes toward imperialism, we cannot escape feelings of ambivalence about any sequel that Spenser might have written. The Thirty Years' War, beginning nineteen years after Spenser's death, was fueled by a similar Protestant activism and devastated parts of Central Europe for a century. In its own time, the sequel would have had to face the discrediting of heroic aggrandizement by humanists, by Rabelais (in his character Picrochole, for instance), by Montaigne, and by Shakespeare.

Shakespeare most programmatically discredits it in his late historical romance *Cymbeline* (c. 1609-10), one of his two excursions (with *Lear*) into the world of Arthur's fabled line. When Arthur's predecessor Cymbeline has escaped the influence of his poisonous second queen and his Picrochole-like stepson Cloten (who is the advocate of the epic of contact sports in the play), then his final position is the same as that of Rabelais' Grandgousier and Gargantua faced with the Picrochole-problem: fight with no holds barred when you have to; but, in the ordinary course of events, paying the tribute in the coin in which it is demanded—cakes in the case of Grandgousier, £3000 in the case of Cymbeline[17]—is preferable by far to bloody heroism.

Another Roman Lucius, in this case a general of Augustus, demands the tribute from Cymbeline, making his case as Malory's Roman ambassadors to Arthur had done, in terms of Julius Caesar's conquest of Britain.   Against his better judgment, Cymbeline is led to refuse it. Lucius attacks with his legions from France and a contingent from Rome. In the greatest extremity, the British overcome them and capture Lucius and the surviving Romans. The empire is seriously strained, for Augustus has committed all his remaining troops to the suppression of revolt in Pannonia and Dalmatia. Cymbeline, however, avoids Arthur's future choice. With Lucius at his mercy, he says he will pay the tribute and let things go on as before. He had already said (III.i.69-70) that his own personal formation as a man in large part derived from the metropolitan center, Rome, where he had lived under the tutelage of Augustus. (Like Shakespeare and us, he was a beneficiary as well as a victim of phenomena associated with Roman imperialism.)

All that the Romans themselves need to yield is another kind of tribute—the bracelet and ring which the other varlet in the play, Jachimo, has stolen from Imogen's bedroom, in the other half of the plot. In the love-feast constituted by this last scene, Posthumus, the husband of Imogen, pardons him freely. It has several times been noticed that Shakespeare repeatedly affirms in this scene a tradition that goes back to Geoffrey: it was in Cymbeline's reign that Christ was born.

The essential elements of Shakespeare's story, however, do not conform to any episodes concerning Cymbeline or any other king in the sources which we feel sure he consulted for the historical side of his plot: Holinshed, the *Mirror for Magistrates*, and Spenser's Book of Briton Moniments. Those elements seem to coalesce only in his imagination. Perhaps his imagination was partly guided by reading of, and reaction against, Malory's tale of Arthur's treatment of the tribute and Spenser's treatment of the subject. A name and role agree: Malory's Emperor Lucius, Shakespeare's general Lucius, who is otherwise completely Shakespeare's invention, unrelated to his recognized sources.[18] If Shakespeare read Malory's tale, he may have noticed not only the entrance of Malory's Rome-conquering Arthur into Spenser's Briton Moniments but also Spenser's unique juxtaposition of sixth-century Arthur and first-century Cymbeline, to the latter's disadvantage. Spenser's stanza citing Arthur's complete defeat of the Romans, quoted above, ends with his predecessors' vigorous yet unsuccessful efforts in the same direction: "Yet oft the Briton kings against them strongly swayd." In the next line, Cymbeline appears as the first of these kings, refusing the tribute in subsequent lines but killed by treachery while fighting a Roman expeditionary force. It is attractive to suppose that Shakespeare, weaving in material from other sources, turned the tables on Arthur's successful imperialism by giving Cymbeline the better part.

My theory needs further confirmation, building as it does upon a new (although apparently indubitable) interpretation of one line of *The Faerie Queene* and upon Shakespeare's supposed reading of *Le Morte Darthur*, for which we have no evidence elsewhere. But the notion that his *Cymbeline* reacts against Malory's and Spenser's British hero has the merit of hermeneutic simplicity in relation to a puzzling play. If the relation is only coincidental, it is at least revealing.

NOTES

1. For Geoffrey's *Historia Regum Britanniae* I cite for convenience the Sebastian Evans translation revised by Charles Dunn: *History*

of the Kings of Britain (New York: Dutton, 1958), pp. 203-32 (IX.xv-X).

2.   Perhaps shadowing and glorifying England's comparatively piddling imperialistic venture on the Continent up to that time. Eugène Vinaver (*The Works of Sir Thomas Malory*, 2nd ed., 3 vols. Oxford: Clarendon, 1967, III, 1367-8) makes a convincing case for the theory that Malory alludes to Henry V's conquests in France in Arthur's French campaign against Lucius.

3.   *The Works of Edmund Spenser, A Variorum Edition*, ed. Edwin Greenlaw et al. (Baltimore: Johns Hopkins University Press, 1932-57), I, 167-70. All quotations of Spenser below follow this edition.

4.   Quoted in *Variorum*, I, 323.

5.   An alternative seems to me less likely. It is that Spenser might refer here to the conquest of Rome, beginning with an allegorization of either the exactions of Catholicism on English soil before the time of Elizabeth or the danger of native Catholicism in her time.

6.   For convenience I cite Caxton's version of Malory in the Everyman edition with modern spelling and punctuation: Sir Thomas Malory, *Le Morte d'Arthur* (London: Dent; New York: Dutton, 1906) I, 130 (V.i). It is of some importance that Malory almost surely got the notion of Arthur's conquest of Rome from a manuscript of the Chronicle of John Hardyng, completed around 1463; and that Spenser was familiar with the form of this chronicle printed by Grafton in 1543. I hope to publish on this additional point soon.

7.   Because the British kings Belinus and Brenius had formerly conquered Rome, and the emperor Constantine was son to Helena, supposed to be British (Malory, 132). Spenser's history increases these interrelations of British and Roman rulers' houses.

8.   Malory, I, 143.

9.   *FQ* I.v.42.8, IV.v.31.9, V.xi.41.5, VI.8.24.3, and the quoted example in *Epithalamion*.

10.   It is a little surprising that none of Spenser's early editors saw even the possibility of a connection between *Morte Darthur* 5 and "Till Arthur all that reckoning defrayd." In the twentieth century, Carrie Harper's intelligent dissertation (*The Sources of the British Chronicle History in Spenser's Faerie Queene* [Bryn Mawr College Monographs, 7], Philadelphia, 1910) did not include Malory in its search. Her account (pp. 108-09) of II.x.47-49 offers no specific explanation of this line, and her list of material for which she found no source includes Julius Caesar's "sword, yet to be seene this day" in stanza 49 but not the defrayment. Perhaps the reference to

Arthur out of chronological order helps to account for her failure to see the resemblance of what is said about him to what appears in Geoffrey. The two most authoritatively annotated editions of *FQ* since 1910 (the Variorum and that of A.C. Hamilton, London and New York: Longman, 1977) simply follow Harper. Hamilton (p. 267) paraphrases the relevant line as "evened the account either by getting revenge or by withholding `tribute,'" which is accurate as far as it goes, and seems to ask for Malory's story.

11. For this and following information, see Malory, I, 133, 140-42, 145-49.

12. Of the works relating Arthur's defeat of the Romans it is certain that Spenser knew Geoffrey and Caxton's Malory and almost equally certain that he knew none of the others (except Hardyng; see note 6). Following his usual practice, he would no doubt have fused details from the two sources he knew, but I dismiss the possibility that he might have followed Geoffrey in aborting the conquest of Rome. The claimed defrayment would not then have occurred. In an epic he needed a successful (even if fictional) conquest here as much as he did in his account of Arthur-Leicester's private fictional conquest of Antwerp in *FQ* V. To identify a patron with an unsuccessful conquest would have been similarly infeasible.

13. As a reigning faery, Gloriana would have had a death, like her father Oberon.

14. For this arrangement, and the subsequent one, see Variorum III, 428-29.

15. Variorum III, 193.

16. As Patrick Cheney pointed out in his "*Prothalamion* and *The Faerie Queene*...," a paper for "Spenser at Kalamazoo," The International Congress on Medieval Studies, Kalamazoo, Michigan, May 1987.

17. The coin of Cymbeline's tribute, like that of Arthur's, is in question. J.M. Nosworthy (in his Arden edition of *Cymbeline* [London: Methuen, 1955], note to III.i.9) says that 3000 pounds means pounds of gold or silver, but I cannot see why Shakespeare's first audience should have heard anything but pounds sterling in the simple enunciation of 3000 pounds, any more than they did when Falstaff said, "Master Shallow, I owe you a thousand pound." £3000 would have been no intolerable burden on Cymbeline's exchequer.

18. J.P. Brockbank, in "History and Histrionics in *Cymbeline*," in *Shakespeare Survey* 11 (1958), 48, suggests that Lucius is named after the British king in Holinshed (*History*, 1587, IV.19) under whom England is supposed to have first become Christian, in the

second century A.D. The connection seems tenuous, but the article is most valuable.   A further, more distant resemblance between Malory's and Shakespeare's accounts is that each contains a dream portending British success against the Romans (in Malory, of Arthur as a dragon overcoming a tyrant as a bear out of the east; in Shakespeare, of Cymbeline as the sun enforcing terms on the empire as an eagle from the south).   See Malory, I, 134-35; *Cymbeline*, Riverside edition, IV.ii.348-50; V.v.467-76.

Arthur, Argante, and the Ideal Vision:
An Exercise in Speculation and Parody

Judith H. Anderson

One of the more luridly colorful figures in *The Faerie Queene* is Argante, the aggressively lustful giantess of Book III. She first appears bearing the Squire of Dames "athwart her horse," bound fast "with cords of wire, / Whom she did meane to make the thrall of her desire."[1] Within stanzas, she has discarded the Squire, replacing him with the mightier Sir Satyrane, whom she plucks by the collar right out of his saddle and evidently hopes to subject to her service, for "ouer all the countrey she did raunge, / To seeke young men, to quench her flaming thrust." Whomever she finds most fit "to serue her lust,"

> She with her brings into a secret Ile,
> Where in eternall bondage dye he must,
> Or be the vassall of her pleasures vile.
> > [III.vii.50]

The reprehensible Argante is also the twin sister of Ollyphant, or elephant, with whom she is said to have been locked in sexual intercourse at birth. These incestuous twins are therefore a nightmarish parody of the immaculate birth of the twins Amoret and Belphoebe two cantos earlier. Incest, from Latin *incestus*, is the supreme expression of unchastity, as A. C. Hamilton notes, and this fact emphasizes the parodic relation between Belphoebe, exemplar of chastity in Spenser's poem, and the lascivious Argante.[2]

Spenser takes Ollyphant, the name of Argante's twin brother, from the giant in Chaucer's *Sir Thopas,* a tale on which Spenser drew frequently and specifically in Book I for Prince Arthur's dream of his beloved elf queen, the Queene of Faerie.[3] In the Letter to Ralegh, Spenser wrote that his own sovereign Queen, Elizabeth, bears two persons, "the one of a most royall Queene . . . the other of a most vertuous and beautifull Lady." "This latter part," he added, "in some places I doe express in Belphoebe," who bodies forth chastity. The former part—"the person of . . . the Queene, and her kingdome in Faery land"—he expresses in the Faerie Queene herself, the idealized figure whom Arthur loves and for whom he searches the length of Spenser's poem.[4] Through both connections, on the one hand, as a parody of Belphoebe's birth, and, on the other, in the shared Chaucerian origin of Ollyphant's name and Arthur's vision of the Faerie Queene, the genealogy of Argante thus touches distantly the person of Queen Elizabeth.

Argante's own name has never been accounted for satisfactorily. Whereas most editors pass over it in conspicuous silence, Hamilton follows Joel Belson in glossing it as a coinage from Greek *argos* (ἀργός), meaning "bright," "shining," "white," or "swift-footed," and related to the Greek words *arges* (ἀργής), meaning "bright," "shining," "white," or "vivid," and *argas* (ἀργᾶς), meaning "shining" or "white."[5] This gloss, as Belson explains it, seems to me somewhat forced, however, since Argante is said to be afire, not alight, with fury and lust; since her "sun-broad shield" suggests enormousness—indeed enormity—not brilliance; and since her dappled horse, not she, accounts for the speed with which she enters the poem.[6] In fact, if we try to base Argante's name on Greek coinages, the word *argos* (ἀργός) or "idle," "yielding no return," seems to me an equally suitable candidate, because we can connect it with Spenser's use of *idle* elsewhere in the poem, meaning "useless" or "degenerate in moral terms" and occasionally punning on *idyll,* or "place of pleasure," a meaning relevant to Argante's island bower, her "secret Ile" of lust.[7]

But I doubt that the primary source of Argante's name is to be found in coinages from the Greek. Instead, it is to be found in Arthurian legend. In Laȝamon's *Brut,* King Arthur, mortally wounded at the battle of Camelford, addresses these words to his successor: "And I will fare to Avalun, to the fairest of all maidens, to Argante the queen, an elf most fair, and she shall make my wounds all sound; make me whole with healing draughts."   Reinforcing Arthur's words, Laȝamon subsequently adds, "the Britons believe yet that he is alive, and dwelleth in Avalun with the fairest of all elves."[8]   While in Laȝamon, two women merely bear Arthur over the sea to Avalon, in Geoffrey of Monmouth, an undoubted Spenserian source, Avalon is specified to be an isle or island and thus the kind of land mass that Spenser's Argante (not to mention Spenser's sovereign) inhabits.[9]

Belson, Hamilton's source in glossing Argante's name, was aware of the occurrence of Argante in Laȝamon's *Brut*, but he refers to it only as an example of his belief that Argante is a variant of the name Morgan in medieval literature, for it is usually Morgan le Fay who reigns in Avalon.   Rather than consider the relation of Laȝamon's Argante to Spenser's, Belson is intent on the relation of Spenser's Argante to the "'morgans' or sea women of Breton folklore who were said to dwell in under-sea palaces" and in French folklore were said to have a "craze for human men" that could never be sated because men died at their touch.[10]   Unfortunately, Belson's bridge from Spenser's Argante to these frustrated morgans is his belief that the names Argante and Morgan were interchangeable and that Spenser and his readers were aware of this possibility.   The only evidence for their interchangeability, however, is the presence of Argante, instead of Morgan, in Laȝamon's *Brut* and the older scholarly speculations of our own century based upon it, which are, to put the matter mildly, highly conjectural.[11]   Moreover, the morgans of folklore do not even match Argante very closely, for she is an island or land creature, not a sea woman, and at her touch men like Satyrane or the Squire of Dames may get bruised but they do not perish.   In view of these difficulties, it is not surprising that Hamilton adopted Belson's Greek etymology of Argante's name and passed over his hypothesis that Argante is really Morgan and therefore based on the morgans of myth.   Yet the facts remain that Spenser uses the name Argante and that the apparent source of this name either is Laȝamon's *Brut* or is represented by it, since a number of scholars argue that La3amon drew on Welsh, Irish, or French sources for his poem, which now are lost.[12]

Before I pursue further the relation of La3amon's Argante to Spenser's, I should raise more directly the question of whether Spenser might have encountered the *Brut*. La3amon's long poem, which contains the first version of Arthur's life in English, is generally considered of thirteenth-century origin. Its subject is the history of the Britons, who are depicted as the descendants of Trojan Brutus; about a third of it treats the story of Arthur. Although La3amon's Middle English is difficult, it is not inaccessible, and the main argument against the likelihood that Spenser knew it is the absence of a printed edition of it during the Renaissance and its survival to this day in only two Cottonian manuscripts, if modern editions are excepted.[13] Indeed, the main reason that few readers have noticed the coincidence of Argante's presence in La3amon and in Spenser is very probably the scarcity of modern editions of the *Brut* until fairly recently.

Yet the provenance of the two known manuscripts of La3amon's *Brut* is English, and La3amon, an English priest in Worcestershire with ties to Ireland, was presumably drawing on oral and written legend in greatly elaborating his major source, the French *Brut* of Wace. Neither La3amon's poem nor his putative sources, therefore, were entirely beyond Spenser's reach, which, Rosemond Tuve has repeatedly assured us, must have extended to manuscript sources.[14] Spenser's demonstrable interests in British history, Arthurian legend, and older poetry in English would surely have recommended La3amon's poem to him, had he met it. Noteworthy here, perhaps, is the fact that Spenser's particular interest in the story of Brute was strong enough for him somehow to have produced five Welsh words in two lines of verse, which actually scan, in the account of Brutus Greenshield that Arthur finds in Alma's chamber of memory, amid "rolles,"

> And old records from auncient times deriu'd,
> Some made in books, some in long parchment scrolles,
> That were all worme-eaten, and full of canker holes.
>
> [II.ix.57][15]

Aside from Spenser's historical interests and the availability or unavailability to him of a manuscript of Laȝamon's *Brut*, there is nothing outside his *Faerie Queene* itself to influence our judgment of the one piece of hard evidence of a relationship between Spenser and Laȝamon that we have—the name *Argante*. Simply assuming this relationship for the present, I would like to explore its potential for significance in *The Faerie Queene*, to see what kinds of meanings it might release and in what kinds of patterns participate, thereby to measure its plausibility on internal grounds.

From what we have seen already, Spenser's perverse Argante is a simple antitype of the chaste Belphoebe and shares, through the origin of her brother Ollyphant's name, a distant tie to Prince Arthur's vision of the elf queen, and in these radically deflected ways parodically approaches the idea of Elizabeth I. This is parody that the origin of Argante's name as Laȝamon's elfish queen of fairies enforces so considerably as to alter its status from tentative suggestion to far-reaching and metamorphic fact. With Laȝamon to hand, the very structure of the episodes surrounding the center of Book III, the Gardens of Adonis, begins to participate in parody. On both sides of the idealized Gardens, there is thwarted love. In the cantos on their far side, such compromised and dishonorable figures as Argante, the Witch and her son, False Florimell, and the Squire of Dames dominate the scene. On their near side and in sharp contrast are the honorable figures of Belphoebe and Timias, who alludes to Sir Walter Ralegh as conspicuously as Belphoebe does to Elizabeth.[16] From the perspective of the thwarted love of Timias for Belphoebe, plus the recognition of Argante as a monstrous parody of the Faerie Queene, Argante's figure can be read as a terrible reflection of and on Elizabeth's notorious exploitation of courtly flirtation with her younger male courtiers. Here I would emphasize that this reading is unlikely to occur merely on the basis of contrast between Belphoebe and Argante, chastity and unchastity. It is simply not a meaning truly available without reference to Laȝamon's *Brut*.

If we once recognize in Argante a distorted reflection of the Faerie Queene, we can make sense of other resonances latent and perhaps suppressed in Argante's figure. For example, should we also choose to derive her name secondarily from the Greek coinages I earlier discussed, we can recover a sardonic commentary on the rewards of the courtier's life that is substantially more detailed and realistic than is an animated fantasy of lust. Greek *argos*, meaning "useless" or "yielding nothing," refers to a lack of return on untilled land or to a lack of return of money—to the absence of yield, then, on land or money. We need only connect this word (as I did earlier) with its Greek homonym *argos*, or "shining" and "bright," and thence with the related *arges* and *argas*, "shining," whose root, *arg-*, shared with the latter *argos*, comes in Latin and French to mean "silver" and "money"— *argentum* and *argent/argenté*, respectively—more nearly to suggest Argante's name and to find in the giantess a sour but typically Spenserian reflection on the niggardly rewards of courtiership under Elizabeth's thumb.[17]

As antitype to an idealized elf queen, Argante correlates more generally with the ambivalent treatment of Arthur, at times throughout Spenser's poem but most conspicuously in Book I, when, paradoxically, the poem also most idealizes him. Here, Arthur's figure, embodying in the poem the perfection of all the virtues, is imprinted with complicating, compromising, and completing elements of meaning and history. In the course of the poem, Argante proves to be just one of the skeletons in Prince Arthur's closet.

When Arthur is first introduced, the poet concludes a lengthy description of him by focusing on the wondrous shield he carries, which can dispel illusion and turn men to stone. The shield, we learn, was made anciently for Arthur by Merlin:

> Both shield, and sword, and armour all he wrought
> For this young Prince, when first to armes he fell;
> But when he dyde, the Faerie Queene it brought
> To Faerie lond, where yet it may be seene, if sought.
>
> [I.vii.36]

The "he" who died refers logically and syntactically in the last two of these lines to Arthur, the "he" who fell to arms in the line immediately preceding, rather than to Merlin, and yet the temporal clause, "when he dyde," is the more unsettling precisely because of its initial unobtrusiveness, its insidious subordination, its failed ambiguity.[18] The poet's use of the word *but* ("But when he dyde"), rather than *and*, points up the discontinuity present in Arthur's death, even as the pronoun *he* momentarily masks it, and the combined influence of the two words further contributes to the oddly emphatic, oddly evasive effect. It is as though the poet were simultaneously inviting us to overlook Arthur's death and refusing to let us do so.

Acknowledged to be dead in time even when first introduced in the poem, the young Prince Arthur is conspicuously an image, a poetic figure tied and not tied to British history. His youth itself, not yet possessed of rule, and his romantic quest for an ideal, distance him both from the mighty king dominant in legendary history and from the very human and fallible warrior of the Arthurian cycles. At the same time, of course, the figure of Spenser's Arthur is conceived in allusion to British history, not only through his name and descriptive details like the dragon on his helmet, but also through the canto-long catalogue of the British rulers who preceded him, a mnemonic event in which Arthur himself participates in the House of Alma. This Arthur exists in the space between history and imagination, between what has been and what might be, between the forces that engendered the Arthur of legendary history and the glimpse, elusive but inspiring, of the Faerie Queene. He is at once a figure of pure and open potential and, insofar as he is in some sense truly Arthur, a figure embedded in the failures of history.

From this point of view, the complicating and potentially subversive elements of parody in Arthur's dream of the Faerie Queene, which have attracted attention of late, make sense. The dream itself alludes to that of Chaucer's comic Sir Thopas; numerous verbal details within it echo the Redcrosse Knight's dream of a false Una earlier in Spenser's poem; and several of its lines recall Chaucer's Wife of Bath's Prologue and his *Troilus and Criseyde*, both tales of humanly vital but immoral or ephemeral love.[19] Even as Arthur expresses the Faerie ideal that motivates him, these echoes and allusions parodically qualify his vision, though they do so without destroying or overwhelming its positive force. They both threaten *and* enrich it by adding dimensions to it undeniably present in human history. Without such dimensions, Arthur's dream would not be moored to what has preceded him, whether in Redcrosse's Christian story, in Chaucer's poetic world, in the Arthurian cycles, or in the consciousness of the race. With them, the dream has a basis in history and human reality, morally mixed for ill and good as these must always be.

The ambivalences that cluster around Arthur's figure when the poet first describes him similarly indicate parody of various sorts.[20] The dragon on his helmet bespeaks his kinship to Uther Pendragon (or "dragon's head") and reflects the fiery dragon in the sky that foretold Arthur's birth, but in a Book in which the cumulative symbols of evil are serpentine forms, it signals as well the demonic force that the figure of Arthur harnesses.[21] In this last sense, Arthur's dragon is like the brazen serpent of Moses in the wilderness, like that in Fidelia's cup, and like those associated with wisdom and healing in classical myth—on the caduceus, for example, or in the figure of Asclepius.

Atop Arthur's crest, "A bunch of haires discoulourd diuersly" exactly replicates a line describing Archimago impersonating the Redcrosse Knight and thereby parodically recalls evil illusion more precisely than is ever the case in Arthur's dream. The replicated line charges Arthur's figure with the ambivalent potency earlier possessed by evil alone. Arthur's figure, taken whole, redirects this potency, rather than being drawn by its presence into alliance with Archimago's disguise. Arthur's crest itself, for example, is said to be comparable "to an Almond tree ymounted hye . . . Whose tender locks do tremble euery one / At euery little breath, that vnder heauen is blowne" (I.vii.32). Throughout Book I—from the Wandering Wood, to Fradubio's grove, to Orgoglio's fountain of lust and beyond—trees, often trembling, are associated with the theme of fleshly nature and, to this point, with temptation and failure. Now, however, the trembling of a tree suggests a world in concert with heaven, and the specification of the tree as an almond alludes to Aaron's rod in Numbers (17.5-8) that budded and yielded almonds as a sign of his election by God.[22] Like the tree of life into whose balm Redcrosse falls in his final fight with the Dragon, the tree and the theme it embodies are here repossessed by a positive power. And yet, even as they are repossessed, allusive parody is present as both threat and human relevance. Nature redeemed, or repossessed, is not *natura impeccabilis*, nature incapable of sinning. But two parodic touches in the description of Arthur take us closer to Argante. Both suggest pride, which from the beginning of Book I participates in the ambivalent potency of the natural world. This ambivalence underlies and accounts for most Spenserian parody and is, indeed, the axis around which Spenserian types and antitypes revolve.

The first of the prideful parodies occurs when Spenser uses the word "haughtie" to describe Arthur's helmet (31). This word recalls Orgoglio's "haughtie eye" some fifteen stanzas earlier and anticipates the Dragon's crest in canto xi (15). Sixteenth-century meanings of *haughty* range from negative, through neutral, to positive ones. It can simply mean "high, lofty," in a literal sense or "imposing in aspect"; more positively, it means "high-minded" and "aspiring," exalted in "character, style, or rank"; and yet its earliest meaning, which persists throughout the period, is the one still current: "high in one's own estimation," "proud," and "arrogant."[23] While Arthur's helmet is defensive armor and thereby implies his haughtiness to foes, it also carries his identifying crest and with it once again the trace of a double potential for evil or good. In this the "haughtie helmet" resembles the word *pride* itself when it first appears in Book I to characterize the trees in the Wandering Wood—those "loftie trees yclad with sommers pride" (i.7). Here, if only for a moment before *pride* is redefined as an obstruction of heaven's light, it carries the natural and innocent meaning, "prime," "flowering," "splendor," and glances at the ambivalence of the natural world for evil or good, pain or pleasure, anarchy or energy.[24]

The second parodic touch of pride in the description of Arthur is more insistent than his haughtiness. It alludes to the House of Pride and specifically to the characterization of Lucifera, that "mayden Queene," whose figure is an early antitype in the poem to that of the virgin Queen, Elizabeth, and therefore potentially a parody of her. Twice in this characterization the phrase "exceeding shone" occurs: thus Lucifera's

> . . . bright blazing beautie did assay
> To dim the brightnesse of her glorious throne,
> As enuying her selfe, that too exceeding shone.
>
> Exceeding shone, like *Phoebus* fairest chylde. . . .
>
> [I.iv.8-9]

Like the "glistring gold" of Lucifera and her throne, which is at once an extension of and rival to her discontented self, the "glistring ray" of Arthur's wondrous shield "so exceeding shone . . . That *Phoebus* face it did attaint" (vii.34). That Arthur's pride is in the shield whose power is God's is a meaning that carries the promise of redemption and the threat of presumption. It is a meaning inscribed in biblical history and in the history of Britain.

My point has been that, from an early stage of *The Faerie Queene*, parody is evident in connection with Arthur's own idealized figure and with the ideal he pursues, the elf queen of his vision. Argante, as a parody of this queen, is an immensely stronger and more destructive instance of the broader parody whose roots spread over Book I, but she is hardly alien to Spenser's methods or to the ambivalence and oppositions of his points of view. The potential parody of the virgin Queen present in Lucifera becomes in Book III more directly a criticism of her "ensample dead"—her lifeless or unworldly example—in the person of Belphoebe, and in Book IV it emerges in the loathsome figure of Slander, "that queane [or queen] so base and vilde" (III.v.54, IV.viii.28).[25] As a monstrous fantasy and a fleeting nightmare not quite suppressed, Argante is a shocking parody of the Faerie Queene in Book III but, sadly, once recognized, one that is hard to ignore or forget. As such a parody, moreover, she is an assault on the object of Arthur's quest, and, if we trust the sequence of cantos and books in *The Faerie Queene*, she is an assault from which this quest never fully recovers. Never, after the final half of Book III, is the possibility of Arthur's finding the Faerie Queene in any sense viable.

NOTES

1. All Spenserian references are to *The Works of Edmund Spenser: A Variorum Edition*, ed. Edwin Greenlaw et al., 11 vols. (Baltimore: Johns Hopkins Press, 1932-57), cited as *Var.*; *The Faerie Queene* is cited as *FQ*. The present reference is to *FQ* III.vii.37.

2. Edmund Spenser, *The Faerie Queene*, ed. A. C. Hamilton (London: Longman, 1977), p. 373. *Faute de mieux*, I use the term *parody* throughout this essay to approximate the phenomenon of reflection in a fun-house mirror—in this case a reflection often more sobering than comic. To my mind, one can parody a person's status or behavior and, indeed, a person's identity or style of life. Indeed, one can parody any manner or form that the mind has fashioned. Parody of Elizabeth I, of the virgin Queen, is the parody of an image, idea, or conception of Elizabeth. Spenserian parody typically and ironically reflects actual texts—Chaucer's or Spenser's own, for example—and textualized ideas, such as the virgin Queen or Belphoebe.

3. In the 1590 *Faerie Queene*, "Chylde Thopas" is the confounder of Ollyphant (III.vii.48, *Var.*, III, 412).

4. *Var.*, I, 168.

5. Hamilton, ed., p. 373; Joel Jay Belson, "The Names in *The Faerie Queene*" (Ph.D. Columbia University), 1964, p. 35. Liddell and Scott, s.v. , ’ΑΡΓΌΣ, ἀργής, ἀργᾶς. On the relationship of these Greek words, see Julius Pokorny, *Indogermanisches etymologisches Wörterbuch*. Bern: Francke, 1959), pp. 64-65, who discusses their proto-Indo-European root, *arg-*. Hamilton, I should note, cites only *argos* to gloss Argante's name. Belson cites both *argos* and *arges* but not *argas*.

6. *FQ* III.vii.39, vs. 8; 49, vs. 8; 40, vs. 4; 37, vs. 3.

7. *FQ* III.vii.50. Liddell and Scott, s.v. ἀργός

8. "Layamon's *Brut*," in *Arthurian Chronicles Represented by Wace and Layamon*, intro. Lucy Allen Paton (1912; rpt. London: J. M. Dent, 1928), p. 264. Laȝamon, *Brut*, ed. G. L. Brook and R. F. Leslie, EETS 227 (London: Oxford University Press, 1978), II, 750:

    And ich wulle uaren to Aualun.' to uairest alre maidene.
    to Argante þere quene.' aluen swiðe sceone.
    & heo s[c]al mine wunden.' makien alle isunde.

al hal me makien.' mid halewei3e drenchen.

. . . .

Bruttes ileue𝛿 3ete.' Þat he bon on liue.
and wunnien in Aualun.' mid fairest alre aluen.

[14277-80, 14290-91]

9.   Galfrido Monemutensi, *Brittannie vtriusq[ue] regu[m] et principium origo & gesta insignia* ([Paris]: Jo. Badius Ascensius, 1517), Fo. xci^v, VII.vii: "in insulam Auallonis"; Geoffrey of Monmouth, *The Historia Regum Britanniae*, ed. Acton Griscom (London: Longmans, Green, 1929), p. 501.

10.   Belson, pp. 35-37; Lewis Spence, *The Minor Traditions of British Mythology* (London: Rider, 1948), pp. 27-28. There is no foundation in Spence for Belson's suggestion that the morgans of Ushant live "on" the island.

11.   For example, Lucy Allen Paton, *Studies in the Fairy Mythology of Arthurian Romance*, 2nd ed. (1903; rpt. New York: Burt Franklin, 1960), pp. 26-28; J. D. Bruce, "Some Proper Names in Layamon's *Brut* Not Represented in Wace or Geoffrey of Monmouth," *MLN*, 26 (1911), 65-68.

12.   J. S. P. Tatlock, *The Legendary History of Britain: Geoffrey of Monmouth's Historia Regum Britanniae and Its Early Vernacular Versions* (Berkeley: University of California Press, 1950), pp. 483-531, esp. pp. 515-29; Spence, p. 27; Paton, pp. 26-34; Bruce, pp. 65-69. For a recent assessment, see *Dictionary of the Middle Ages*, ed. Joseph R. Strayer (New York: Scribner's Sons, 1983), II, s.v. *Brut.*

13.   *Dictionary of the Middle Ages*, II, s.v. *Brut.* Cf. Carrie Anna Harper, *The Sources of the British Chronicle History in Spenser's Faerie Queene* (1910; rpt. New York: Haskell House, 1964), p. 24-27.

14.   Rosemond Tuve, "Spenser and Some Pictorial Conventions" and "Spenserus," in *Essays by Rosemond Tuve*, ed. Thomas P. Roche, Jr. (Princeton: Princeton University Press, 1970), pp. 112-62, esp. 112-18.

15.   The Welsh words occur in *FQ* II.x.24: "That not *Scuith guiridh* it mote seeme to bee, / But rather *y Scuith gogh*, signe of sad crueltee." See also Charles Bowie Millican, *Spenser and the Table Round: A Study in the Contemporaneous Background for Spenser's Use of the Arthurian Legend* (Cambridge: Harvard University Press, 1932), p. 202, n. 5; cf. p. 78.

16.   On the allusion to Ralegh, see James P. Bednarz, "Ralegh in Spenser's Historical Allegory," *SSt*, 4 (1983), 49-70.

17. Edmond Huguet, *Dictionnaire de la langue française du seizième siècle* (Paris: Didier, 1925), s.v. *Argente, Argenté*. Lewis and Short, s.v. *Argentum*, relate *arges* and *argas* etymologically to *argentum*. Henry Gibbons Lotspeich, *Classical Mythology in the Poetry of Edmund Spenser* (1932; rpt. New York: Gordian, 1965), s.v. *Giants*, suggests that Argente, "an alternative name for Luna, daughter of Hyperion," in Boccaccio's *De genealogia deorum gentilium* (IV.16) may account for the name and size of Spenser's Argante. But the name remains Argente, not Argante, in Boccaccio, and, as Belson observes, the incidental size of Argente does not persuasively account for "the psychotic lustfulness which Argante typifies [for this] is, by nature, of monstrous and gigantic proportions" (35-37).

18. Cf. the reference to Merlin's death in *FQ* III.iii.10.

19. I have treated this dream in greater detail in "'A Gentle Knight was pricking on the plaine': The Chaucerian Connection," *ELR*, 15 (1985), 166-74, esp. 172-73. See also Patricia A. Parker, *Inescapable Romance: Studies in the Poetics of a Mode* (Princeton: Princeton University Press, 1979), pp. 83-86.

20. On these ambivalences, see Kenneth Gross, *Spenserian Poetics: Idolatry, Iconoclasm, and Magic* (Ithaca: Cornell University Press, 1985), pp. 128-43, esp. p. 133. In Gross's reading, parodic elements reflect the poet's concern with idolatry, with the threat and power of the image as image. Wonderfully perceptive and persuasive as I often find Gross's ideas and analyses, I consider this meaning too specialized fully to account for the widespread use of parody in *The Faerie Queene*.

21. On the dragon, see Hamilton, ed., p. 103. On serpentine forms, cf. Jane Aptekar, *Icons of Justice: Iconography and Thematic Imagery in Book V of "The Faerie Queene"* (New York: Columbia University Press, 1969), pp. 87-107, esp. p. 103; pp. 125-39.

22. For a similar view, see Kathleen Williams, *Spenser's Faerie Queene: The World of Glass* (London: Routledge & Kegan Paul, 1966), p. 22. Gross, pp. 133-34, gives short shrift to the positive force of the description of Arthur. The suggestion that a positive reading is moralistic obfuscates the fact that the moralism, if that's what it is, is Spenser's. *The Faerie Queene* is much more than simply moralistic, but moral it sometimes—indeed, more than sometimes—is.

23. *OED*, s.v. *Haughty*, 1-3.

24. *OED*, s.v. *Pride sb*[1], II.7, 9.

25. On Belphoebe's "ensample dead" and the "queane" Slander, see my essay "'In liuing colours and right hew': The Queen of

Spenser's Central Books," in Maynard Mack and George deForest Lord, eds., *Poetic Traditions of the English Renaissance* (New Haven: Yale University Press, 1982), pp. 47-66.

"Beauties Chace":
Arthur and Women in *The Faerie Queene*

Sheila T. Cavanagh

... by my side a royall Mayd
Her daintie limbes full softly down did lay
[I.ix.13.7-8]

Was neuer hart so rauisht with delight,
Ne liuing man like words did euer heare,
As she to me deliuered all that night
[I.ix.14.6-8]

When I awoke, and found her place deuoyd,
And nought but pressed gras, where she had lyen,
I sorrowed all so much, as earst I ioyd.
[I.ix.15.1-3]

Arthur's account of his first encounter with the Faerie Queene who then becomes the focal point of his quest leaves many unresolved questions in the mind of the reader. If the meeting actually took place outside of the Prince's dreams, one is left to suppose that, as A.C. Hamilton notes, "either the fairy rose with her virginity intact or she did not."[1] Even if the pair came together only in Arthur's imagination, however, one remains puzzled about the moral implications of such an erotic dream for the personified embodiment of all virtue, since lustful thoughts can be as morally suspect as illicit actions. As the figure in Faery Land who generally rescues the other knights from their battles with temptation, Arthur's actions are normally considered exemplary, but his responses to women greatly problematize his status as superior knight and frequently unsettle the reader's understanding of the modes of appropriate behavior toward women. As one progresses through the epic, this discomfiture increases, until it becomes impossible not to acknowledge that the established boundaries between "good" and "evil" often do not apply for issues concerning gender. Although the virtue receiving primary attention changes in each book, with the respective temptations shifting accordingly, disturbing sexual encounters remain a constant. Women, especially beautiful ones, continue to provoke suspicious responses from Faery Land's heroes, no matter which virtue is the nominal focus of the volume under scrutiny.

The question of Arthur's sexual behavior, for example, arises again in Book III, where the passage providing the title for this essay occurs. At the opening of the legend, Arthur, Guyon, and Britomart are riding together through the forest, exchanging stories about their quests and adventures. When they have gone a short distance, their calm is interrupted by the appearance of the ever-fleeing Florimell, manically pursued by the evil foster:

> Lo where a griesly Foster forth did rush,
> Breathing out beastly lust her to defile:
> His tyreling iade he fiercely forth did push,
> Through thicke and thin, both ouer banke and bush
> In hope her to obtain by hooke or crooke,
> That from his gorie sides the bloud did gush:
> Large were his limbes, and terrible his looke,
> And in his clownish hand a sharp bore speare he shooke.
>
> [III.i.17.2-9]

Arthur and Guyon immediately join in the chase, but there is a disturbing suggestion that their motives might not be in the best interest of Florimell's virtue:

> The Prince and Guyon equally byliue
> Her selfe pursewd, in hope to win thereby
> Most goodly meede, the fairest Dame aliue,
>
> [III.i.18.6-8]

especially since the description of Britomart's response indicates that she assumes they are acting in lust:

> The whiles faire Britomart, whose constant mind,
> Would not so lightly follow beauties chace,
> Ne reckt of Ladies Loue, did stay behind.
>
> [III.i.19.1-3]

Arthur's and Guyon's intentions remain enclosed in mystery and Florimell eventually escapes all the men who are following her, but the perplexing implications of Arthur's participation here never fully dissipate, particularly since the incident occurs in the only book of *The Faerie Queene*—the Legend of Chastity— in which Arthur does not rescue the titular knight. His failure to intervene in the book could be interpreted as related to Britomart's inability to fall and need rescue, but the two episodes considered here suggest that Arthur's own relationship with the virtue of chastity is too dubious for him credibly to educate others in its essential properties. Despite a lack of conclusive evidence against the Prince, the hints of something amiss are too strong to be repressed, although the reader understandably hesitates before directing accusations of reprehensible concupiscence at the knight ostensibly representing Magnificence in the epic. Nevertheless, Arthur's relationship with the women in *The Faerie Queene* demands more attention than it is normally given. The questions it raises help illuminate the problems attendant upon portraying women in the epic generally, as well as emphasizing the problems impeding attempts to reconcile chastity with sexual desire.

Reading the episode in conjunction with modern theories of gender relations helps to place in the foreground the vexed issues concealed in the epic when women disappear into the forest or out of the text. In *Dissemination* and *Spurs*, for instance, Jacques Derrida discusses women from a perspective which can offer the confused reader a way to understand the sexual and textual strategies explored in these episodes with Arthur. One of the most notable—and puzzling—aspects of the Prince's sexual adventures is their repeated tendency to occur somehow off the page. Guyon and Arthur disappear into the folds of the text when they pursue Florimell, just as the Faerie Queene appears only in the shadows where her presence as well as her behavior is suspect. The reader never gets a good view of the proceedings, and must therefore surmise what happened from the most tangential evidence.

Derrida's description of the text and its parallels with virginity resonates with echoes of the questions surrounding Arthur, and suggests an explanation for the amount of activity which occurs in obscure spaces:

> The fold is simultaneously virginity, what violates virginity, and the fold which, being neither one nor the other and both at once, undecidable, *remains* as a text, irreducible to either of its two senses.[2]

Here, the fold of the text becomes the space representative of the hymen, the membrane whose contradictory connotations surpass even the questions enveloping Arthur. Symbolizing both marriage and virginity, the hymen is the physical manifestation of the virtue the Faerie Queene and Florimell presumably seek to preserve. Allied closely with the text, "the closed, feminine form of the book,"[3] the hymen becomes incorporated with what cannot be known; accordingly, characters such as Arthur manifest such unclassifiable responses to its simultaneous presence and non-presence. The hymen presents a challenge to masculinity, but demands protection at the same time. Hence, male knights face an apparently irreconcilable dilemma. As Derrida notes: "The hymen 'takes place' in the 'inter-', in the spacing between desire and fulfillment, between perpetration and its recollection."[4] Arthur's relationship with Gloriana seems perpetually situated in just this space; he forever desires her, but the quest which would enable him to return to Faery Court and potential fulfillment is never complete. Similarly, he inhabits the area bound by real or imagined penetration and by his inability to recreate the moment except through recollecting it for the knights he meets on his journey. There can be no present moment for the hymen or for Arthur and his Queen; therefore, the frustration engendered for the reader by her entrapment in the margins of the text ineluctably replicates the role of woman within the epic. As *Dissemination* suggests:

> The interim of the hymen differs (defers) from the present, or from a present that is past, future, or eternal . . . [it] belongs neither to reality nor to the imaginary.[5]

Applying Derrida's analysis of the hymen is less anachronistic than it may seem, since it considers concepts of virginity which confused writers long before *The Faerie Queene* was being composed, and because it offers a useful vocabulary for discussing the prevalent distantiation in the text of issues concerning licit adult female sexuality. Derrida confronts a recurrent theoretical inability to reconcile ideas of virtue with active sexual involvement, consonant with that which pervades Spenser's text. In *The Faerie Queene*, the disparity between the governing presumptions of knightly conduct and the demands of physical desire remains unarticulated, though dominant. Within the epic, the physical expression of sexual attraction is repeatedly withheld from virtuous couples, suggesting an insuperable discomfort with the possible spiritual and psychic ramifications of sex with honorable women.

A similar question, concerning the status of sexual intercourse in Eden, stymied the Church Fathers for centuries. Numerous disputes raged over the moment of Adam and Eve's first sexual engagement.[6] Some thinkers, such as Jerome, contend that sexuality belongs solely to postlapsarian humanity, arguing that such physicality is one mark of the Fall. Others, such as Augustine, however, assert that the first couple had physical intimacy in Eden also, but that it took a different form than the one it acquired after the original sin was committed. According to this theory, had Adam and Eve remained in Paradise, Eve would have been able to have had sex, conceived, and given birth without the rupture of her hymen. In Eden, therefore, virgin births would have been the norm and the apparent contradiction which demands that chastity be both innocent and fecund would merely represent the physical reality of female physiology.

There is a possibility, therefore, that the confusing encounter between Arthur and the Faerie Queene enacts a return to this prelapsarian sexuality. Since the pair presumably represent the highest fulfillment of virtue possible for humanity, their access to a form of sexuality only available to those of the purest chastity could be a further manifestation of their places at the zenith of human perfectibility. Their union would thus still always be deferred because such perfection must be impeded on earth, but the suggestion that it is attainable could stand as an additional whisper, however soft and indistinct, of the ecstasy to be achieved if Gloriana and the Prince were ever actually joined. Since such transcendent sex cannot even be imagined by the "unworthy," nor recaptured once past, Arthur can only try to refashion it fleetingly through further dreams or retellings of his tale. At the same time, since it remains forever unclear whether the encounter ever took place, neither Arthur, his auditors, nor the reader are forced to contend with those aspects of sexuality which disturbed the church patriarchy. Erotic thoughts may require censure, but they are not as compromising for virtuous knights as erotic actions could be.

Hélène Cixous' discussions of masculine dreams and the so-called "enigma of woman" suggest a complementary reading of this episode. The incident, whether real or imagined, could be transformed into a dream in order to keep Gloriana less threatening for Arthur, while narrating the memory of her empowers him. In Cixous' terms:

> Man's dream: I love her—absent, hence desirable. . . Because she isn't there when she is. . . Where is she, where is woman in all the scenes he stages within the literary enclosure?. . . she is in the shadow. In the shadow he throws on her; the shadow she is.[7]

Gloriana's image on the shield and the pressed grass where she only might have rested restrict her representation to images and shadows. Knights work hard to preserve virtuous women in *The Faerie Queene* as objects for quests and inhabitants of domestic spheres of learning rather than daily companions; therefore, encapsulating Gloriana in a dream or in an emblem ensures that love will remain, as Cixous calls it, "a threshold business"[8] which will not interfere with male domains or adventures. In addition, Arthur can openly talk about his "dream" without compromising his own or Gloriana's integrity or reputation. Any questions concerning Gloriana's virtue remain unanswerable. Gloriana, with other virtuous women, thereby occupies the place of the trace; forever deferred and yet endlessly sought, even though she is neither truly obtainable nor even actually sought directly.

Even if the reader's hesitations undermining the Prince's encounter with the Faerie Queene can potentially be defused from this perspective, however, the reader must still confront the knots created by Arthur's seemingly lecherous pursuit of the beleaguered Florimell and his failure to participate as an exemplum of virtue in the Legend of Chastity. It seems unlikely that the episode's placement in Book III is accidental, since it so clearly dramatizes a significant attack against chastity— by the foster without question, even if some dispute is possible concerning the knights' intentions.

Unfortunately, however, Arthur's pursuit of the regrettably magnetic beauty, which pointedly constitutes his only activity in Book III, can be readily perceived as one repercussion emanating from the suppression of his erotic feelings for Gloriana. In a dramatic departure from the consistent pattern established in the other books, Arthur does not arrive to rescue the titular knight in the eighth canto of the Legend of Chastity. Instead, he is already present when the tale begins and he devotes all of his energy to this fervent chase after the woman whose haste "scarse them leasure gaue, her passing to behold" (III.i.15.9). Although the narrative occasionally attempts to deflect accusations of unseemly Princely ardor, claiming, for instance, that Arthur's praiseworthy motive is "To reskew her from shamefull villany" (III.i.18.5), such assertions lose credence when Timias is left alone to pursue the source of Florimell's distress, while Arthur and Guyon "Her selfe pursewd, in hope to win thereby / Most goodly meede" (III.i.18.7-8). The emphasis throughout this interlude remains with male "leasure" and desire, and Florimell's fate is left fixed within its usual perilous space. Thus, although the definition of "meede" as "reward" may dominate, the secondary sense, that of "unlawful gain" (OED) cannot be completely suppressed and the "reward" need not be virtuous.

As Arthur approaches Florimell, the erotic nature of his quest comes into sharper focus—"Then gan he freshly pricke his fomy steed" (III. iv: 48. 2)—and she renews her efforts to escape, "With no lesse haste, and eke with no lesse dreed, / That fearefull Ladie fled from him" (III. iv: 50. 1-2). A.C. Hamilton's gloss on the passage suggests that her continued flight emanates from "the apprehension of women in love,"[9] but the pitch of Arthur's sexual frenzy and his method of reassuring her of his honorable intent rightly fail to calm this perpetual prey. While Florimell's demonstrated powers of discernment do not always enable her to distinguish between worthy and suspect offers of assistance or sanctuary, here her refusal to tarry seems warranted, despite the narrator's assertions to the contrary.

Not only does his lustful chase introduce ample cause for caution, but the Prince's "Many meeke wordes" (III. iv: 48. 9) do little to assuage the atmosphere of erotic intent when the reader recalls the meaningful collaboration between words and sexual intimacy displayed in my opening epigraphs. Since the potential rescuer has already established his strong belief in a sensual association between language and sex, his unavoidable panting here—from his sustained haste, if not completely from sexual arousal—merely increases the suspicion he incurs when "Aloud to her he oftentimes did call" (III. iv: 48. 6). With the foster long gone, Florimell has no immediate need of Arthur's aid, and she receives ample warning to fear the kind of assistance he might be preparing to offer. Proteus' parallel "speeches milde" (III. viii: 34. 1) later prove to be the prelude to an attempted "bold assault" (III. viii: 36.1), thereby justifying the tremulous maiden's caution in this episode.

When Florimell's phenomenal riding ability and the onset of night allow her finally to lose her pursuer, the strikingly lustful origin of the Prince's chase becomes even more apparent. As soon as he realizes that he will not be able to overcome her, he falls to the ground, clearly hoping to induce a dream such as the one he experienced earlier in the poem: "Downe himselfe he layd / Vpon the grassie ground, to sleepe a throw" (III. iv: 53. 7-8). The scene contrasts harshly with the previous situation, however. Here, instead of the rapturous words and embraces of his faerie lover, "The cold earth was his couch, the hard steele his pillow"

(III. iv: 53. 9). His overwhelming interest in his own erotic loss, rather than Florimell's safety, becomes evident as he tosses and turns, bemoaning his hard fate. It seems unlikely that he would be so distraught if he had merely desired a pleasant chat or wanted primarily to comfort the frightened lady. The substance of his anguished thoughts indicate how completely, though unsuccessfully, he had hoped to conflate the two women he desired:

> Oft did he wish, that Lady faire mote bee
> His Faery Queene, for whom he did complain
> Or that his Faery Queene were such, as shee.
>
> [III.iv.54.6-8]

Subsequently, the vehemence of the aubade which replaces his slumber and his "heauvie looke and lumpish pace" the next morning, reinforce our awareness of Arthur's strongly disappointed sexual desire for the lady.

The Prince's lament here renews the reader's hesitation at the mode of male sexual behavior apparently being sanctioned. Although Florimell safely eludes her eager pursuer, she cannot escape her status as the object of Arthur's deflected lust for the Faerie Queene's amorous embraces. The Prince is drawn to Florimell in an attempt to relocate the locus of his desire in order to preserve Gloriana's position as the unsullied site of future, licit, consummation. His vast, residual sexual energy needs to be diverted, therefore (seven years of celibacy is apparently a bleak prospect for a young knight, no matter how august he might be), and Florimell's renowned beauty becomes the object of his quest to release his excess libido.

Arthur's subsequent absence during Britomart's adventure supports the suggestion that chastity is, as it is often considered, primarily a female virtue. The Redcrosse Knight's ability to recover from sexual lapses in Book I is not apparently available to Britomart, whose chastity needs to remain unscathed and unquestioned, since it is irredeemable if lost. Thus, although Arthur and the titular knights throughout the rest of the epic display moments of sexual weakness, Britomart never wavers from her quest for Artegall, except, significantly, when she suspects him of misdealings with another woman.

The men, however, weaken regularly, and as we have seen, the Prince is no exception. Although Artegall is able to dissuade Arthur from continuing to let Duessa soften his princely "tender hart" (V. ix: 46. 1)—"All which when as the Prince had heard and seene, / His former fancies ruth he gan repent" (V. ix: 49. 1-2)—Guyon fails to perform a similar restraining function when he and the Prince take off in "envy and gealousy" after the hapless Florimell. The duo's participation in the endless pursuit of the "chased, yet chaste" woman quickly leads them into the hidden folds of the text, while also focusing the reader's attention on elements of female characterization in *The Faerie Queene* which might help elucidate the conundrum manifest through their presentation, namely, that women can be held up as icons to be protected, yet can concurrently be placed in danger by the same knights.

Women are rarely truly "present" in the epic. Perpetually iconic, demonic, in disguise, or in flight, women remain at the distance which Derrida claims is essential, securing their identification as the *pharmakon*, that is, something simultaneously beneficial and poisonous:

> Distance is the very element of [a woman's] power. Yet one must beware to keep one's own distance from her beguiling song of enchantment. A distance from distance must be maintained. Not only for protection (the most obvious advantage) against the spell of her fascination, but also as a way of succumbing to it, that distance (which is lacking) *is necessary*. . . . Perhaps woman—a non-identity, a non-figure, a simulacrum—is distance's very chasm.[10]

Woman's continual deferral in *The Faerie Queene* anticipates and enacts this warning, but never directly confronts its sentiment. Despite this silence in the epic, however, the theories of woman which Derrida articulates correllate with the fear of women manifest throughout the poem. Normally, the knights have extended close contact with women only when they are in the dangerous company of an illusory beauty such as Duessa or the

False Florimell or when they visit an honored woman like Mercilla, whose pronounced psychological distancing and iconic status eradicate the threat emanating from ordinary persons of her gender. Chaste, virtuous women who are worthy and capable of the knight's affections are either fleeing or fleeting, with Britomart as a notable exception, whose disguise, however, reduces her erotic danger for the knights. Nonetheless, when her thoughts turn from questing to love, even Britomart is sent away, enabling Artegall to continue with his mission unimpeded by female distractions.

Women confuse the knights in *The Faerie Queene* because they elicit such conflicting responses. Arthur, for instance, is in the precarious position of being strongly tempted by the crimes of concupiscence he is bound by his knighthood to prevent; in his own iconic position, he cannot openly succumb to his lust. At the same time, however, there is no appropriate model available for "lawful lust." Marriage could lead to commitments antithetical to knightly responsibilities, but premarital engagements would jeopardize the worthiness of the woman contracted. Thus, worthy consummations are forever postponed and virtuous ladies who arouse erotic interest must disappear or enter the category dominated by wanton women. In addition, as Derrida notes, the sexual act involved in ending a woman's virginity can engender a contradictory and complex set of emotions which a knight could have considerable trouble reconciling with the ordinary tenets of his quest:

> It is the hymen that desire dreams of piercing, of bursting, in an act of violence that is (at the same time or somewhere between) love and murder. . . With all the undecidability of its meaning, the hymen only takes place when it doesn't take place, when nothing *really* happens, when there is an all-consuming consummation without violence. . . . There is only the memory of a crime that has never been committed.[11]

Arthur's pursuits and possibly his consummations remain in the margins, therefore, in order to shield him, though not excuse him, from accusations of untoward concupiscence as he struggles to contend with his erotic responses. Women's perpetual undecidability undermines knightly attempts to differentiate between good and evil women and obscures efforts to discern the proper way to deal with both groups. Hence, all women fall within the definition Catherine Clément offers for a sorceress: "She is innocent, mad, full of badly remembered memories, guilty of unknown wrongs; she is the seductress, the heiress of all generic Eves."[12] Women who thus refuse to remain clearly demonic or iconic introduce such a jumble of emotions that they cannot be contended with openly. On such occasions, therefore, they glide into the irretrievable folds of the text, where their fates and Arthur's activities with them remain just outside the sight of the reader.

NOTES

1. Edmund Spenser, *The Faerie Queene*, ed. A. C. Hamilton (London: Longman, 1977), p. 121. All references to Hamilton and all quotations from *The Faerie Queene* come from this edition.
2. *Dissemination*, trans. Barbara Johnson (Chicago: University of Chicago Press, 1981), pp. 258-59.
3. p. 259.
4. p. 212.
5. p. 231.
6. For an account of this controversy, see John Bugge, *Virginitas: An Essay in the History of a Medieval Ideal* (The Hague: Martinus Nijhoff, 1975), esp. pp. 20-26.
7. Hélène Cixous and Catherine Clément, *The Newly Born Woman*, trans. Betsy Wing (Minneapolis: University of Minnesota Press, 1986), p. 67.
8. p. 67.
9. Hamilton, p. 344.
10. *Spurs: Nietzsche's Styles*, trans. Barbara Harlow (Chicago: University of Chicago Press, 1979), p. 49.
11. *Dissemination*, pp. 213, 214.
12. *The Newly Born Woman*, p. 6.

The Pastness of Arthur in the Victorian Era

Tennyson and the Passing of Arthur

John D. Rosenberg

Every great poem springs from some single generative moment that gives rise to all the rest. The generative moment of *Idylls of the King* comes at the very end of the poem as we now read it, although the lines are among the first that Tennyson drafted in his elegy to the fallen Arthur. We all recall the scene—if not from Tennyson, then from Malory—as the three Queens receive the wounded king into the barge and Bedivere, bereft of his lord, cries aloud,

"Ah! my Lord Arthur, whither shall I go?
Where shall I hide my forehead and my eyes?
For now I see the true old times are dead, . . .
Such times have been not since the light that led
The holy Elders with the gift of myrrh.
But now the whole Round Table is dissolved
Which was an image of the mighty world,
And I, the last, go forth companionless,
And the days darken round me, and the years,
Among new men, strange faces, other minds."

["The Passing of Arthur," 396-406]

I sometimes believe that the great world of Arthurian myth came into being solely to memorialize this primal scene of loss, the loss of a once-perfect fellowship in a once-perfect world. Malory tells us that Merlin "made the *Round Table* in token of the roundness of the world." [1] Circles are emblems of inclusive perfection, microcosms that, in a fallen world, are made in order to be broken. In the springtime of Arthur's realm, Tennyson's Vivien, seductress of Merlin and the *femme fatale* of the *Idylls*, prophesies that her ancient sun-worship

> . . . will rise again,
> And beat the cross to earth, and break the King
> And all his Table.
>
> ["Balin and Balan," 451-53]

Much later, in the bleak winterscape of Arthur's passing, her prophecy is fulfilled. Bedivere carries the King's shattered body to the water's edge, beside a ruined chapel topped with a broken cross ("The Passing of Arthur," 174-77). In this landscape of apocalyptic desolation—

> A land of old upheaven from the abyss
> By fire, to sink into the abyss again—
>
> ["The Passing of Arthur," 82-83]

the three Queens arrive for Arthur's uncertain embarkation to Avalon. There, the "flower of kings" may perhaps find a land of eternal spring, a heaven-haven

> Where falls not hail, or rain, or any snow,
> Nor ever wind blows loudly.
>
> ["The Passing of Arthur," 428-29]

There, healed of his grievous wound, Arthur may perhaps re-embark for his second coming to Camelot.

"FLOS REGUM ARTHURUS": Tennyson took the epigraph for the *Idylls* from Joseph of Exeter. But if Arthur is the very Flower and Epitome of Kings, the bright epithet conceals a dark underside, for flowers, like all flesh, wither and die. From the first line of his Coming to the last line of his Passing, it remains a great open question whether Tennyson's Flower of Kings is an annual or a perennial.

More equivocal even than the question of Arthur's return is the question of whether he ever really walked among us in the first place. I raise here more than the vexed issue of Arthur's historicity, about which Tennyson read everything in print. I mean to suggest that the *idea* of Arthur as Tennyson envisioned him carries with it a strong supposition of non-being, of a ghostly presence made all the more vivid by virtue of its very absence. For the grand peculiarity of Tennyson's Arthur is that the shadow he casts is more real than his substance. In so penumbrating his hero, Tennyson remained true to that most memorable of epitaphs, carved on Arthur's purported tomb at Glastonbury: HIC JACET ARTHURUS, REX QUONDAM, REXQUE FUTURUS—*The Once and Future King*. The phrase haunts us less for what it says than for what it leaves out, its total elision of an Arthurian present. The quick iambic trimeter—the once and future King—propels us from Arthur's remote past directly to his return in an unspecified future; it is tight-lipped about Arthur here and now.

So, too, is Tennyson. At once the central and most elusive figure in the *Idylls*, Arthur exists in time and transcends time; he exists in time because we who imagine him live, move, and have our being in time; and he transcends time by virtue of inhabiting a perpetual past and an eternally promised future. Malory's Arthur is born after the normal nine-month term at an unspecified season. Tennyson's King, both a Christ figure and a solar deity, is born "all before his time" ("The Coming of Arthur," 210)— *prematurely*—on the night of the New Year, in the season of Epiphany. His Coming is a kind of Incarnation; his Passing evokes the Passion: a shadow in a field of skulls, the mortally wounded Arthur exclaims,

> "My God, thou hast forgotten me in my death:
> Nay—God my Christ—I pass but shall not die."
> ["The Passing of Arthur," 27-28]

Malory's Arthur is killed in early summer, eight weeks and a day after Easter Sunday. Tennyson's Arthur passes as he comes, in mid-winter, when "the great light of heaven / Burned at his lowest in the rolling year" ("The Passing of Arthur," 90-91).

His birth, like his death, is shrouded in mystery. That mystery is deepened, not dispelled, by the genealogical riddling of Merlin: "From the great deep to the great deep he goes" ("The

Coming of Arthur," 410). According to one account in "The Coming," Arthur's purported parents are the dark-haired, dark-eyed Uther and Ygerne; but Arthur, as befits a sun-king and the Son of God, "is fair / Beyond the race of Britons and men" ("The Coming of Arthur," 329-30). Of uncertain pedigree, he is also without progeny. Arthur, that is, exists outside genealogy; outside history; perhaps also outside humanity—"beyond the race . . . of men." [2]

Tennyson more than once hints that Arthur is illusory, conjured into being by magicians like himself, just as Merlin, Arthur's architect and wizard, conjures Camelot into being. We first see Camelot through the dazzled eyes of Gareth, the spires of the dim rich city appearing and disappearing in the shifting mists. Gareth rides through city-gates that depict

New things and old co-twisted, as if Time
Were nothing, so inveterately, that men
Were giddy gazing there . . . .
["Gareth and Lynette," 222-24]

A great peal of music stops Gareth dead in his tracks, and Merlin's mystifications compound his confusion:

"For an ye heard a music [says Merlin], like enow
They are building still, seeing the city is built
To music, therefore never built at all,
And therefore built forever."
["Gareth and Lynette," 271-74]

Tennyson here draws on the myth, old as cities themselves, of the city as a sacred center, an *axis mundi* where heaven and hell intersect. Camelot is supernatural in origin, supertemporal in duration. Like Troy, which rose to the music of Apollo's lyre, Camelot is "built to music." But since, as St. Paul warns, we can have "no continuing city" here on earth (Hebrews 13:14), Camelot is never finally built. Yet the ideal that animates it predates its founding and will survive its fall, and hence the city is "built forever." Camelot embodies in stone the same paradox that Arthur embodies in flesh. A Byzantium of the artist-sage's imagination, Camelot, like its king, triumphs over time by never having entered time; its fall is as purely illusory as its founding. Arthur is the point of focus at which the idealisms of all other characters in the *Idylls* converge; as their belief in Arthur's authority and reality breaks down, the king and his fair city vanish into the mists from which they first emerged. Bedivere, the last believer, companionless on the desolate verge of the world, watches Arthur dwindle to a mere speck on an empty horizon, his death-pale, death-cold king departing for a paradise that can never be, in the faint hope of returning to a kingdom that never was.

Bedivere's lament, like much else in Tennyson's "The Passing of Arthur," finds its source in the final book of Malory's *Morte Darthur*. But Bedivere's last three lines, spoken as he goes forth companionless, have no source in Malory; nor could they have, for they arise from direct personal experience—the poet's own—of overwhelming loss at the death of Arthur. Not the death of the mythical king, but of Arthur the flesh-and-blood friend of Alfred Tennyson—Arthur Henry Hallam, to whom Tennyson dedicated his *other* great Arthur poem: *In Memoriam: A.H.H.*

Arthur Hallam's death was the single most important event in Alfred Tennyson's life. In Section VII of *In Memoriam*—

> Dark house, by which once more I stand
> Here in the long unlovely street,
> Doors, where my heart was used to beat,
> So quickly, waiting for a hand,
>
> A hand that can be clasp'd no more—

Tennyson pictures himself as a ghost, guiltily haunting Hallam's empty, tomb-like house, until the blank day breaks on the bald London street. At the end of *Idylls of the King*, Tennyson again stands alone and Arthurless, this time on the desolate verge of the world, the sole survivor of the last dim weird battle of the West, an alien compelled to

> "... go forth companionless,
> And the days darken round me, and the years,
> Among new men, strange faces, other minds."

Tennyson's profoundly personal quest for reunion with Hallam in *In Memoriam* becomes, in *Idylls of the King*, a profoundly impersonal despair for the passing not only of a hero, but of civilization itself.

In a moment, a word about why Arthurian myth exerted so powerful a hold on Tennyson's imagination and on Victorian culture at large, but I still can't quite let go of Bedivere. Holding on, after all, is what Arthur's story is all about. Perhaps we are all Bediveres in our need to preserve some relic of an idealized past, be it the sour shards of our infant blanket or the bejeweled hilt of Excalibur. The special pathos of Bedivere's Peter-like betrayal of his lord's command—to return the sword to the great deep—is that Arthur mistakes heroic loyalty to his memory for vulgar theft. The literal-minded Bedivere cannot see that it is the words of poets, not the hilts of swords, that memorialize the past. To Bedivere is left the burden of perpetuating the King's story after all living witness to his presence is gone. In the "white winter" of his old age, Bedivere narrates "The Passing of Arthur," serving as both actor and chronicler in the idyll in which he figures. As the poem draws to a close, its various narrators themselves seem to age, like the poet himself, who began the *Idylls* in his early twenties and made the last of his myriad additions and revisions fifty-eight years later, within months of his death. In the later idylls, the legend of Arthur becomes self-perpetuating and cannot be confined to any single teller, be it Bedivere or that nameless Bard—"he that tells the Tale," Tennyson calls him—who is at times Malory, at times Tennyson himself, at times the great chain of Arthurian chroniclers and poets who came before him.

Self-reflexive in virtually every line, the *Idylls* not only recounts Arthur's story but also recreates the process by which myths are made. We see the process at work in scenes that recall the former splendor of the Round Table even as it goes up in flames. Thus Arthur, alone with the repentant Guinevere at

Almesbury Convent, recalls the glorious world he believes her sin has wrecked:

> "... that fair Order of my Table Round,
> A glorious company, the flower of men,
> To serve as model for the mighty world,
> And be the fair beginning of a time."
>
> ["Guinevere," 460-63]

In the idyll that immediately follows "Guinevere"—"The Passing of Arthur"—Bedivere, as if he had overheard Arthur at Almesbury, incorporates Arthur's description of the Round Table into his own lament. You recall the words—the ones I can't let go—

> "But now the whole Round Table is dissolved
> Which was an image of the mighty world,
> And I, the last, go forth companionless ..."

Arthur's very words—the Round Table as image of the mighty world—have now become canonical, a part of his own story, transmitted whole, like verbal relics, from character to character and place to place. Bedivere suffers a kind of anxiety of posterity, for if he discards Excalibur,

> "What record, or what relic of my lord
> Should be to aftertime, but empty breath
> And rumours of a doubt?"
>
> ["The Passing of Arthur," 266-68]

The dying Arthur is himself preoccupied in arranging, like the folds of a shroud, his own afterhistory. He commands Bedivere to fling Excalibur into the mere; then shapes through prophecy the legend of which he is himself the subject:

> "And, wheresoever I am sung or told
> In aftertime, this also shall be known."
>
> ["The Passing of Arthur," 202-03]

Characters within the larger fiction of the *Idylls* generate lesser fictions within it—mirrors within mirrors that reflect the whole. The result is that as the realm sinks ever deeper into the abyss, it reemerges in retrospective glory. Tennyson's most daring use of retrospect for this purpose occurs in "Guinevere," the idyll least indebted to any source. Before Arthur arrives at the Convent, cruelly to denounce, then to forgive, Guinevere, a naive young novice keeps vigil with the contrite Queen. Unaware of Guinevere's identity, the novice prattles about magical signs and wonders that, years ago, accompanied the founding of the Round Table "before the coming of the sinful Queen" ("Guinevere," 268). The novice's father, now dead, had served as one of Arthur's first knights, and her account of his recollections, although dating back only one generation, takes on the aura of a garbled legend barely recoverable from the past. The mystery of the King's birth, invested with the highest powers of Tennyson's imagination in "The Coming of Arthur," is here lowered in key to a folktale. Divinity lapses into popular superstition; and for an instant the city built to music threatens to become a Victorian Disneyland, with fairy palaces and magical spigots gushing wine. The novice's fantastical, vulgarized account of the wonders of Arthur's coming serves, by contrast, to authenticate the "original" wonders, themselves of course no less fictional than the novice's. So too her morally simplistic indictment of the "sinful Queen" and of Lancelot enlarges our sympathy for the adulterous lovers, who are "marred . . . and marked" ("Lancelot and Elaine," 246) by their sin but, uncannily, grow in grace because of it. The ruins of Camelot recall the city arising in its initial splendor, just as Arthur's passing contains the possibility of his return. The reciprocal movements of rise and fall are held in perfect poise by the seasonal cycle to which all twelve idylls are linked: the founding of the Round Table in earliest spring, its flourishing to the point of rankness in the long summer idylls, its falling into the sere and yellow leaf in the autumnal "Last Tournament," its ruin in the chill mid-winter of "The Passing," with a distant hope of renewal to come. Incorporating this cycle into its narrative structure, *Idylls of the King* is itself a kind of literary second coming of Arthur, a resurrection in Victorian England of the long sequence of Arthuriads extending back centuries before Malory and forward through Spenser, Dryden, Scott, and Tennyson. The poem takes on the quality of a self-fulfilling prophecy and validates itself, like Scripture, by foretelling in one idyll what it fulfills in the next, until at the end the nameless narrator foretells the survival of his own poem, a prophecy which our gathered presence here today triumphantly confirms.

Tennyson drafted his "Morte d'Arthur" late in 1833, under the first terrible shock of Arthur Hallam's death, at age twenty-two, of a cerebral hemorrhage. They had met four years earlier, as undergraduates at Trinity College, Cambridge, and at the time of his death Hallam was engaged to Tennyson's sister Emily. Dead too young to have shaped a life in public, the gifted Hallam lived on posthumously as a prince of friends, a king of intellects, among his remarkable circle of acquaintance. The draft of "Morte d'Arthur," which Tennyson later incorporated verbatim into the completed *Idylls* as "The Passing of Arthur," appears in the same notebook that contains the earliest sections of *In Memoriam*. This first-composed but last-in-sequence of the *Idylls* is sandwiched between Section XXX of *In Memoriam*, which commemorates the Tennyson family's first desolate Christmas at Somersby without Hallam, and Section XXXI, which depicts Lazarus rising from the dead. The physical placement of the "Morte" graphically expresses the poet's longing. [3] At the end of his life, in the autobiographical "Merlin and the Gleam," Tennyson wrote:

Clouds and darkness
Closed upon Camelot;
Arthur had vanish'd
I knew not whither,
The king who loved me,
And cannot die . . . .
[stanza VII]

The "king who loved me" is the friend who died on the fifteenth of September, 1833, and whose passing left the young Tennyson stranded "among new men, strange faces, other minds."

Poets, I believe, are impelled to write the same poem over and over again, in myriad different guises, just as Dante Gabriel Rossetti painted the same face again and again. At first glance, *In Memoriam* and *Idylls of the King* could not appear more unlike: the one is a deeply personal elegy, about the death of an actual friend, set in the contemporary moment and concerned with contemporary issues, like the conflict of science and faith; the other is a consciously archaic recreation of mythical figures from a world that never was. But at bottom elegy and idyll are, if not the same poem, variations on the same theme—Tennyson's single overriding theme—the theme of loss; or, as he phrased it to himself in early boyhood, the "Passion of the Past." [4] It is a singularity of Tennyson's nature that absence was more vivid to his senses than presence: "It is the distance that charms me in the landscape," he told a friend, "the picture and the past, and not the immediate to-day in which I move." [5] If poets are born, not made, then Tennyson was a born Arthurian. His eldest son, Hallam Tennyson, namesake of Arthur Hallam, writes in the *Memoir* of his father, "What he called 'The greatest of all poetical subjects' perpetually haunted him." [6] Tennyson himself tells us that "the vision of Arthur as I have drawn him . . . had come upon me when, little more than a boy, I first lighted upon Malory."[7] Malory's *Morte Darthur* assuredly "influenced" the *Idylls*, just as Arthur Hallam's sudden death assuredly "inspired" Tennyson to write *In Memoriam*. But causality in the psyche is quite unlike causality in external nature. What ultimately determines what we do and become are those external accidents that are in accord with our inner nature. Malory matters less than the antecedent disposition that drew Tennyson so early and so powerfully to the myth of Arthur; Hallam matters less than the antecedent disposition that caused Tennyson to mourn so obsessively and so long for his absent friend, until poetry sprouted from his grave.

In Memoriam begins with a funeral and ends with a marriage-feast; the *Idylls* opens with a marriage—Arthur's to Guinevere—and ends with a funeral. Elegy and idyll are bound by a deep inner complementarity. Hallam Tennyson was the first to point out the curious sandwiching of the "Morte d'Arthur" between two of the earliest sections of the elegy to Arthur

Hallam. Mourning, at which Tennyson was something of a professional, is the ritual by which we learn both to hold on and let go, to clasp the dead and to live without them. *In Memoriam* and *Idylls of the King,* each written over a period of decades, and then revised for decades more after their publication, are the most exquisitely protracted holdings-on and lettings-go in our literature. Late in *In Memoriam* Tennyson compresses a lifelong trauma into a phrase:

> . . . and my regret
> Becomes an April violet,
> And buds and blossoms like the rest.
> [Section 115]

Tennyson learned to fashion his greatest poetry out of the corpse of his friend, a process that quickened his guilt and preserved his sanity. Within months of Hallam's death in Vienna—the bad tidings reached Tennyson early in October, 1833—he had begun *In Memoriam;* drafted "Le Morte d'Arthur"; composed the originating lyric of *Maud*—

> Oh! that 'twere possible,
> After long grief and pain,
> To find the arms of my true-love
> Round me once again!—[8]

written "Break, Break, Break"; and drafted his two greatest dramatic monologues, "Ulysses" and "Tithonus," all centering on the experience of loss.

In the same year that Tennyson wrote his "Morte d'Arthur," Coleridge opined, "As to Arthur, you could not by any means make a poem national to Englishmen. What have *we* to do with him?"[9] With a simplicity surprising in this subtlest of English critics, Coleridge took the common position—as common in 1833 as it is today—that Arthurian literature is escapist, irrelevant to the real concerns of the modern world. To this day the prejudice persists that Tennyson's doom-laden prophecy of the fall of the West is a Victorian-Gothic fairytale. The majority of Tennyson's contemporaries believed that the modern poet's proper business is to portray modern life, a position whose logic would have disbarred Shakespeare from dramatizing the plight of King Arthur's ancient British neighbor and colleague, King Lear, or prevented Homer from depicting a war "far on the plains of windy Troy" that had ended centuries before Homer was born. Tennyson was urged to write an epic not about knights in armor but Work or Sanitation. He had to create the audience by which his poem came to be appreciated. And that is precisely what he did in the long intervals between drafting the "Morte" in 1833-34, prefacing it with the embarrassingly apologetic frame-poem of 1842, and waiting another seventeen years before publishing the 1859 *Idylls of the King*.

Of course, the audience was latently present—Arthurians have always been among us—but they took awhile to come out of the Victorian-Gothic closet. Arthur underwent a revival in the nineteenth century, particularly during the reign of Victoria, because England had become so quickly and radically *un*-Arthurian. St. Augustine wrote *The City of God* as the barbarians were storming the gates of the earthly city; so, too, Camelot rose again as the railroads tore out the heart of ancient cities, as the streets of Coketown shook with machines and the misery of exploited labor, the skies darkened with factory smoke, rivers ran foul with industrial wastes, and God most alarmingly disappeared from England's once green and pleasant land. The medieval revival, of which Arthurianism was a part, was not so much an attempt to escape the hard new world of industrial capitalism as a radical attempt to reform it. Tennyson's *Idylls*, Pugin's advocacy of Gothic architecture in *Contrasts*, Carlyle's *Past and Present*, Ruskin's "Nature of Gothic"—all recreate the medieval past in order to remake the English present. The Victorian medievalizers are not idle dreamers but social critics, zealots, prophets. Reading Malory's *Morte Darthur* or the *Mabinogion* helps us understand Tennyson's *Idylls*, but so too does Lyell's *Principles of Geology* or Carlyle's *On Heroes*.

Perhaps the surest road to Tennyson's Camelot is via another great Victorian epic that appeared in the bookshops alongside the *Idylls* in 1859, Darwin's *Origin of Species*. Evolution is an idea with two faces. One is smiling and beckons us onward and upward to ever-higher forms; the other face is a death's head, bones encased in stone, a struggle ending in extinction. Tennyson's two Arthur poems, in addition to their deeply personal content, are also profound meditations on the leading idea of his century: evolution. In *In Memoriam*, Hallam figures as "the herald of a higher race," a "noble type" of the perfected humanity into which we will ultimately evolve (Section CXVIII, 14; Epilogue, 138). In *Idylls of the King*, evolution undergoes a catastrophic reversal; mankind, in Arthur's anguished words, "reel[s] back into the beast" ("The Last Tournament," 125). Evolution has been tinged by Apocalypse. That three of the more notable long poems of the later nineteenth century—*The Wreck of the Deutschland*, *The City of Dreadful Night*, and *Idylls of the King*—a r e apocalyptic in design and imagery is no more coincidental than that Yeats, who came to maturity at this time, is the great modern poet of Apocalypse. The *fin de siècle* became a type of the *fin du monde*. "The blood-dimmed tide is loosed" might serve as epigraph for *Idylls of the King*, and Christ the Rough Beast slouching towards Bethlehem is the perfect heraldic emblem for Arthur's Last Battle, which Tennyson himself eerily glossed as "a presentment of human death,"—of human *extinction*. [10] The Battle is fought in a landscape literally as old as the hills but as imminent as nuclear winter:

A land of old upheaven from the abyss
By fire, to sink into the abyss again;
Where fragments of forgotten peoples dwelt,
And the long mountains ended in a coast
Of ever-shifting sand, and far away
The phantom circle of a moaning sea

. . . .
Nor ever yet had Arthur fought a fight
Like this last, dim, weird battle of the west.
A deathwhite mist slept over sand and sea:
Whereof the chill, to him who breathed it, drew
Down with his blood, till all his heart was cold
With formless fear . . . .

[size=0.9]["The Passing of Arthur," 82-98][/size]

The Apocalypse is an ancient idea; evolution, when Tennyson wrote, a new one. The marriage of the two he entitled *Idylls of the King*.

NOTES

1.   See *La Mort d'Arthur*, ed. R. Wilks (London, 1816), 3 vols., III, chap. 50, and David Staines, *Tennyson's Camelot: The "Idylls of the King" and Its Medieval Sources* (Ontario: Wilfred Laurier University Press, 1982), p. 173. Staines assumes that Tennyson followed the Wilks edition, and not that of Walker and Edwards (2 vols., 1816) when writing the draft of the "Morte d'Arthur."

2   See Elliot L. Gilbert, "The Female King: Tennyson's Arthurian Apocalypse," *PMLA* 98 (1983), 868.

3.   See Hallam Tennyson, *Alfred Lord Tennyson: A Memoir*, 2 vols. (London, 1897), I, 109, and *The Poems of Tennyson*, Christopher Ricks, ed. (London: Longman, 1969), pp. 889, 891. All quotations from Tennyson's poetry have been taken from this edition.

4   See "The Ancient Sage," 219.

5.   Quoted by Sir James Knowles, "Aspects of Tennyson," *Nineteenth Century* 33 (1893), 170.

6.   *Memoir*, II, 125.

7.   *Memoir*, II, 128.

8   See Ricks, ed., pp. 598-99 and 1082.

9.   *Table Talk*, 1835, 1836; cited in Staines, p. 1.

10. *Memoir*, II, 132.

Ideological Battleground:
Tennyson, Morris, and the Pastness of the Past

Jonathan Freedman

To discuss the endurance of Arthur is obviously to perform an act of cultural preservation and redemption, to pay tribute to the power of the past and seek to make that past a palpable presence in the present. But it is also to participate in that process of remodeling the past which lies guiltily at the heart of any effort of commemoration. The history of the nineteenth-century Arthurian revival reinforces this lesson, for the revival brought with it a reinvention of the Arthurian.[1] Men and women, acting out of different motives and responding to different needs, rearranged the bundle of narratives that compose the Arthurian cycle to mirror their own images, to resemble their own desires and fears. Thus Arthurianism entered Victorian culture as many things at one and the same time: for Rossetti and the Pre-Raphaelites, it embodied an exoticism at once native and strange; for Tennyson, it provided a parable of ideal imperial order and an image of that order's decadence; for Morris, it represented a haven of intense, vital experience in a world which seemed bereft of such experience, and a reflection of the cruelty and violence intrinsic to the exercise of social authority.

What is most striking about this list is its resolute doubleness. To each of these poets or painters, the Arthurian legend itself was deeply contradictory. Thus for Tennyson, the Arthurian cycle was simultaneously a narrative of creation and dissolution, of an ideal community whose very principles of organization undermined it, of an imperialism which brought order without but fell to a greater chaos within. For Rossetti, its legends provided at once images of restraint and indulgence, passion and destruction, sexual freedom and chaste purity. And for Morris, Arthurianism conjured forth a romance-world whose authenticity, intensity, and vitality stood in vivid contrast to the industrial ugliness of Victorian England, and at the same time evoked a privileged heterocosm whose squalor and violence ironically mirrored that of his contemporary world.

A phenomenon such as this—the revival of a set of narratives to serve similar, but contradictory, ends—calls for a cultural as well as a formal analysis. One can easily imagine the lines on which such an analysis would be conducted. A structural anthropologist, for example, would want to speak of the ways that the Arthurian narratives served the classic function of myth—mediating cultural conflict, recounting and thus reconciling the antinomies of experience: the conflict between civilization and violence on the one hand and ordered and destructive sexual passion on the other. Indeed, we could hypothesize that in a good Lévi-Straussian manner the two sets of antinomies speak to, and release the tensions created by, each other. Thus the contradiction of a violence intrinsic to the civilization which conquers violence is displaced into the epic's erotic plot—it is the violence unleashed by sexual betrayal which brings down Camelot. Similarly, the fear of sexuality inherent in the Guenevere plot and enhanced by the Galahad plot upon which Victorians fixated with particular fervor is released by the demonization of the bestial heathen that the Arthurian knights battle and (intermittently) conquer.

Alternatively, one could imagine an ideological critique of this doubleness. The Arthurian revival, one could say, provided a way of criticizing the dominant presuppositions of the contemporary order—imperialism, capitalism, patriarchy—but also provided a way of managing those criticisms: it safely suffused them with the musty odor of nostalgia, the aura of loss and regret, in order to forestall their transformation into principles of belief and incitements to action.

Both of these approaches seem to me to be reasonable and cogent. But I want to take another approach to this phenomenon. I want to suggest that the battlegrounds of Arthurian romance served not only as the field upon which competing ideologies clashed by night, but also as the locus of a deeper, more intense (if equally ideological) struggle: the struggle to shape the random collocation of narratives that compose our experience of the past into an order—any order at all. The desire and the difficulty of doing so, I want to suggest, is the story these Victorian narratives tell, and the narrative we participate in as we speak about them.

As we all know, the Arthur cycle, lying as dormant as the enchanted Merlin for most of the eighteenth century, was revived in the early nineteenth century as part of the general renewal of romance that accompanied the rise of British romanticism. "Let us have the old Poets and robin Hood," cried Keats, and Arthurian romance provided both the archaic poetic diction and the native British subject-matter Keats demanded.[2] But from the first, discovering the correct formal vehicle for the Arthurian proved problematic. Trying to write verse-romance in a disenchanted age proved difficult enough for Spenser, for whom it meant a turn to conscious archaism. The difficulty could only multiply exponentially in an age for which the quest-romance had been transformed into mock-epic on the one hand and low-mimetic, realistic narrative on the other. Many of the first Arthurian efforts of the nineteenth century reflect this difficulty. The initial efforts of Victorian Arthurianism are formally awkward; the material does not fit easily into even the most flexible formal structures. Arnold's *Tristram and Iseult* (1853), for example, giddily alternates between poetic forms: at once poetic drama, dramatic monologue, and philosophical lyric, the poem seeks to pour itself into one formal vessel or another, but can never wholly do so. "If I republish that poem," Arnold wrote his friend Arthur Clough, "I shall try to make it more intelligible. . . . The whole affair is by no means throroughly successful."[3] Arnold to the contrary, however, the result is far from displeasing. The formal difficulties of the poem testify to the power of the narrative it inscribes; the incommensurability between the love of Tristram and Iseult and the social conventions or forms that fail to contain or restrain that love is reflected in the very awkwardness of Arnold's verse.

Similar problems are posed by Tennyson's first efforts in the Arthurian mode. Indeed, the elaborate framework within which he felt it necessary to enclose the "Morte D'Arthur" in his 1842 *Poems* vividly demonstrates the problems Victorian poets faced when translating these narratives into a contemporary idiom: the difficulties, that is, of finding an appropriate way to appropriate the Arthurian. The relation between frame and poem is one of carefully wrought echo. In the frame, a group of young men a few years out of college, having sent the women off to bed ("The game of forfeits done—the girls all kiss'd / Beneath the sacred bush and past away"), gather round the wassail bowl to hear one of their number, "the poet Everard Hall," read the eleventh book of his Arthuriad, which his friend Francis had saved from the fire.[4] The scene represents, in other words, a diminished parody of the Arthurian scene, here tidily enclosed within a domestic framework: it is no coincidence that two of the characters have the domestic monickers of "Holmes" and "Hall." These young modern knights, well on their way to becoming old fogeys (they listen to the parson denouncing modernity—the Higher Criticism, geology, the Oxford Movement) gather to celebrate a rite analogous to the rite of the Round Table, a rite of male bonding which here centers on the experience of art, not warfare.

What is most interesting about this faintly comic scene, however, is the hesitancy with which Hall (like Tennyson himself, who felt compelled to erect this elaborate scaffolding) adverts to the Arthurian. Hall burned his epic, he tells his audience, out of a certain anxiety about the decorousness of his attempt to rework the matter of Arthur:

"Why take the style of those heroic times?
For nature brings not back the mastodon,
Nor we those times; and why should any man
Remodel models?" [35-38]

These lines express two somewhat contradictory notions about the heroic narratives of the past, and therefore the past itself. On the one hand, there is the sense that the heroic is no longer efficacious or possible in the modern world—that it represents a previous stage of evolutionary development which, like the mastodon, has been surpassed in a world tidily enclosed and domestically ordered. But on the other hand, the attempt to import the heroic idiom into a contemporary venue is seen as transgressive; to attempt to "remodel models" is to display one's own inauthenticity vis-à-vis those models—as a poet, doubtless, but also as a human being.

And this anxiety is not groundless. The frame-poem never fully encloses the "Morte d'Arthur"; the Arthurian epic disrupts the elaborate setting in which it is placed. For at the very end of the poem, we hear the reactions of all the members of its audience; all but one are, in their way, inadequate to it. (That one, I should say here, is Everard Hall himself, who lets his poem speak for him.) The parson, fast asleep during the performance, wakes himself amidst silence to utter "Good," as if to reembed the poem in a moral framework which is also the moral equivalent of deafness. Francis, the host, "mutters, like a man ill-used, / `There now—that's nothing,'" as if speaking to a child waking from a bad dream; yet the bad dream is the poem he has just heard, and the child he is speaking to is himself (285). The narrator finds a richer revery. He falls into a troubled sleep and dreams of "King Arthur, like a modern gentleman / Of stateliest port . . . ," sailing down the river, hailed by throngs of Englishmen, to whom he promises peace on earth, good will to men (294-95). He awakes to the tune of Christmas bells in the distance.

This final reponse is obviously intended to triumph, yet it remains, to my eye, the most inadequate of all. This dream-vision of Arthur seems to accommodate the past, and all that it embodies for Tennyson—social order, peace, stable criteria of value—into a contemporary world by means of the imagination. But such a project is self-defeating. Tennyson's language here performs at one and the same time two contradictory acts: it translates Arthur and the Arthurian into a contemporary idiom yet suggests the inadequacy of that idiom in comparision to the historical wholeness it is measured against—and therefore calls into question the possibility of performing the very act of integration between past and present that Tennyson has attempted. Tennyson accomplishes this complicated work because, like Milton, he makes us hear the echoes of language past in the language of the present. Underneath the word "gentleman" chimes the notion of "gentle-man," of the participant in and subscriber to the code of gentilesse; underneath "stately" echoes first, perhaps, "state," then its etymon "estate," with its associations of proper social order and hierarchy. But although they resonate, these terms ring hollow, serving only to suggest the gap between the code of gentilesse and the code of the Victorian gentleman, between a world of hierarchical estates and one of "stately port"—a term which, wittingly or not, has the unfortunate effect of making this Victorian Arthur sound something like a well-fed banker. These lines seek to resurrect the image of Arthur for the Victorian audience; they succeed merely in measuring the fullness of his loss.

It might be argued that Tennyson himself eventually wrote his way out of these difficulties, especially in *Idylls of the King* in which, as Henry Kozicki has suggested, he found in Hegelian dialectic a solution to his problems.[5] My own view is that the *Idylls* fail to relate past and present even dialectically. Even at those moments in which Tennyson sought to do so—in the vague gestures toward a progressivist dialectic launched within the cyclical theory of history the poem affirms, and in the embarrassing compliment to Prince Albert, which evades but therefore reminds us of the fact that Albert played a manifestly unheroic role, played in fact a more complacent Guenevere to Queen Victoria's Arthur—his attempt to integrate past and present remains incomplete. The Arthurian past remains for Tennyson either embedded in a mythic past or an equally mythic apocalyptic future; when it enters the present it does so with a resounding thud.

I must confess here a certain ambivalence about this failure; perhaps inadvertently, it pays a tribute to the pastness of the past, to its resolute difference from the historical situation of those experiencing it in the present. Perhaps Everard Hall's sense of transgressiveness of "remodeling models" is ultimately justified. But I want to turn now to a work in which this work of historical translation is performed with a certain amount of giddy abandon—William Morris' "Defence of Guenevere," published in 1859, the same year that Tennyson's first *Idylls* were published. I want to look at what happens when the model is remodeled without the lingering guilt and sense of inauthenticity

Tennyson displays. For here that model is reconstituted as a site of otherness itself: Guenevere stands in the same relation to her accusers as does the past to the present in Tennyson's poem. She does so because she stands the relation one might have assumed between subject and audience on its head; she accuses her accusers, both in the immediate context of the poem, and in the larger, extended context of the Victorian public to which it is addressed. And in doing so, she provides an entirely different model of relating past to present, historical myth to the realities of the moment.

Morris' remodeling of models here is dual. On the one hand, he remakes or reimagines the account he is given in Malory; on the other hand, however, he simultaneously adopts but subverts the conventions of the Victorian dramatic monologue. Beginning with the latter act of subversion will allow us to note the true audacity of the former. For Morris is particularly interested, I think, in the ways the monologue interacts with its audience—the audience within the poem and the audience beyond, for whom that inner audience stands. In most dramatic monologues, the audience within the poem remains silent. In the classic examples of the form, we have no way of knowing what the audience's response might be, nor do the characters within the dramatic monologue always know what the object of their address thinks of them. Yet—like the silence of a rigorous psychoanalyst—the very lack of response and participation from these implicit audiences challenges the speakers. It forces them into revelations of memories or of aspects of their experience they wish to hide. And beyond this implicit audience stands the actual audience, ready (as Robert Langbaum has shown) to approve and to reject, to judge these characters or to sympathize with them.[6] By so revealing themselves to implicit others, Browning's characters also reveal themselves to those who exist beyond the imaginative life of the poem—that is, to its readers, who, isolated from yet drawn into contact with these self-revealing *personae*, form opinions and judgments about them.

Morris enters into this tradition as he enters into all traditions: to demonstrate and then demolish from within its hidden assumptions. Like Browning's monologists, Guenevere presents a series of specious casuistries. She offers in her own defense a dizzying series of arguments, ranging from threats (Lancelot killed Mellyagraunce, her last accuser; he may do the same to you) to blandishments, an appeal to what she calls the "gracious proof" (I.241) of her own beauty, to manifestly false analogies, to direct appeals to the pity of her audience.[7] But unlike Browning's monologists, in doing so Guenevere does not open herself up to the "sympathy" and "judgment" of her audience. Rather, she turns that audience's desire to judge her back upon themselves. Guenevere challenges the very terms her audience applies to her—not only those of the fictive historical audience to whom she speaks directly, but more powerfully and more importantly, those of the contemporary Victorian audience that stands behind Arthur's court. Like a good lawyer, she performs this transvaluation by shifting the very ground on which judgment is to be passed. Although it is true that Arthur is at best an inadequate helpmeet—

> "bought
> By Arthur's great name and his little love
> . . . .
> . . . for a little word
> Scarce ever meant at all, must I now prove
> Stone cold for ever?"
> [82-83; 86-88]

she asks—although it is true that she loves Lancelot, and he at least defends her honor; although it is true that it was his blood that was found on her bed; although it is true that he was found in her bedchamber, with Guenevere's head resting on Lancelot's breast; though all these things be true, nevertheless, she insists, theirs was what Henry James would call a virtuous attachment:

> "Nevertheless you, O Sir Gauwaine, lie,
> Whatever may have happen'd these long years,
> God knows I speak truth, saying that you lie!"
> [283-88]

Guenevere's assertion here is enormously complex, and well worth pondering. It has usually been taken to be an outrageous prevarication. Her claim is frequently understood to be that she and Lancelot have not committed adultery, or if they have, have done so only in spirit, in which case she is indeed lying. But this is not, of course, what she says. "Whatever may have happen'd during those long years," Gauwaine cannot tell the truth about it: such is the substance of her claim. And on those terms, her assertion is clearly true: Gauwaine does not, cannot pierce the mystery of the love she and Lancelot share. In that sense, her assertion is perfectly correct; God knows she speaks the truth—but only when she says that Gauwaine lies.[8]

This is a brilliant equivocation, yet one also feels, at least in dramatic context, that it is a fundamentally irrelevant one. As a legal defense, even in a medieval court, it is flimsy at best; and as an emotional defense, in front of Arthur's own knights, it is less than politic. How then can it be said to constitute a "defense" at all, at least under the criteria Guenevere's audience brings to the process of judgment? The answer lies at the end of the poem. Guenevere turns sideways from her accuser, "listening, like a man who hears / His brother's trumpet sounding through the wood / Of his foe's lances" and, at that moment, Lancelot arrives "at good need" to carry her off (288-90). We now recognize that Guenevere's performance here is to be taken as a defense in a different sense: a knightly defense, a parrying, by the use of language, of the thrusts of her accusers—a holding action, while she awaits the intervention of Lancelot.

Guenevere's language, then, evades the categories that her immediate audience—and the audience beyond the poem for whom they stand—bring to the task of judgment. Truth, like the "troth" Guenevere has pledged in the "little words" of the marriage ceremony, is extraneous to the language she employs. Her language is tactical: it is to be judged by the canons of rhetoric rather than by those of empirical verification or logic. That is, her arguments, her analogies, her threats, her use of evidence, are to be evaluated not on the basis of their truth and falsity, but rather for their effectiveness. Her words are her weapons. And as such, they serve to challenge the notion of judgment on the basis of truth and troth alike—the notion that language has an objective grounding in an overarching "reality" which lies behind it, the notion that this reality is embedded in a larger network of values (being true to one's vows, one's word) which lies behind and authenticates that reality. Guenevere's defense issues a challenge to both the fallible epistemology and moral assumptions of *all* the audiences she faces.

There are many things to say about this dimension of Morris' poem, for it helps to place Morris in the context of literary theory as well as literary history. What I want to point to here, however, is the way that Guenevere's redefinition of the possibilities of language alters the ways that Morris can deploy the matter of Arthur. I suggested earlier that Morris' Guenevere explicitly stands to the judging court just as Tennyson's sense of the Arthurian past implicitly stands to his sense of the present. I want to conclude by suggesting that Morris' Guenevere also stands in the resonant relation to her author that Tennyson erects his elaborate framework to escape. As Guenevere rewrites her own history in the trial, so Morris rewrites the character and legend that is Guenevere (indeed, he creates the entire scene, which is never mentioned in Malory). As she conceives of language as a weapon, as an instrument analogous to, indeed allied with, Lancelot's arms, so too Morris seizes upon the narrative of Guenevere for a polemical purpose—in this case, to make full subversive use of the Arthurian legend in an indirect but nevertheless powerful statement to his contemporary audience.

In Morris' hands, what Guenevere reminds the Victorian audience—and a twentieth-century one as well—is this: that narratives such as Guenevere's are always written from the point of view of Gauwaine; that history is not a value-neutral set of facts or even a privileged set of myths expressing universal human truths, but a trial, a contestation, a clash of interpretations which the more socially powerful always wins; that from the point of view of the present, all narratives, even (especially) the privileged narratives which speak of and come to represent the past, are ideologically determined; that rich and resonant as they may be, they represent history only as it is experienced from the point of view of a censorious court. Morris' point here is not, however, to bemoan this fact, but to reappropriate, remake, rework, and respeak the Arthurian, a respeaking which is analogous to his character's more effective form of speaking because it is, actually or potentially, a weapon in his arsenal of power.

Let me conclude ambivalently. Each of these models for deploying the Arthurian possesses an attraction for the twentieth-century critic, particularly at the historical moment of a turn—or return—to historical criticism. Although the Arthurian cycle is notoriously more "myth" than "history," Tennyson's and Morris' attempts to embed the narratives of the past in the context of the present possess a clear relevance to the concerns of an historicist criticism. Although he may reach it by a circuitous and ideologically suspect route, Tennyson's sense of the otherness of the past, his invocation of the past as the site of difference itself, is one that many historically-minded scholars and critics aspire to—even if, like Tennyson himself, they inevitably reveal their interests, their fears, and their desires in the very terms by which they image that difference. Morris' gleefully ideological appropriation of the narratives of the past serves as a corrective to this view. For Morris reminds us of the tactical and political dimensions of these narratives and, more importantly, of the political nature of the acts of judgment we inevitably perform as we encounter them and transform them into narratives of our moment. Morris thus effects, in the words of Jean Howard (writing of the failures of Stephen Greenblatt and Louis Montrose to politicize their historicist criticism), "a move into history [as] an *intervention,* an attempt to reach from the present moment into the past in order to rescue both from meaningless banality."[9]

But in doing so Morris also forcefully demonstrates the problematics of a fully *engagé* historicism of the sort Howard advocates. For the historical "intervention" perfomed by Morris is too easy and too powerful—and, finally, too ahistorical. Morris' reworking of the matter of Arthur, unlike Tennyson's recountings of Arthurian legends, swallows these narratives up with dizzying ease; one finds no acknowledgment of the possibility that these narratives can resist his "interventions," can fail in any way to conform themselves to the expectations and judgments he brings to them. In this sense, Morris is not to be identified with Guenevere, as he probably would have wished, or even with Lancelot, whose rescue-mission might also have served as an acceptable model for his historical poetics, but rather with the kangaroo court Guenevere addresses. And in *this* judgment, to follow the allegory through, the Arthurian narrative has no defense against its accusers. It can only stand humbly before its audience and respond to their charges with silence.

Neither Tennyson's nor Morris' deployment of Arthurian narratives is finally satisfactory, then, for both lead to positions that prove, by their own logic, untenable. Tennyson's evocation of the pastness of the past conduces to an utter detachment of past from present—a detachment which denies the very impulse that had impelled this turn to the historical. The impulse of Everard Hall—and the Everard Hall side of Tennyson—to find in the past a locus of value has the paradoxical effect of blocking any avenue of communication between historical narratives and contemporary concerns. The former recede into pure myth, and the latter empty themselves of any sense of historical connection or meaning. Morris' ideological appropriation of the Arthurian narratives reestablishes the network of communication between past and present that Tennyson had disrupted, but the fervor with which he accomplishes this task reduces the narratives themselves to silence. Guenevere herself may be given full voice by Morris' subversive text, it is true; but as she speaks, the difference between the narrative which encloses her and Morris' own is effaced, stilled. And past and present alike may thereby be rescued from (in Howard's phrase) "meaningless banality," but only at the cost of eliminating the gap between the two, only at the price of eliding the sheer otherness of Arthurian narrative. It is true that one could easily seek to unify these strategies and say that Tennyson's vision of the past demands Morris' and Morris' Tennyson's, and that both, when taken together, provide a satisfactory way of bringing the narratives of the past to the consciousness of the present. But rather than perform this tactical maneuver, I remain content to let these two visions clash with each other on the ideological battleground we all inhabit as we reexperience and reimagine the Arthurian.

NOTES

1. The most accessible account of the Arthurian revival in Victorian England is Mark Girouard, *The Return to Camelot: Chivalry and the English Gentleman* (New Haven: Yale University Press, 1981), esp. pp. 178-96. For Victorian medievalism in general, see A. Dwight Culler, *The Victorian Mirror of History* (New Haven: Yale University Press, 1985), pp. 152-84 and 218-40. The early history of nineteenth-century British Arthurianism is surveyed by James Merriman, *The Flower of Kings: A Study of the Arthurian Legend in England Between 1485 and 1835* (Lawrence: University of Kansas Press, 1973), pp. 113-77.

2. Keats, *Letters* (New York: Oxford University Press, 1935), p. 97.

3. Arnold, *The Letters of Matthew Arnold to Arthur Hugh Clough* (Oxford: Oxford University Press, 1933; repr. New York: Russell and Russell, 1967), pp. 135-36.

4. *The Poems of Tennyson*, ed. Christopher Ricks (London: Longman, 1969), pp. 582-98. Further citations in the text refer to this edition. The frame-poem was originally published in the same 1842 edition in which the "Morte d'Arthur" first appeared, but was separated from its companion-piece, thus reinforcing the hesitancies and ambivalences the frame-poem thematizes.

5. Kozicki, *Tennyson and Clio: History in the Major Poems* (Baltimore: Johns Hopkins University Press, 1979), pp. 112-45.

6. Robert Langbaum, *The Poetry of Experience: The Dramatic Monologue in Modern Literary Tradition* (New York: Norton, 1963), esp. pp. 73-108.

7. William Morris, *The Defence of Guenevere and Other Poems* (London, 1858), pp. 1-17. Further citations in the text refer to this edition.

8. My argument here diverges from more traditional readings of this famous crux. Angela Carson and Carole Silver have persuasively argued that these lines create the central irony of the poem, the contrast between the falseness of Gauwaine's specific charges and their more general truth; while Guenevere is innocent of the two acts of adultery of which Gauwaine accuses her, there can be no doubt that she has slept with Lancelot on (numerous) other occasions. My own view of the poem suggests, by contrast, that the truth or falsity of either Gauwaine's argument or Guenevere's casuistical response is irrelevant to the poem; Morris is not interested in the question of truth, but rather that of power, and his vision of language here moves beyond questions of reference to

questions of rhetorical effectiveness or failure. This view also diverges from Jonathan Post's attempt to redirect critical focus from Guenevere as defense-witness to Guenevere as artist. While I agree with Post that Guenevere, like Sidney's poet, nothing affirmeth, I think as well that Morris' own views of art and language are more subversive than Post recognizes. Angela Carson, "Morris's Guenevere: A Further Note," *Philological Quarterly* 42 (1963), 131-34; Carole Silver, "'The Defence of Guenevere': A Further Interpretation," *Studies in English Literature* 9 (1969), 695-702; Jonathan Post, "Guenevere's Critical Performance," *Victorian Poetry* 17 (1979), 317-27.

9.   Jean Howard, "The New Historicism in Renaissance Studies," *English Literary Renaissance* 16 (1986), 43. Although I am somewhat uneasy with the implications of Howard's argument, I consider this essay the best single response to the issues raised by the New Historicism. Howard, to be fair, prefaces the remarks I quote with a demurral: "I am not suggesting that it is desirable to look at the past with the willful intention of seeing one's own prejudices and concerns." Yet it is difficult to see how, if one believes that the critic must acknowledge the non-objectivity of his or her own stance and the inevitably political nature of interpretive acts, that critic can see anything other than his or her own "prejudices and concerns." My point here is not to quarrel with Howard's premises, however, but rather with her conclusions— particularly with her assertion of the *desirability* of "interventionist" reading. Tennyson's and Morris' examples suggest to me that another model of historical reading, that of Dominick La Capra's "dialogue" between past and present, provides a more acceptable paradigm of historical interpretation, for that model allows both the critic and the text at hand some scope of action. But finally, unlike either Howard or La Capra, I think that the question of the viability of historicist reading is undecidable—which does not in any way suggest the undesirability or the unimportance of the attempts to decide it.

Victorian Spellbinders:
Arthurian Women
and the Pre-Raphaelite Circle

Carole Silver

"The shadow of another cleaves to me, / And makes me one pollution,"[1] cries Tennyson's Guinevere, echoing the word "polluted," Tennyson's epithet for her. To many Victorians, the very name "Guinevere" meant adulteress and fornicatrix. Yet members of the Pre-Raphaelite Circle saw Malory's queen as hero or, at the least, as sympathetic sinner and depicted her and her sisters-in-sin, Iseult and Nimue, with admiration. How was it that Dante Gabriel Rossetti, William Morris, Edward Burne-Jones, and Algernon Charles Swinburne painted and wrote of these sullied females with such respect and understanding? Why did they read and apply Sir Thomas Malory's *Morte Darthur* in ways different from Tennyson's more prevalent and socially approved interpretation?

The answer is not that these Pre-Raphaelites were more liberal and liberated than most Victorian men, for, in the mid-1850's, when they first encountered Guinevere and her sisters, they fully shared the social and sexual mores of their culture. Morris and Burne-Jones had contemplated High Church priesthood and were exploring the formation of a monastic brotherhood with Sir Galahad as its moral model. Rossetti was immersed in Dante and his ideal of spiritual love and not uninterested in Roman Catholic practice. Even Swinburne, still in adolescence, was more conventional than he would later be.

In fact, the reasons for the Pre-Raphaelites' glorification of medieval fallen women were not directly personal. Instead, their defenses of Guinevere's sisters stemmed from their study of Malory, their views of chivalric love, and their perceptions of Arthurian women as beings of another time and order who therefore functioned under different moral laws.

For Morris, Burne-Jones, and Rossetti and, later, for Swinburne, the Malory-Caxton *Morte Darthur*, published in 1817 with a long introduction and copious notes by Robert Southey, was the central text. Malory's crucial view of Guinevere seemed to them to be the proleptic summary of her life at the end of Book 18: "While she lived she was a trewe lover, and therfor she had a good ende."[2] The twenty-fifth chapter, "How true love is likened to summer,"[3] with its comparison of the noble *fin amor* of Arthur's day and the light, unstable passion of the fifteenth century, provided them with a model for permissible extramarital love and, especially, the important concept of "stability" or steadfastness in love. Swinburne, for example, alludes to the phrase "green summer" in an Arthurian poem,[4] thus drawing upon the implications of Malory's analogy: "For like as winter rasure [destruction] doth always erase and deface green summer, so fareth it by unstable love in man and woman" (2:362). Burne-Jones titles an apparently subjectless painting of 1864 *Green Summer*, expecting others—who did not get his point—to catch his allusion to Malory. For this study of a circle of green gowned ladies sitting on the verdant grass beside a lake made green by the full-foliaged trees reflected in it is far more than a "harmony in green."[5] The ladies' flowing medieval robes, their chaplets of flowers, and the coif on the head of the woman who reads from an early printed book all place them in a world not far removed from Malory's. The book from which the lady reads aloud may be the Caxton *Morte Darthur*; the listeners' pensive faces suggest their comprehension of its message and perhaps their sense that "winter rasure" will inevitably come.[6]

Moreover, Southey's edition was the authentic Malory to Burne-Jones, Morris, and Rossetti. They absorbed Southey's introductory remarks as well as the elaborate notes he provided—notes that offered summaries of and quotations from Malory's sources and thus made otherwise inaccessible romances available to them. Most important, they were deeply influenced by Southey's treatment of illicit love. For example, quoting extensively from the *Romance of Merlin* and the *Prophecy of Merlin*, Southey explains and justifies Nimue's beguiling of the wizard. Chivalrously, if chauvinistically, he blames knights rather than their ladies for adulterous relationships. He suggests that Launcelot "might be considered as the ideal of a perfect knight . . . if it could be forgotten that he lives in adultery with the wife of the King he serves" (1: xiv). Yet he never directly speaks of Guinevere as an adulteress. Instead, Southey comments that her "courtesy when Arthur first saw her"— courtesy her father ordered her to demonstrate—"seems to have been designed to win" the King's heart (2: 461). In a similar vein, Southey declares himself "frequently disgusted" (1: xv) by one of the sources of Malory's account of Tristram. Yet he is not distressed by the source's "making the hero, or rather both the heroes, live in adultery," since "these are the conditions of romance, which must be taken with it for better for worse" (1: xv). Instead, he is offended by the author's insensitivity, inconsistency of characterization, and denigration of other heroes.

Still more telling are Southey's more general statements on sexual morality, the implications of which were not lost on the Pre-Raphaelites. Southey distinguishes between "our ordinary morals which are conventional and belong to our age . . .[and] those feelings which belong to human nature in all ages" (1: xv). Separating the temporal from the eternal and the artificial from the natural enables him to indicate, though indirectly, that adultery (as opposed to murder, for instance) may be pardoned. He argues that female chastity is not a major virtue in chivalric romance, citing *Amadis of Gaul* as "the first romance in which the female character was made respectable" (1: xxix). Even in that romance, he comments, the author thought "the virtue of chastity might be dispensed with, provided they [women] were constant in their love" (1: xxix). Thus, on the basis of their reading of Southey's edition of Malory, the Pre-Raphaelite Circle either selected those sources which would extenuate Arthurian women or developed such materials themselves. As they reinterpreted the figures they derived from the *Morte Darthur*, they made constancy and passion in chivalric love replace marital fidelity as a test of virtue.

Southey's distinction between natural and merely conventional morality helps shape William Morris' attitude toward Arthur's queen in "The Defence of Guenevere" (1858) and *Guinevere* (1858), his only completed oil painting. I have commented elsewhere on how, in the poem, Morris' Guenevere both admits and denies her adultery, always defending her behavior on the grounds of a life-sustaining love that transcends ordinary prohibitions.[7] Morris' admiration—expressed through such descriptions as "she stood right up, and never shrunk, / But spoke on bravely, glorious lady fair!"[8] (the sole authorial intrusion in this dramatic monologue)—is clearly with Guenevere; his characterization of her stresses her force. Morris' queen is like the Victorian fallen woman described by Nina Auerbach: "alone in her world, she seems to embody all the defiant powers of all womanhood in the face of little men who would disown them."[9] Far from feeling abased, she is proud and unapologetic, full of "un-Victorian" movement, sexuality, and verbal assertiveness.   Her sensuous gestures, whether the "passionate twisting of her body" (2) or the subtler lifting of a "long hand" (5) to show how beautiful—hence good—it is, are designed to reinforce her rhetorical appeals.   Calmly, she dismisses her marriage as one of convenience; she has been "bought by Arthur's great name and his little love" (3).   Her voice itself is an important weapon; initially soft, it rises to "a windy shriek in all men's ears, / A ringing in their startled brains" (2). Hints of supernatural power appear in her curse upon her accusers. If they execute her, she warns, she will be forced to haunt them: to "scream out" or "shout" in the dark night, to let her "rusting tears" make their swords "light" in battle (6).

Guenevere's silence is as potent as her speech, for when she refuses to continue her defense, she is really informing her judges that their evaluation is meaningless. She accepts only her own and God's verdict, insisting that "all I have said is truth, by Christ's dear tears" (10). In the course of the poem she identifies herself with Christ (her own "dear tears" have flowed), while her power over her accusers becomes equated with that of the angel who tested her in the incident of the "choosing cloths"; he too *seemed* to be issuing "God's commands" (2). To the authority of Christ and that of an angel, she adds (through her threat to haunt her judges) that of the medieval "fay" or fairy—the possessor of occult or preternatural power.[10]

Lancelot, in "King Arthur's Tomb," Morris' companion piece to the "Defence," further testifies to Guenevere's supernatural qualities when, musing on a night of love, he remembers that

> the moon shone like a star she shed
> . . . .
> When she dwelt up in heaven a while ago,
> And ruled all things but God. [12-13]

In this poem, Guenevere becomes equated with Saint Margaret, Eve, and the repentant Mary Magdalene.[11] Thus, by the end of the paired works, she has assumed the stature of a more than human figure. Enchantress, saint, and deity, she cannot be judged by ordinary standards.

Guinevere (1858), Morris' visual portrait, again emphasizes the queen's heroic force and transcendence of conventional morality, while it is even more explicit than the poems about her sexual passion (fig. 1). Critics have so busily explored the painting's biographical content (the model is Jane Burden, Morris' bride-to-be) or examined its composition for evidence of Morris' later brilliance in design, that they have ignored its obvious iconographic and narrative elements.[12] The power of the queen is manifest, for example, in the strong vertical lines of her body which almost break through the patterns that enclose her. Guinevere's head almost touches the top of the canopied bed; she appears larger than life.

The subject of the painting is a pensive moment after love. Guinevere refastens her golden girdle, but has not yet rebuttoned the cuff of one of her "bright sleeves" (5) nor replaced the golden necklace that lies upon the table. Her eyes may or may not be on the illuminated book before her, but ours should be focused on the rumpled bed behind her. The dog that dozes on the bedsheets may symbolize fidelity (either the queen's troth to Launcelot or her sleeping faith to Arthur), but, whatever its symbolism, its position forces recognition on us. We are to notice that both pillows have been used and that both sides of the bed have been occupied. The oranges and wine decanter alongside the bed are further indications that the queen has been with someone—most probably her lover. Yet her dignity and calm make us perceive her not as "fallen" but as risen, albeit from a bed of love.

Significantly, Dante Gabriel Rossetti's depiction of another moment from the love of Launcelot and Guinevere, this time based on Malory's account of "Sir Launcelot in the Queen's Chamber" (1857),[13] shares both the same model (Jane Burden) and the same image of a powerful, mysterious Guinevere (fig. 2). While her three ladies cower and weep and Launcelot bends to scowl out the tower window at the knights who have trapped him, Guinevere stands erect, entirely regal in her dress and bearing. In Malory's account, she is about to swoon; in Rossetti's drawing, only the way her clasped hands touch her neck reveals her tension. The queen's very stillness in a drawing full of motion, her lifted face and half-closed eyes (a pose later recapitulated in Rossetti's "holy" portrait of *Beata Beatrix*) make her resemble a saint or spirit sustained, if separated, by her special vision.

Sir Launcelot's Vision of the Sanc Grael, Rossetti's mural (of which only studies survive) for the Oxford Union project of 1857, is another treatment of Guenevere as enchantress and deity (fig. 3). The queen stands against an apple tree, almost fused with it as if she were its dryad;[14] in an outstretched hand, she holds one of the golden apples—the fruit of temptation—with which she is surrounded. According to Rossetti, who described his subject as "Sir Launcelot prevented by his sin from entering the chapel of the San Grail," the knight

has fallen asleep before the shrine full of angels, and between him and it rises in his dream the image of Queen Guenevere, the cause of all. She stands gazing at him with her arms extended in the branches of an apple-tree.[15]

However, the most illuminating description of the mural is by Swinburne, who embedded his visual impressions of it in a fragment of a poem called "Lancelot," closely imitative of Morris' Arthurian poems. In Swinburne's dramatic monologue, Lancelot's vision of the grail is obscured by an image of the queen:

Lo, between me and the light
Grows a shadow on my sight
A soft shade from left to right,
Branchéd as a tree.

.   .   .   .

And against it seems to lean
One in stature as the Queen
That I prayed to see.[16]

As the new vision brightens, Lancelot can see the queen's
miraculous beauty, "All her shapeliness and state," and "the
apples golden-great [that] / Shine about her there" (69). Her
eyes literally stare him out of grace and he seems:

To be hidden in a dream,
To be drowned in a deep stream
Of her dropping hair. [70]

Significantly, both Rossetti's mural and Swinburne's poem
portray the queen as a powerful goddess who rivals Jesus.
Deliberately placed in the posture of the Crucifixion, Rossetti's
Guenevere suggests an alternative to Christian worship. Not
only is she a type of Christ, but she is also a figure for Eve, as
indicated by the apple tree and its fruit; moreover, she is
identified with Venus by the fact that the apples are golden.[17]
The unearthly power her image has over Launcelot explains the
look of sorrow on the face of the kneeling grail angel. Swinburne's
depiction of the queen echoes Rossetti's. Again, Guinevere is
beyond conventional morality. Although she engages in
adulterous love, she can still hear and see the angels. While
Lancelot's eyes are earthbound (in token of his sin), hers can
"pierce / Thro' the colours vague and fierce / That a sunset
weaves and wears" (71).

While the figures of Guinevere and Iseult were often
interchangeably used by members of the Pre-Raphaelite Circle,
the primary enchantress, for Swinburne, was Iseult. Swinburne's
fascination with her dated from his days at Eton, but his most
significant Arthurian apprentice work, "Queen Yseult," was
written when, participating in the Oxford Union project, he came

to know Rossetti, Morris, and Burne-Jones. His treatment of
Arthurian women is closely linked to theirs.

However, Swinburne's main source for "Queen Yseult" was not
Southey's Malory but another compendium of Tristram materials,
Sir Walter Scott's edition of the *Tristrem* of Thomas of
Ercildoune. Although Scott criticizes the morality of *fin amor*,
he too skirts the issue of the ladies' culpability,[18] while
Swinburne emphasizes the superhuman courage and vitality of
women who choose love outside of marriage. Queen
Blanchefleurs, Tristram's mother, is one of them, "a Lady free"
(10) who takes Tristram's father as her paramour. In the
"stability" and intensity of her erotic passion, Blanchefleurs
prefigures Yseult, while Yseult herself is a physical and psychic
sister to the Guenevere of Morris' poems. Resembling Morris'
queen in her defiant, turbulent nature as well as in her long limbs,
"arrow hand" (61) and "corn-ripe"(62) red-gold tresses, Yseult
uses her "bright hair" (23) as a net of enchantment. Tristram,
like the Lancelot of "King Arthur's Tomb," is entangled by it and
the earthly love it symbolizes.[19] Closely following his medieval
sources, Swinburne exonerates Yseult from the charge of adultery
in every way possible: the love potion is drunk by accident; the
lovers are already almost married (since Tristram serves as proxy
for King Mark); Swinburne's Mark, like Morris' King Arthur, does
not deserve his bride. A drunkard and a coward, he is so
unappealing that his own subjects whisper: "Great pity is / He
such queen should ever kiss" (32).

Another spellbinder, Yseult appeals through her incredible
beauty, her magical voice, and her implied skill in necromancy.
Daughter of the Irish sorceress who brewed the love potion, she
has miraculously healed the wounded Tristram. Her mixed
natural and preternatural traits and the power that emanates
from them are revealed in an incident Swinburne invents.
Barefoot herself, she carries Tristram across a courtyard filled
with snow so that the presence of two pairs of footprints will not
reveal their assignation.

Later in his career, Swinburne felt the need to counterbalance
Tennyson's "Last Tournament" with its portrait of a cynical Iseult
and dismissal of a mitigating love potion. The purpose of his
Tristram of Lyonesse (1881), he said, was to present the story

not diluted and debased as it has been in our own time by other hands, but undefaced by improvement and undeformed by transformation, as it was known to the age of Dante wherever the chronicles of romance found hearing from Ercildoune to Florence.[20]

In the poem's "Prologue," separately published in 1871, Iseult is entirely mythic and immortal, the opalescent April sign in the eternal zodiac of love. In the poem itself she is both human and transcendent in her passion and determination. Her relationship with Tristram is paralleled by Guinevere's with Launcelot and, as we shall see, by Nimue's with Merlin; Swinburne finds all the lovers guiltless and noble. Again, "stability" not chastity is virtue, and Iseult, arguing with God (like Guenevere in "King Arthur's Tomb"), refuses to renounce her lover or repent her love. Implicitly comparing herself to the Virgin Mary, she announces that her passion has made her "Blest" [blessed] . . . *beyond* women" (4:96, my emphasis). Through allusions to Mary, Psyche, Eve, and the goddesses of earth, Swinburne not only pardons but deifies Iseult—without denying or obscuring her rich human sexuality.[21]

What Iseult was to Swinburne, Nimue was to Burne-Jones. Almost haunted by her image, Burne-Jones painted her with Merlin in 1857—contributing a mural called "Merlin imprisoned beneath a stone by the Damsel of the Lake" to the Oxford Union project—and again in 1861, 1870, 1874, and 1884. The paintings constitute a continuing "defense of the enchantress" and it is not surprising that their painter begged Tennyson not to call the vicious harlot of the *Idylls* by the name of Nimue. An obliging Tennyson renamed his enchantress Vivien.[22]

Burne-Jones' Nimue is preternatural by birth, a descendant of a goddess of the sea, a Lady of the Lake or "fay," and a skilled practitioner of magic. Utilizing several versions of the tale he found redacted in Southey as well as Malory's account, Burne-Jones depicts her as a maiden striving to preserve her virtue, a lover struggling to retain the love of her philandering beloved, or the protectress of a worthy knight (Launcelot) whom Merlin would otherwise unwittingly destroy. In a watercolor of 1861, which originally bore Malory's text upon its frame,[23] Merlin is depicted as a wizened, small, and somewhat sinister figure. Nimue's massive form, clothed in voluminous robes of orange and gold, dominates the painting's foreground and controls its composition. Hers is the only vitality in the rugged, barren landscape that represents the Cornwall of Malory's account. Her compelling gaze reaches out of the painting, inviting viewers to participate in the spell she weaves.

Even in the intense *Beguiling of Merlin* (1874), Burne-Jones portrays Nimue less as a demonic villainess than as an anguished deity (fig. 4). The enchantress wears the clinging garments of a Greek goddess (her drapery was copied from classical sculpture) and the serpent headdress of a Medusa or Lamia. Standing in the position of dominance Burne-Jones usually reserves for men, she establishes the vertical plane in a cruciform painting[24]— literally becoming the upright of this cross of passion. Because of the writhing branches of the hawthorn tree behind her, she appears almost as tangled in enchantment as the weaker Merlin; yet she retains both sexuality and vital force. The literary source of this painting, Southey's redaction of the *Romance of Merlin*, identifies the setting as Broceliande and the tree as "white thorn"[25]—the favorite haunt of witches and fairies. It also explains that Merlin, knowing what will be, has chosen to succumb to Nimue. When she has triumphed, gaining both his magic powers and her own freedom, she will not utterly desert him.

In Burne-Jones' last depiction of the tale, a small watercolor roundel entitled "Witch's Tree,"[26] the enchantment has been completed. The aged Merlin, a self-portrait of the painter, lies amid the hawthorn blossoms peacefully asleep. A youthful Nimue, her fairy's crown now made of gold, stands near him gazing mildly at his face. In this gentle visitation, Nimue seems free of evil; she has become a spirit, muse, or benign dream.

Thus, Burne-Jones joins Morris, Rossetti, and Swinburne in the exaltation of morally questionable medieval women. All not only exonerate their ladies, but, by investing them with multiple orders of being, render them potent. By utilizing allusion rather than direct statement, by depicting them in poems and paintings (media less accessible than novels to a morally cautious public), and by describing them as existing in a legendary past, thus further distancing them from ordinary sanctions, the Pre-Raphaelites succeeded in glorifying these spellbinders and the code of extramarital love they personified.

Moreover, these intensely portrayed Arthurian women stand in striking contrast to Victorian depictions of King Arthur himself.[27] Whether the king is seen as the tepid lover of the "Defence" or as the ghostly ideal of Tennyson's *Idylls* or even as the fallen hero of Burne-Jones' *Sleep of Arthur in Avalon* (1890-98),[28] he lacks the passion and vitality, the sheer mobility, of the enchantress figures. Both in his person and as a symbol, he seems a fixed, flat element in the literary and visual designs ostensibly centered on him. The ideals he represents—fidelity and continence, among them—seem sane but colorless and weakened, if not dying; the moral virtues he epitomizes are the products of a closed, conservative social order. If, as Tennyson argues, enchantresses helped rend that order and assisted in destroying Arthur's realm, they did not perish with it.

Instead, the spellbinders lived on to represent new and morally turbulent attitudes and acts. To the artists (and Rossetti, Morris, and Burne-Jones sought love outside of wedlock), Guinevere and her sisters personified ideal mistresses or fantasies of them. They were alternatives or supplements to maiden-mother wives and family-centered marriages. Yet, despite the fact that images of them often signaled male obsessions, that they were touched and sometimes tainted by woman-fear or woman-worship, they may have also served subtly to inspirit a Victorian female audience. Guinevere, Iseult, and Nimue were depicted as heroic in their courage, cleverness, and love. Since they were "fays" or preternaturally powerful women who followed the laws of their being, they could not be despised as fallen wives or unchaste maidens. Perhaps for Victorian women to know that such characters, great in stature and rising in their fall, could be envisioned, was comforting and freeing. Clearly, for romantics of both sexes, the appeal of spellbinders was vast. However dangerous they were, they represented other possibilities in a world too often lacking in enchantment.

NOTES

1.   Alfred, Lord Tennyson, "Guinevere" in *Idylls of the King, Poetical Works* (London: Oxford University Press, 1953), p. 432.

2.   *The Byrth, Lyf, and Actes of King Arthur* (*Le Morte Darthur*), ed. Robert Southey, 2 vols. (London, 1817), 1: 363. All further references to this edition are cited parenthetically, by page, in the text.

3.   The Southey edition is without chapter headings. For headings and a corrected modern text, I have used Sir Thomas Malory, *Le Morte D'Arthur*, ed. Janet Cowen, 2 vols. (Harmondsworth: Penguin, 1969), 2: 425. All further references to this edition are cited parenthetically, by page, in the text.

4.   Algernon Charles Swinburne, *Tristram of Lyonesse* in *The Complete Works of Algernon Charles Swinburne*, ed. Sir Edmund Gosse and Thomas J. Wise, 20 vols. (London: Heinemann, 1925-27), 4: 33. All further references to this volume are cited parenthetically, by page, in the text. See also Southey, 2: 362.

5.   The painting is so decribed in *Burne-Jones: The Paintings, Graphic and Decorative Work of Sir Edward Burne-Jones* (London: The Arts Council of Great Britain, 1975), p. 32. The painting exists in two versions, gouache and oil, both in private hands.

6.   Among the models for the painting are Jane Burden Morris and Georgiana Burne-Jones, the wife of the painter. The ladies' innocence is perhaps symbolized by the somewhat incongruous small white lamb resting on the folds of one lady's green robe. The reader, whose dark robe and coiffed head may denote the fact that she is married, appears to be teaching her audience the lesson of experience.

7.   See Carole Silver, *The Romance of William Morris* (Athens: Ohio University Press, 1982), pp. 19-25.

8.   *The Defence of Guenevere and Other Poems* in *The Collected Works of William Morris*, ed. May Morris, 24 vols. (London: Longman, 1910), 1:2. All subsequent references are cited parenthetically, by page, in the text.

9.   Nina Auerbach, *Woman and the Demon: The Life of a Victorian Myth* (Cambridge: Harvard University Press, 1982), p. 163.

10. Lucy Allen Paton, in *Studies in the Fairy Mythology of Arthurian Romance*, 2nd ed. (New York: Burt Franklin, 1960), originally published in the 1920s, described the medieval "fay" as "Essentially a supernatural woman—always beautiful, untouched by time, unhampered by lack of resources to accomplish her pleasure," and, in effect, "unlimited in her power" (pp. 4-5).

Although Paton centers her book on Morgan le Fay, Niniane (Nimue), and the Lady of the Lake, her definition does illuminate aspects of Pre-Raphaelite depictions of Guinevere and Iseult.

11. Silver, p. 29.

12. See, for example, Philip Henderson, *William Morris: His Life, Work and Friends* (New York: McGraw-Hill, 1967), pp. 48-49; James Harding, *The Pre-Raphaelites* (New York: Rizzoli, 1977), p. 95; and Tate Gallery, *The Pre-Raphaelites* (London: Tate/Penguin, 1984), pp. 169-70. The painting seems originally to have been called *Guinevere* but was later catalogued among Dante Gabriel Rossetti's possessions as *La Belle Iseult*. The latter identification better suits the picture's iconography and may well reflect Morris' intention. The dog on the bed may represent Tristram's Petitcreu; the harping knight in the background may suggest Tristram. However, whether the figure is Guinevere or Iseult, the subject matter of the painting—a woman dressing after love-making—is the same.

13. See Virginia Surtees, *The Paintings and Drawings of Dante Gabriel Rossetti: A Catalogue Raisonné*, 2 vols. (Oxford: Clarendon, 1971), 1:51-55. Surtees notes that this design's original frame had inscribed in gold upon it: "How Sir Launcelot was espied in the Queen's Chamber, and how Sir Agravaine and Sir Mordred came with twelve knights to slay him" (p. 54).

14. The same iconography links the queen to Eve in Rossetti's *Arthur's Tomb* (1855). Here, Guinevere is surrounded by apple trees from which fruit hangs and a snake and an apple lie in the lower lefthand corner.

15. Quoted in Surtees, p. 52, from a letter of Rossetti's to Charles Eliot Norton, July 1858.

16. Swinburne, *Complete Works*, 1:68. All further references to this volume are cited parenthetically, by page, in the text.

17. In Rossetti's *Venus Verticordia* (1864-68), Venus holds the golden apple that Paris has awarded her and which, in Rossetti's version of the myth, he eats—thus engendering his passion for Helen.

18. *Sir Tristrem; A Metrical Romance of the Thirteenth Century by Thomas of Erceldoune, called the Rhymer*, ed. Walter Scott, 3rd ed. (Edinburgh, 1811), pp. 340-42. Swinburne takes the names of the characters and many of his incidents from this version of the legend.

19. Both ladies are depicted as having the red-gold hair of Elizabeth Siddal, Rossetti's early model and future wife. Both Lancelot (in

"King Arthur's Tomb," 1: 11-22) and Tristram (in "Queen Yseult," 1: 24-25) are depicted as willing to die for their ladies' hair.

20. Quoted in George Benjamin Woods and Jerome Hamilton Buckley, eds., *Poetry of the Victorian Period*, rev. ed. (Chicago: Scott, Foresman, 1955), p. 1036.

21. For Swinburne's treatment of female sexuality in the poem, see John D. Rosenberg's "Introduction" to *Swinburne; Selected Poetry and Prose*, ed. John D. Rosenberg (New York: Modern Library, 1968), xii-xiv.

22. Penelope Fitzgerald, *Edward Burne-Jones: A Biography* (London: Joseph, 1975), p. 84. Fitzgerald retells the incident about Tennyson as part of her argument that the enchantresses are not "sinister" or "depraved" themselves; instead, they represent the weakness of the males involved with them.

23. The frame probably bore the subheading of Book IV of Malory: "How Merlin was assotted and doted on one of the Ladies of the Lake, and how he was shut in a rock under a stone and there died" (Cowen, ed. 1:117). Burne-Jones also illustrated *A Book of Verse*, William Morris' illuminated manucript of 1870, with a small roundel of Morris and Jane Morris as Merlin and Nimue. The poem this picture illustrates, "Love and Death," is a *carpe diem* poem which utilizes the hawthorn tree associated with the lovers in several versions of the legend.

24. Martin Harrison and Bill Waters, *Burne-Jones* (New York: Putnam, 1973), p. 113. They interpret the painting as a study of "the eternal struggle between the sexes" (p. 110). The model is Mary Zambuco, with whom Burne-Jones was having a somewhat torrid affair.

25. This version of the painting derives from Southey's quotations from the *Romance of Merlin* (2: xliii-xlviii): "At length it fell out that as they were going one day hand in hand through the forest of Broceliande, they found a bush of white thorn which was laden with flowers . . . and they disported together and took their solace" (2: xlvi).

26. The watercolor is from Burne-Jones' *Flower Book*, now in the British Museum. The model for Nimue is probably the painter's daughter, Margaret.

27. I am indebted to William Sharpe for the main ideas of this paragraph.

28. In one version of the painting, the face of Arthur was that of William Morris, who had recently died. Significantly, another of Burne-Jones' last works was *The Dream of Launcelot at the Chapel*

of the San Graal. The painting is, in effect, a recapitulation of
Rossetti's mural of 1857 for which Burne-Jones sat as Launcelot.

Fig. 13.1. William Morris. *Guinevere* (1858). Reproduced courtesy of the Tate
Gallery.

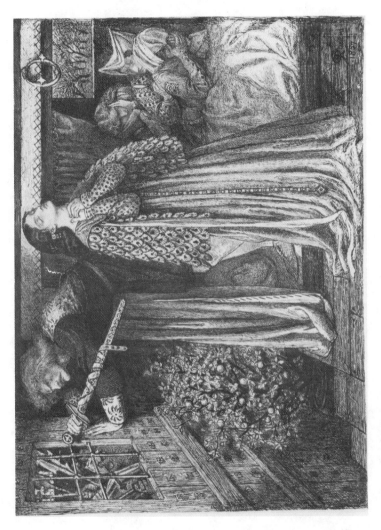

Fig. 13.2. Dante Gabriel Rossetti. *Sir Launcelot in the Queen's Chamber* (1857). Reproduced courtesy of the City of Birmingham Art Gallery.

Fig. 13.3. Dante Gabriel Rossetti. Study for *Sir Launcelot's Vision of the Sanc Grael* (1857). Reproduced courtesy of the Ashmolean Museum.

Fig. 13.4.　Edward Burne-Jones. *The Beguiling of Merlin* (1874). Reproduced courtesy of Lady Lever Art Gallery.

The Last Idyll: Dozing in Avalon

William E. Fredeman

In the broader context of the nineteenth century's fascination with medievalism, the Arthurian legend had widespread appeal for both writers and artists. In "The Arthurian Century: A Chronology of Significant Arthurian Publications in the Nineteenth Century," an appendix to his *King Arthur's Laureate*, Phillip Eggers has traced most of the literary works of the period treating the matter of Arthur, but there has been no comparable examination of the visual interpretations of this material, which are equally numerous. (Citations in this article and the accompanying Appendix refer to the Selected Bibliography beginning on page 303.) The death of King Arthur is a particularly prominent icon in the paintings and illustrations of the Victorians, recurring in at least a dozen major pictures and in several illustrated books, the most famous of which is the celebrated Moxon *Tennyson* of 1857.

Tennyson's role in the Arthurian revival has long been recognized, but it is not always possible to determine whether Tennyson or Malory is the immediate source of a particular drawing or painting. As David Staines has noted, although "Tennyson's poetry did not stand behind all the Arthurian art and literature of Victorian England, . . . it did serve to raise the subject matter to a new level of literary respectability" (156); and many Victorian Arthurian pictures are "either illustrations of Tennyson's poems or depictions of incidents which originated in Tennyson's Arthurian world. . . ." What Staines says of the Pre-Raphaelites is equally true of many other Victorian artists: "Tennyson became the source of their understanding of the legends"; "their medievalism owed more to Tennyson than to the medieval world and the *Idylls of the King* came to hold the inspirational force that Malory occupied for Tennyson" (158). There was unquestionably a renewal of interest in Malory in the 19th century, commencing with Southey's edition of 1817, and continuing with Thomas Wright's three-volume edition of 1858, but most of the publications appeared after the first installment of the *Idylls* in 1859. Tennyson, as Staines rightly observes, "opened the door to the wealth of the Arthurian legends" (159), and it was the Laureate who "brought the Arthurian legends to the consciousness of the English people; his poetry that re-established their literary eminence" (163).

While these points are important in assessing Tennyson's influence on the evolution of Victorian ideas about King Arthur, it is also essential to recognize the personal levels on which Tennyson's treatment of Arthurian themes operates. The death of Arthur in particular had an intensely personal and symbolic, if not an allegorical, significance for Tennyson. Closely related to his preoccupation with the themes of loss and despair and to his firm commitment to a belief in immortality, it becomes, in its blending of pictorial and narrative elements, a central and dramatically visual icon, which had wide appeal for the artists and illustrators of the period.

I

Tennyson's earliest-composed idyll, the "Morte d'Arthur," which, with only slight revisions and the addition of 198 lines, became "The Passing of Arthur" in *Idylls of the King*, was clearly conceived, from the evidence of the domestic frame-poem, "The Epic," which introduces both the poem and the second volume of *Poems* 1842, not as the last, but as the penultimate, idyll in the heroic work by Everard Hall, who is a thinly disguised mask for Tennyson himself. Following Hall's "deep-chested" musical reading—"mouthing out his hollow oes and aes"—of Book 11 of his epic, which Francis Allen had rescued from the hearth to which the poet had once consigned it, "The Epic" concludes with the narrator's dream-vision of the resurrection and return of King Arthur:

                                                    I seem'd
To sail with Arthur under looming shores,
Point after point; till on to dawn, when dreams
Begin to feel the truth and stir of day,
To me, methought, who waited with the crowd,
There came a bark that, blowing forward, bore
King Arthur, like a modern gentleman
Of stateliest port; and all the people cried,
"Arthur is come again: he cannot die."
Then those that stood upon the hills behind
Repeated—"Come again, and thrice as fair;"
And, further inland, voices echoed—"Come
With all good things, and war shall be no more."
At this a hundred bells began to peal,
That with the sound I woke, and heard indeed
The clear church-bells ring in the Christmas morn.

The fictional context provided by the frame-poem for the "Morte d'Arthur" has always been tantalizing, for if Book 11 of Hall's epic treats the death of Arthur, the last idyll must deal with his return, a closure that Tennyson does not attempt in *Idylls of the King*, choosing instead to depict, as he does in so many of his works, what elsewhere I have referred to as "the penultimate moment." The dream-vision in "The Epic" is, thus, Tennyson's only attempt to portray the apocalyptic conclusion of the Arthurian legend, which Malory, after exhausting all his sources in authorized books, addresses only in his postlude on the death of Arthur:

Yet some men say in many parts of England that King Arthur is not dead, but had by the will of our Lord Jesu into another place; and men say that he shall come again, and he shall win the holy cross. I will not say it shall be so, but rather will I say: here in this world he changed his life. But many men say that there is written upon his tomb this verse: *HIC JACET ARTHURUS, REX QUONDAM REXQUE FUTURUS.* [Pollard 2: 494]

Tennyson's fascination with the thematic possibilities of Arthur's return, however, is evident in the first brief reference in his poetry to Arthur's death and afterlife, that stanza describing the Arthurian room in "The Palace of Art," which Rossetti illustrated so effectively for the Moxon *Tennyson* (fig. 1):

> Or mythic Uther's deeply-wounded son
> In some fair space of sloping greens
> Lay, dozing in the vale of Avalon,
> And watch'd by weeping queens.

Tennyson began experimenting with Arthurian materials as early as 1830 in "Sir Launcelot and Queen Guinevere" and published both "The Lady of Shalott" and "The Palace of Art" in *Poems* 1833, but none of the earlier poems has the strong autobiographical redolence of the "Morte d'Arthur," which, composed in 1833-34, must have been at least partially written under the impress of Arthur Hallam's death. Together with its pendant frame-poem, "Morte d'Arthur" can be read on an analogical and symbolic level, perhaps even as a mini-*In Memoriam*, in which King Arthur anticipates that larger-than-life, transcendent other Arthur who dominates so many of the visionary vignettes in the later poem. And the concluding line of "The Epic"—"The clear church-bells ring in the Christmas morn"—echoes the several Christmas turn-sections of *In Memoriam*, which reinforce the Hallam-Christ comparisons made in that poem. That King Arthur assumes an even greater symbolic Christ-like stature is too patent to require elaboration; and both Arthur-Man and Arthur-King confirm, when Tennyson finishes with them, his firm and life-long commitment to a belief in immortality.

In all, Tennyson wrote five Arthurian poems in the 1830's, but only "The Lady of Shalott," the seed-poem for "Launcelot and Elaine," and "Morte d'Arthur" were incorporated into the final scheme of the *Idylls*. The three poems share a common iconographical image in the boat or barge that conveys the respective corpses to Camelot and Avilion. A conventional romantic metaphor for internal and external quest or search, the barge plies either the mysterious waterways of the inner self or the broader spans of river, mere, and sea in search of the well-springs of man's origins and the teleological meanings of life itself. A recurring image or device in "Ulysses," "The Lotos-Eaters," *In Memoriam*, "De Profundis," "The Voyage," and "The Voyage of Maeldune," besides the two poems already mentioned, the barge is central to both Tennyson's symbolic and personal world views: transporting Arthur in and out of life—"from the great deep to the great deep" (in Merlin's "weird rhyme")—with the promise of return, on the symbolic level in *Idylls of the King*; affirming immortality on the personal level, in "Crossing the Bar," the concluding lyric, after 1889, of all editions of Tennyson's works; and merging the symbolic and personal—the heroic and the domestic—in the "parabolic drift" of his thinly veiled "autopsychology" (to use Rossetti's term), "Merlin and the Gleam" (1889).

Although Tennyson only twice employs images involving paintings or pictures in the *Idylls*—first, to describe the "painted battle" in "The Coming of Arthur" (122); second to portray the look in Arthur's "wide, blue eyes / As in a picture" in the "Passing" (338)—the style of the entire work can be characterized as "painterly." In its dramatic settings and landscapes, the richly textured and colorful descriptions of the accoutrements of knighthood surrounding Arthur's court, the minute attention paid to dress and design and architecture, and the set-piece vignettes within the narrative, the *Idylls* contains a wealth of natural, artificial, and symbolic pictures that early on attracted painters and illustrators to translate into visual terms its vivid, verbal details. Tennyson's poetry generally has inspired widespread artistic interpretation, but few poems have elicited the response of the death scenes of Elaine, "The Lady of Shalott," and King Arthur, whose passing is rendered either literally or symbolically, anticipating that "Last Idyll" treating the apocalyptic promise of his return. The appeal of Arthur's death and departure in the nineteenth century is heavily dependent on the mystical ornateness and ambiguity that dominates Tennyson's treatment of the event in the *Idylls*.

II

Notwithstanding the claim of the anonymous *Athenaeum* critic reviewing the first installment of the *Idylls* in 1859 that Tennyson's poetry contained an "excess of the pictorial," most artists were attracted either to the scene of Arthur on the barge or to projections of his aestivation in Avalon. In fact, only two drawings have been located that treat any other scene associated with Arthur's death, both from an extensive unpublished series illustrating the *Idylls* in the Tennsyon Research Centre, by Hugh J. Reveley. The first represents Bedivere casting Excalibur into the mere where it is received and brandished by the arm of the Lady of the Lake, "Clothed in white samite, mystic, wonderful." The second depicts Bedivere carrying the wounded Arthur to meet the barge in which the tallest queen stands on deck with open arms to receive the king (fig. 2). Unlike other works, which focus either on the decorative or symbolic details of Arthur's death, Reveley's picture concentrates on the bleakness of the naturalistic landscape, the perspective of which dwarfs the narrational context associated with the figures on the shore and on the barge. The emphasis in the picture is on the atavistic and elemental aspects of a world returned, or returning, to wasteland after the collapse of Arthur's civilization symbolized by the rocky crags down which Bedivere, the last of the surviving knights loyal to Arthur, struggles with his burden. The pathetic fallacy inherent in the picture is also carried by the storm clouds gathering in the distance and by the expanse of water which almost trivializes the barge by deflecting attention to the forces of nature which dominate the setting. While Reveley's drawing lacks the polish and emblematic density of Rossetti's and Paton's illustrations and the rich luxuriance and color of James Archer's or Burne-Jones's paintings, all to be discussed later, it captures in its starkness and intensity the emptiness and decline of the Arthurian world, in a style reminiscent of Martin or Doré.

Reveley's picture conveys accurately the mood or tone of Tennyson's lines, but it is not, like Maclise's illustration for the "Morte d'Arthur" in the Moxon *Tennyson* (fig. 3), literally faithful to Tennyson's text, in which the decks of the barge, "like some full-breasted swan," are "dense with stately forms." In the illumined prow, the stately queen nestles Arthur in her arms, while the two other queens, standing by the mast, in the darkened half of the barge, stare down on the wounded king. The whole scene has about it a staged and funereal quality that contrasts dramatically with the most elaborate depiction of the barge-scene produced by a Victorian artist: Noel Paton's *The Death Barge of King Arthur* (fig. 4).

What distinguishes Paton's picture from more conventional representation of the barge scene is the intensity of emotion, the pervasiveness of grief that animates the scene and, no less than the wind that puffs the sail, seems to propel the barge through the water. Everything about the picture conveys a sense of almost cinematic, or operatic, movement missing from more stereotypical portrayals, in which the barge appears frozen in the manner of a still photograph. These static and posed illustrations convey only the trappings, not the iconography, of grief. By contrast, Paton succeeds in capturing a feeling of cosmic loss; his picture is loss-laden in its symbolism: the ornateness of the barge, the histrionic emotions registered on the faces of the eight queens, the sweep of the prow through the water, the decorative overloading of Christian and pagan heraldic symbolism on the stern and on Arthur's shield and helmet, the puffed sail enlivening the pendragon motif, the hectic activity of the cowled oarswomen, the verisimilitude of the nautical effects, the sublimity of the natural forms in the background, contrasting with the sparseness of the carefully drawn vegetation on the shore from which the barge has just pushed off, including the uprooted stump of a great tree, which, like Arthur, has been felled—all suggest a style even more Pre-Raphaelite in its concern with the accuracy of minute detail than Rossetti's drawing for the Moxon *Tennyson, Watched by Weeping Queens* (fig. 1).

Rossetti's picture is static by comparison with Paton's, but intentionally so; and of course it is truer to the artist's than to the poet's vision, for not even the "Morte d'Arthur," which elaborates on the meager description of the Arthurian quatrain in "The Palace of Art," contains the iconographic details found in Rossetti's illustration.

The picture is dominated by female forms who occupy the whole of the foreground: Arthur, almost obscured, is surrounded by a circle of ten queens with flowing hair, each wearing a different emblematic crown, perhaps intended to underscore the mythic nature of the king's heritage. One of the queens supports Arthur's visor; another has her hand on the hilt of Excalibur, mysteriously restored to the dozing king by the Lady of the Lake, to whom Bedivere had returned it. In the background, occupying roughly the top sixth of the drawing, the barge seems both at anchor and under full sail, its deck emblazoned with what appear to be eight shields. From a tall Celtic cross in the prow flows a pennant; the sail is decorated with a barely discernible design, suggestive rather than particular. Aft is a deck-house topped by a cross and a small belfry; off the stern is another angled cross from which is suspended a lantern. On the far shore, across a narrow inlet into which a tributary river empties, is a barren landscape with scattered trees and a small chapel that may house Arthur's tomb, with its enigmatic, but non-Tennysonian, inscription. Although predominantly dark in its shades and tones, the drawing skillfully highlights the faces, dresses, and crowns of the queens attending Arthur, conveying more effectively the ambiguity of Arthur's suspended condition between life and death.

Produced during Rossetti's Arthurian period, in which he orchestrated the decorations of the Oxford Union murals and painted those half-dozen jewel-like watercolors that constitute his finest mini-corpus, *Watched by Weeping Queens* is characterized by the poet-painter's recreation of medieval trappings as he imagined them rather than by a strict adherence to symbols associated with any specific text. Preferring to "allegorize on his own hook," he introduces into this picture details, such as the ten queens, which, while they have no authority in Tennyson or Malory, adequately convey the natural and supernatural dimensions of Arthur's symbolic role.

Rossetti's *Queens* provides a convenient transition to the two located Avalon paintings from the six identified works treating this subject. The earliest, James Archer's *La Mort d'Arthur*, exhibited at the Royal Society in 1862, combines an allegorical treatment with a realistic representational style (fig. 5). Arthur, lying effigy-like in a circle of ladies, within a green clearing, is being attended by two queens, one of whom, on whose lap his head rests, his eyes open, holds a globed talisman against his bandaged wound. The other, robed in black with an embroidered golden cape, and wearing a black wimple under her crown, balances in her lap an open book, perhaps the book of secrets Merlin describes in Book VI of the *Idylls*, the text of which no mortal, not even Merlin, can read, and the likely source of the potion she offers the king with her right hand, while her left clutches what appears to be another talisman. In the immediate background, natural counterparts to the five foreground figures, are five apple trees, appropriate to the Hesperian orchard isle that Loomis identifies as at least one source of the name Avalon. Hovering in mid-air, seemingly an extension of the tree at the furthest right, an opaque and opalescent angel tenders a golden Grail-like chalice, one source of the decline of Arthur's earthly kingdom, but here a symbol of Grace, embodying the promise of renewal and return. On either side of the central and largest tree, which bifurcates the picture, and against which a beautiful and madonnaesque lady kneels overseeing the ministrations to Arthur, are framed two seascapes: on the right, the barge, with an enormous but indistinct human figurehead, rests at anchor, its sail furled, anticipating the voyage out; to the left, on the strand, two standing figures converse, one a cowled and bearded old man, reminiscent of Merlin, the other a lady, perhaps the Lady of the Lake, who gestures toward the recumbent Arthur. Beyond, in the distance, a moutain-ranged isthmus looms, projecting into the sea, beckoning. The scene is dominated by silence and suspense, as if Arthur, the queens, the barge, nature, and the supernatural are caught up in a temporal hiatus—suspended in a frozen present between a world that was and one that yet shall be.

In terms of size alone, the most impressive Arthurian work painted during the century is unquestionably Burne-Jones' *The Sleep of King Arthur in Avalon*, a painting on which he and his studio assistant, T. M. Rooke, worked for nearly two decades (fig. 7). The picture proved, both in its conception and execution over its long history, a trial for Burne-Jones; and in the final year of his life the subject assumed a biographical dimension as the artist, pressing to complete his last major work, addressed his letters to Georgie at Rottingdean from "Avalon" (Penelope Fitzgerald, *Burne-Jones* [1975], 281). Introduced to the magic of Camelot by Rossetti during the "Jovial Campaign" at Oxford in 1857, Burne-Jones found in Arthurian materials an imaginative world beautiful and seductive enough to serve as a personal dreamland from which he could escape the horrors of Victorian industrial England. He would, he said, paint another angel every time they built another factory; and his angels, or their epicene counterparts, dwell as often in Camelot and Avalon as in Arcady. The scope of Burne-Jones' Arthurian canon is more extensive than any other Victorian artist's, ranging from a single panel for the Union murals, to individual watercolors, to tapestries, to murals for Red House, to stained glass, to the stage designs for J. Comyns Carr's play *King Arthur*, produced by Henry Irving.

Besides his *Avalon*, which most critics regard as his masterpiece, Burne-Jones also produced one other work specifically treating Arthur's death, *Meadow Sweet*, reproduced in *The Flower Book* (1905; fig. 6). Measuring only six inches in diameter, the picture is dominated by the enormous ship, which appears to be grounded and on whose aft deck three figures stand. Attended by two ladies positioned at his head and feet, Arthur reclines in the foreground. The focal scene is foreshortened by a surround of rolling hills underscoring the isolation of Avalon. The rigging of the ship, which is dominated by a large mast, is bare, with no hint of imminent departure. The very presence and massive size of the ship, and its dramatic juxtaposition with the recumbent king, do convey a stark sense of static urgency; yet while this miniaturized rendition is thematically consistent with the artist's treatment of the subject in *The Sleep of King Arthur in Avalon*, *Meadow Sweet* has little of the symbolic force apparent in the larger work.

Penelope Fitzgerald notes Burne-Jones' concern that in *Avalon* (fig. 7), "Arthur must be lost, the picture must give a sense of loss, but also the possibility of return" (175). In its complex imagery, though the viewer tends to be overwhelmed by the profusion of luxuriance and symbolism, there is a sense of imminence in the *tableau vivant* of female forms—both queens and fairy ladies, damsels with dulcimers, horns, and other musical instruments—

who ring the sleeping Arthur. Indeed, the picture bears many resemblances to a stage set when the curtain has just been raised and the action is yet to commence. Visually, the glory of Arthur's past is portrayed emblematically in the Grail legend on the panels of the golden canopy beneath which Arthur lies in state, Morgan cradling his head in her lap; the promise of renewal and impending return is conveyed by the queen at his feet, who holds his massive crown at the ready. But the picture also has a subtle musical subtext that interacts with the visual arrangement, surfaces, textures, and patterns and harmonizes the whole. More suggestive of celebration than lament, the silent music has a thematic redolence that recalls those "unheard melodies" of Keats' piper, or the "mournful melodies" played by "accomplished fingers" in Yeats' "Lapus Lazuli." And the keystone of that later poem—"All things fall and are built again, / And those that build them again are gay"—echoes poignantly Tennyson's lines describing the mystical and ambiguous continuity of Arthur's Camelot, where

> They are building still, seeing the city is built
> To music, therefore never built at all,
> And therefore built forever.
> ["Gareth and Lynette," 272-74]

III

But what of the "The Last Idyll"—the ostensible topic of this essay? Apocalyptic prophecy is of course difficult to depict convincingly, and no artist known to me, ancient or modern, has ever attempted the subject of Arthur's return, which, like the Trinity in Christian theology, is the *sine qua non* of most versions of the Arthurian legend. Certainly, it is for Tennyson; and even a parodist, like Mallock, who, after recommending that his apprentice poet-chefs catch a prig as an alternative to an epic hero (available only to Carlyle) and dust the broken fragments of his wife's reputation over him as he simmers, concludes his "recipe" for "writing an epic like Mr. Tennyson," with the sentence: "Then wound slightly the head of the blameless prig;

remove him suddenly from the table, and keep in a cool barge for future use" (18).

Idylls of the King was for Tennyson his *Paradise Lost*: as personally elegiac and, in its "parabolic drift," as autobiographical in its concern with questions of faith and immortality, as *In Memoriam*. Tennyson said to James Knowles, in defining his elegy as a "sort of Divine Comedy, cheerful at the close," that the poem "begins with a funeral and ends with a marriage—begins with a death and ends in the promise of a new life." The *Idylls*, reversing the pattern of *In Memoriam*, begins with a birth and a marriage and ends with a death. But, paradoxically, his epic also "ends in the promise of a new life"; and while Tennyson addressed the theme of Paradise Restored only in "The Epic" frame to the "Morte d'Arthur," Arthur's speech to Bedivere from the barge—"The old order changeth, yielding place to new, / And God fulfills himself in many ways, / Lest one good custom should corrupt the world"—seems to me prophetic rather than stoical, and it must refer, not to the world of Mark and darkness that Arthur, as *Rex quondam*, leaves behind but to that new Jerusalem where Arthur as *Rex futurus* will once again take his place in a universe "Bound in gold chains about the feet of God."

Philosophically, of course, neither *In Memoriam* nor the *Idylls* is unequivocally optimistic: T. S. Eliot found the doubt of *In Memoriam* more convincing than its faith; and Kathleen Tillotson rightly points to the deepening pessimism that characterizes the later serial installments of the *Idylls*. But these strictures notwithstanding, the promise of a "Last Idyll" is at least reservedly optimistic and consistent with those tentative commitments to the "larger hope" of *In Memoriam* (LIV), to the "sunnier side of doubt" of "The Ancient Sage," and to the "one clear call" and expectation of meeting the Master Pilot in "Crossing the Bar." Even Tenniel's caricature (fig. 8) cannot quite expunge the sentiment and the faith; and Tennyson in the punt recalls, albeit unintentionally, those other barge-bound figures in the poetry who have embarked on the quests for their respective Avalons: "The Lady of Shalott," Elaine, "the lily maid of Astolat," and Arthur, "the once and future king."

If *Idylls of the King* is not Tennyson's major work, it must be regarded as his most seminal, and the one toward which his entire poetic career was directed. The Arthurian materials were for Tennyson a life-long obsession, from 1830 to that last-composed, synthetically descriptive line on King Arthur, which he instructed Hallam in 1891 to insert into the Epilogue of his epic: "Ideal manhood closed in real man." Fittingly, his intensely personal involvement with the symbolic themes inherent in the Arthurian story was commemorated on the occasion of his own death in a sensitive and powerful visual interpretation by A. Forestier, appropriately entitled *The Last Idyll* (fig. 9), which expresses far more succinctly than any analysis, the essence of this paper's intent. The colorful and moving description of this work made by the late G. W. Whiting, whose monograph on *The Artist and Tennyson* led me to Forestier's picture, provides a fitting close to this iconographic analysis:

> . . . Tennyson lies peacefully on his bed, with his arms resting on the coverlet and his eyes closed. He is obviously dreaming. At his feet watch the relatives. In the bright moonlight which pours through the window and lights up the poet's face there appears a vision; a host of characters from the *Idylls of the King*. In their midst is King Arthur, and he is surrounded by a fair company of ladies and knights, with helmet, shield, and banner. Nearest to the dying poet, almost bending over him, and bearing in her left hand a lily is the maid of Astolat, who when she came to Camelot:

did not seem as dead
But fast asleep, and lay as tho' she smiled,
and who now comes to bid her poet the last farewell. . . . [81]

APPENDIX:
THE LAUREATE AND THE KING:
AN ICONOGRAPHIC SURVEY
OF ARTHURIAN SUBJECTS IN VICTORIAN
ART

William E. Fredeman

The artistic works listed in this appendix have been gathered from a number of scattered sources, there being to date no iconography of Arthurian-inspired works of art. The list is by way of a prolegomenon, and no claim is made for its completeness; however, the number of items identified gives a clear indication of the imaginative appeal the subject had for Victorian artists. Many of the works cited have not been located in modern collections, but for each, full, if not always complete or totally consistent, documentation is provided. One of the most interesting discoveries made in preparing the catalogue is how widespread was the use of Arthurian narrative in the applied arts. Besides paintings, watercolors, and drawings based on literary sources— often Malory but more frequently Tennyson's *Idylls*—book illustrations, tapestries, murals, embroideries, illuminations, and even stage sets and costumes drew heavily on Arthurian subjects. No designs for tiles were uncovered, but an Arthurian tile surround by Morris & Co. can easily be imagined. The number and variety of works taken directly from Tennyson suggest that his prominence in the Arthurian revival of the nineteenth century had a far greater influence on the art of that period than previous commentators realized.

Contents

I.   Arthur Dead: The Passing of Arthur
      A.   Paintings and Watercolors
      B.   Book Illustrations
            1.   Victorian
            2.   Two Modern Examples

II.   Related Pictures and Drawings
      A.   The Lady of Shalott
            1.   Paintings and Watercolors
            2.   Selected Book Illustrations
      B.   Elaine, the Lily Maid of Astolat
            1.   Elaine on the Barge
                 a.   Paintings and Watercolors
                 b.   Book Illustrations
            2.   Other scenes
                 a.   Paintings
                 b.   Sculptures
      C.   Other Arthurian Subjects
            1.   Paintings and Watercolors
            2.   Tintagel
            3.   Book Illustrations

III. King Arthur and the Pre-Raphaelites
      A.   Dante Gabriel Rossetti
      B.   Edward Burne-Jones
            1.   Paintings and Drawings
            2.   Other Media
      C.   Arthur Hughes

IV.   Miscellaneous Works: Photographs and Curiosa

V.   Tennyson Live and Dead
      A.   Caricatures
      B.   Tennyson Dead

                              *   *   *

I. Arthur Dead: The Passing of Arthur

A. Paintings and Watercolors

James Archer, *La Mort d'Arthur* (1860; RA 1861:615; Manchester City AG).

> See J. A. Blaikie's two sonnets on "Arthur in Avalon," in *Love's Victory: Lyrical Poems* (1890), originally published in the *Magazine of Art* (7 [1884]: 433-34) and subtitled "For a Picture by T. Archer." The poem, Eggers says, "extols Arthur as the Victim of low jealousy but a hero transcending human failure. Blaikie sees Arthur as an eternal inspiration to his `spiritual family'" (p. 244).

i.

Stricken of man, and sore beset of Fate,
  He lies amid the green of Avalon;
  What comfort met ye unto Uther's son,
O mournful Queens? What styptic to abate
Life's eager stream? Alas, not theirs to sate
  His soul with earthly vision! he hath done
  With mortal life, and chivalry's bright sun
Is darkened by the powers of hell and hate.

Lo! now, the garden of his agony
  Is very sweet, though dread the hour, and drear
With utterless spell of horrid potency;
The barred east beyond the brightening sea,
  Thick with portentous wraiths of phantom fear,
Is flushed with triumph, stirred with melody.

ii.

"Glory of knighthood, that through Lyonesse
  Was a lamp, O selfless soul and pure,
  What though thy visionary rule endure

So ill the assault of envy? Not the less
Thy victory, though failure thee oppress;
Not sterile thy example, and most sure
The seeded fruit; with might thou shalt allure
For evermore through life's embattled press

Thy spiritual sons to follow thee;"
The mystic Four their solemn vigil keep
Until day break, and eastward silently,
Over the kingless land and wailing deep,
The sacrificial symbol fire the sky;
Then they arise, no more to watch and weep.

Edward Burne-Jones, *The Sleep of King Arthur in Avalon* (1881-98; 111 x 254 inches; Museo de Arte de Ponce).

Originally intended as a triptych and commissioned by George Howard to hang in the library of Naworth Castle, the work is generally regarded as EBJ's masterpiece. A number of "modellos" survive (Ponce and National Museum of Wales, Cardiff, reproduced in Martin & Waters) which help to trace the evolution of this enormous work: in one the island situation of Avalon is pronounced (fig. 251); in another the wings depict battle scenes, later rejected (fig. 250); a contemporary photograph has hill fairies and rocks in the wings (fig. 254). For EBJ's other Arthurian subjects, see IV.B.

E. H. Courbould. *Morte d'Arthur* (Institute of Painters in Watercolors 1864; unlocated).

Illustrates Tennyson's "Passing of Arthur" (361-89). "King Arthur lies stretched upon the barge, attended by the knights and the three queens. `The color and texture of the robes and other accessories, and also the lustre of the jewels in the crowns, are realized with infinite care.' [*AJ* 1864: 171] But there are too many black shadows. Another observer adds the information that the painter secured `a tremendous effect by introducing a blazing pitch-pot, or lampion, swinging from the tackle overhead, and which, firing with partial glare the lamenting Queens and pallid King lying at full length bleeding upon the deck, makes by the violence of the contrast, the further forms haunting the barge more like shapes of Erebus, the midnight sky more ebony black.' [*ILN* April 23, 1864: 399] This device affords scope for a display of technical power; but, the critic thinks, it is less appropriate than the effect, suggested by the poet, of the `long glories of the winter moon' on the level lake. The painter's scenic contrasts do not have that mysterious and indefinite quality that awakens the imagination." (Whiting pp. 72-73).

Frank Dicksee, *The Passing of Arthur* (RA 1889:150; unlocated).

". . . a transcription, `in the truest spirit of reverence and poetry,' of the launching of the dead King on the Sea of the Great Unknown. Fully armed, Arthur lies prone in the `dusky barge, dark as a funeral scarf from stem to stern,' with the wailing queens around him and his pale face illumined by the `long glories of the winter moon.' The picture is mysterious in its stealthy light and prismatic shadows." [citing *MA* 1889: 271]. Whiting quotes the critic in *AJ* (1889: 186) who feels that, though the work is impressive, its weak point is that the face of Arthur is "too effeminate and young for an Ideal Arthur and too orderly for `one whose curls were parched with dust' and clotted with blood," a point with which the *Athenaeum* critic agrees (1889: 638), seeing Arthur as feebly designed and surrounded by queens "of still weaker invention": only the weeping Queen who "placed against the sheeny space of the moon's light upon the water, is half lost to sight amid the splendour which dazzles our eyes," is outstanding. Whiting continues: "The face of Arthur `bears no trace of the romance and poetry which belongs to him.' The queens `are but genteely sorrowful.' The whole picture is characterized by a pretentious, easy-going pathos." (Whiting p. 73).

Arthur Hughes, [*Morte d'Arthur*] (oil-on-board version of *The Knight of the Sun*, 10 x 16 inches, signed; sold at Sotheby's Belgravia November 11, 1975, lot 57; unlocated). Pen & ink studies for the Oxford mural entitled *The Queens in the Barge* (Bottomley Bequest, Carlisle) are illustrated in the *Burlington Magazine*, July, 1970: 453 and on fiche in Christian, but the drawing is too faint to illustrate. For AH's mural sketch for Alice Boyd, see III.C.

John W. Inchbold, *King Arthur's Island* (RA 1862:572; unlocated).

Joseph Noel Paton, *The Death Barge of King Arthur* (sepia, 1862; Glasgow Art Gallery and Museum); engraved by the Glasgow Art Union in 1866 for prize distribution.

William B. Scott, *King Arthur Carried to the Land of Enchantment* (RA 1847:1184; unlocated).

For this picture, Scott wrote a poem, published in *Poems* (1875), entitled "I Go to be Cured in Avilion." It begins: "Silently, swiftly the funeral barge / Homeward bears the brave and good, / His wide pall sweeping the murmuring marge, / *Flowing to the end of the world.*"

B. Book Illustrations

1. Victorian

Daniel Maclise, *Arthur on the Barge to Avalon*. Wood-engraved illustration for "Morte d'Arthur" in the Moxon *Tennyson*, 1857.

Hugh J. Reveley, [*Bedivere casting Excalibur into the mere*] and [*Bedivere carrying Arthur to the barge*]. Drawing Nos. 29-30 in "Illustrations of Tennyson's *Idylls of the King,*" 1864-72; unpublished original pen & ink wash drawings (*Tennyson in Lincoln* 2: 6052).

D. G. Rossetti, *Watched by Weeping Queens.* Wood-engraved illustration for "The Palace of Art" in the Moxon *Tennyson,* 1857. For DGR's other Arthurian pictures, see III.A.

2. Two Modern Examples

Morte d'Arthur: A Poem by Alfred Lord Tennyson. Designed, calligraphed, and illuminated by Alberto Sangorski. Oxford: Blackwell, 1937. Original ed. 1912. Full-page illustration of Arthur in the barge.

The Death of King Arthur: Being the Twenty-first Book of Sir Thomas Malory's Book of King Arthur and of His Noble Knights of the Round Table. With Illustrations designed and engraved on Wood by Catherine Donaldson. London: Macmillan, 1928. Twelve woodcut illustrations, including Arthur on the barge and Arthur's tomb.

II. Related Pictures and Drawings

A. The Lady of Shalott

1. Paintings and Watercolors

Entry or page numbers below prefixed *LS* refer to reproductions in the *Ladies of Shalott* exhibition catalogue; those prefixed W are page references to Whiting's monograph.

G. H. Boughton, *The Road to Camelot* (RA 1898:216): W 56.

H. Darvell, *The Lady of Shalott* (Society of British Artists 1855): W 54.

William Maw Egley, *The Lady of Shalott* (oil, n.d.): *LS* 8 (LS with back to loom).

Shela Horvitz (1960-), *"I am Half-Sick of Shadows"* (pencil, 1981; see "My Lady of Shalott," *JPRS* 3 (1983): 64-68: *LS*   17.

Edward Hughes, *The Lady of Shalott* (oil, n.d.): *LS* 14.

William Holman Hunt, *The Lady of Shalott* (two versions; see also Moxon *Tennyson*):

   1) Pen & ink, 1850: *LS* 63

   2) Oil, 1886-1905 (two versions):
       a) Wadsworth Athenaeum (Sumner Collection): *LS* 23
       b) City Art Gallery Manchester.

John Lafarge, *The Lady of Shalott* (oil, c. 1872): *LS* 29.

R. S. Lauder, *The Lady of Shalott* (Portland Gallery 1854): W 54.

Peter MacNab, *The Lady of Shalott* (Society of British Artists 1887): W 55.

Sidney Harold Meteyard (two versions):
1) *"I am Half-Sick of Shadows" Said the Lady of Shalott* (oil, 1913): *LS* 7

2) *The Lady of Shalott* (gouache, n.d., from photo): *LS*   10.

John Byam Leston Shaw (oil, 1898): *LS* 57.

Elizabeth Siddal (pen & ink & pencil, 1853): *LS* 58.

John William Waterhouse, *The Lady of Shalott* (three versions):
1) Oil, RA 1888:500: *LS* 12; W 55 (most famous LS sitting upright in boat)

2) Oil, RA 1894:245: *LS* 9; W 56 (LS in web)

3) Oil, 1915, *"I am Half-Sick of Shadows" Said the Lady of Shalott*: *LS* 66 (LS at loom).

2. Selected Book Illustrations

Jas. Fagan, in *One Hundred Illustrations of Tennyson*. Boston: Estes & Lauriat, 1895. (*LS* 15).

William Holman Hunt, in Moxon *Tennyson*, 1857. (*LS* 21-22).

Charles Howard Johnson, in *Complete Works of Tennyson*. 2 vols. New York: Stokes, 1891. (*LS* 27).

Henry Marriott Paget, in *Works of Tennyson*. London: Kegan Paul, 1881. (*LS* 35).

Howard Pyle. *Tennyson's "The Lady of Shallot."* New York: Dodd, Mead, 1881. (*LS* 36).

Dante Gabriel Rossetti, in Moxon *Tennyson*, 1857. (*LS* 41-42).

Edward J. Sullivan, in *A Dream of Fair Women*. London: Grant Richards, 1900. (*LS* 60).

Inez Warry, in *Tennyson's Heroes and Heroines*. London: Tuck, c. 1894. (*LS* 65).

* * *

The Lady of Shalott. ("Illustrated by a Lady.") Nottingham: R. and M. H. Allen. Printed for the benefit of the Midland Institute of the Blind, by permission of the author, 1852. No pagination; text and illustrations printed on one side only. (*Tennyson in Lincoln* 2: 4039).

B. Elaine, the Lily Maid of Astolat

1. Elaine on the Barge

a. Paintings and Watercolors

E. H. Courbould, *Elaine the Lily Maid of Astolat* (New Society of Painters in Watercolors 1861): W 57.

Picture a flagrant sin against poet's text: Elaine depicted as a "vulgar-faced, sensual-lipped female, in a boat, laden with the mere upholstery and gewgaws, instead of the `black decks' and grave trappings of the Maid of Astolat's last voyage." The dumb old servitor is as faithless to the character as the background is to nature. *Athenaeum* April 27, 1861: 565.

Charles Edward Fripp, *Elaine* (watercolor, repro. Sotheby's Belgravia April 18, 1878, lot 34).

Inscribed on label on reverse: "And when she was dead the corps and the bed and all was led the next day unto the Thamse, and there a man and the corps and all were put into a barge on the Thamse"—*La Mort d'Arthur.*

C. Goldie, [Head of Elaine] (French Gallery 1861): W 57.

Close-up of Elaine, depicted as "lying back, dead, with lilies upon the breast, and deep golden hair spread out upon a pillow." *Athenaeum* November 23, 1861: 693.

Edward Blair Leighton, *Elaine* (RA 1899:544): W 60-61 (Illus. *AJ* 1889: 166).

Corpse on a "quaintest-fashioned bier": depicts E's arrival at Camelot, the oarsman presents her to King and Queen while Launcelot, conscience stricken, gazes on in awe, and the knights and ladies of the court gather round.

William Millais, *Elaine the Lily Maid of Astolat* (1862; Collection of William E. Fredeman).

Ernest Normandm, *Elaine*, design for a frieze (RA 1904:901): W 61 (Elaine dead; quotes lines from boat scene. Illus. *ILN* May 7, 1904: vii).

Henry Wallis, *Elaine* (RA 1861:492): W 57.

> Excess of color in imitation of stained glass. Picture is a "blaze of color" (profusion of yellow hair) inconsistent with quiet description of poem. The critic calls Wallis a "screaming colorist" (*AJ* 1861: 196).

b. Book Illustrations

Gustave Doré. *Illustrations to Elaine* (London: Moxon, 1867). Nine plates:

> Frontis. *The Body of Elaine on its Way to King Arthur's Palace* (Plate 7 in the List of Plates)
>
> 1) *King Arthur Discovering the Skeletons of the Brothers*
>
> 2) *Launcelot Approaches the Castle of Astolat*
>
> 3) *Launcelot Relating his Adventures*
>
> 4) *Launcelot Bids Adieu to Elaine*
>
> 5) *Elaine on her Road to the Cave of Launcelot*
>
> 6) *Torre and Lavaine Bid Farewell to the Body of Elaine*
>
> 7) Frontispiece
>
> 8) *King Arthur's Reading of the Letter to Elaine*
>
> 9) *The Remorse of Launcelot*

Julia Margaret Cameron. *The Death of Elaine* (posed photograph [*Tableaux Vivants*] 1875). See IV. Miscellaneous Works.

2. Other scenes:

a. Paintings

R. Gibbs, *Elaine* (Royal Scottish Academy 1875): W 58 (content uncertain).

Mary L. Gow, *Elaine* (International Exhibition 1876): W 58 (chamber scene).

Ellen Montalba, *Elaine* (French Gallery Winter Exhibition 1880): W 60 (Elaine at window, watching Lancelot ride away).

R. Norbury, *King Arthur and the Diamond Crown* (Liverpool Society of Water Colour Painters 1874): W 71.

J. M. Strudwick, *Elaine* (New Gallery 1891): W 60.

> Imitation of EBJ. Interior scene with Elaine sitting on richly ornamental chest gazing at shield or mirror. Illus. *MA* 1891: 263.

b. Sculptures

Thomas Woolner, *Elaine with the Shield of Launcelot* (RA 1868:949): W 58.

F. W. Williamson, *Elaine* (International Exhibition 1874): W 60 (maiden in tower).

C. Other Arthurian Subjects (principally from Tennyson's *Idylls*)

1. Paintings and Watercolors

James Archer:

> 1) *How King Arthur, by means of Merlin, gate his Sword Excalibur from the Lady of the Lake* (RA 1862:483): W 70
>
> 2) *The Sancgreall, King Arthur* (RA 1863:581)
>
> 3) *Sir Launcelot and Queen Guinevere* (RA 1864:428).

John Bates Bedford, *Enid Hears of Geraint's Love* (RA 1862:476): W 64.

E. H. Courbould, *Enid's Dream* (Society of Painters in Watercolor 1873): W 64.

John Duncan, *The Taking of Excalibur* (decoration in Common Room of Ramsay Castle Lodge, Edinburgh 1897): W 70.

Jame Hayllar, *"and the sweet voice of a bird, etc"* [Geraint listening to the voice of Enid] (RA 1860:215): W 63.

Charles Edward Johnson, *Sir Galahad* (RA 1888:479).

William Morris, *Queen Guenevere (La Belle Iseult)* (oil, 1853; Tate; repro. Wood 111).

H. M. Paget, *Enid and Geraint* (RA 1879:396): W 64-65.

Joseph Noel Paton:
  1) *How an Angel Rowed Galahad over the Dern River* (oil c. 1885-86): title later altered in large version to *Beate Mundo Corte*

  2) *The Vision of the Holy Grail* (?): W 67.

Frederick Sandys:

  1) *Morgan Le Fay* (RA 1864; Birmingham City AG; repro. Wood 129)

  2) *Vivien* (RA 1863:707; Manchester City AG; repro. color Treuherz, Plate VII): W 65.

George Frederick Watts, *Sir Galahad* (RA 1862:141; two versions, one at Eton College, the other at Yale; frequently reproduced).

2. Tintagel

Whiting (74) also lists three paintings of Tintagel: 1) John Mogford, *Vestiges of the Past: King Arthur's Castle, Tintagel* (RA 1871:630); 2) Gilbert Munger, *King Arthur's Castle, Tintagel* (RA 1880:535); 3) William Clarkson Stanfield, *Tintagel Castle, Coast of Cornwall* (RA 1866:58).

3. Book Illustrations

(Beardsley) Sir Thomas Malory. *Le Morte D'Arthur*. Introduction by John Rhys. London: Dent, 1893-94. With some 350 designs, including sixteen full-page and four double-page illustrations by Aubrey Beardsley. Issued in twelve parts and in book form. Ten designs (of eleven) omitted from the first edition were published in the 2nd ed., 1909; all eleven in the 3rd ed., 1927. For a list of the major drawings, see Item 59 in Robert Ross' *Aubrey Beardsley* (London: John Lane, 1909), p. 78. Contains no Arthurian death subject.

Amy Butts. *Sixteen Illustrations to the Idylls of the King.* London: Day, 1863. (*Tennyson* in Lincoln 2: 5366).

Idylls of the King. Illustrated by Gustave Doré. London: Moxon, 1868. Combined reprint of four separate volumes illustrating the "lady-books" of Tennyson's *Idylls*: *Enid, Elaine, Vivien,* and *Guinevere,* each with nine plates. For details of *Elaine,* see II.B. Writing to B. B. Woodward on March 6, 1867, Edward Moxon provides interesting background both on Doré's illustrations and on the publication of the volumes:

Doré was quite mistaken as to the motives that led to his having a commission for "*Idylls of the King,*" of which "*Elaine*" is the first instalment. Our literary partner, J. Bertrand Payne, who has studied art as applied to book illustration rather deeply, was long of opinion that the Frenchman's talents would be profitably employed in the depicture of those grandly chivalric scenes so abundant in these epical episodes. He discussed the subject with the Laureate and Mr. Palgrave very fully: the former, who is friendly, on principle, to no artistic or musical illustration of his text, was sometime before he consented to the project. Then the difficulty arose that Doré knew not one word of English, and had never seen the country. Both these were overcome by the energy of the editor and projector of the volume, and Doré set to work in earnest. His original drawings, now at Colnaghi's, and exhibited on Saturday at the Conversatzione of the Royal Society, shew a greater regard for finish and delicacy of tone than anything he has ever before done. These drawings are for sale, and are twice the size of the Engravings. The French edition published for Messr. Moxon in Paris, by Hachette et Cie, was so much approved by the Emperor, that through the intervention of

Lord Cowley he accepted its dedication from the Editor, and is about to confer upon him the Cross of the Legion of Honour.

"Vivienne" and "Guinevere" will be the next published portion of the "Idylls."

The copy presented to the "Queen" was bound, and the proofs selected for it chosen by Mr. Payne's special care, as Mrs. Tennyson desires that Her Majesty should have the opportunity of seeing the result of his labours. (Unpublished letter in collection of W. E. Fredeman.)

Paola Priolo. *Illustrations of Alfred Tennyson's Idylls of the King*; produced expressly for the Art Union of London. London: Art Union, 1863. (No text; *Tennyson in Lincoln* 2: 6027).

III. King Arthur and the Pre-Raphaelites

The Moxon Tennyson (1857):

1. William Holman Hunt: *The Lady of Shalott*

2. D. G. Rossetti: *The Lady of Shalott*

3. D. G. Rossetti: *The Palace of Art (Watched by Weeping Queens)*

4. D. G. Rossetti: *Sir Galahad.*

The other two Arthurian illustrations in the volume were done by Daniel Maclise for the "Morte d'Arthur": *Arthur Receiving Excalibur from the Lady of the Lake* and *Arthur on the Barge to Avalon.*

The Oxford Union Murals (1857); initial titles follow Holman Hunt; major variants in Christian (JC) and Renton (JR) are also cited:

1. William and Briton Reviere: *Education of Arthur by Merlin*

2. William and Briton Reviere: *Arthur's Wedding, with Incident of the White Hart* (JC: *King Arthur's Wedding Feast*)

3. D. G. Rossetti: *Sir Launcelot's Vision of the Sangreal* (JR: *Sir Launcelot Prevented by His Sin from Entering the Chapel of the San Grail*; JC: *The Failure of Launcelot to Achieve the Holy Grail*)

4. Valentine Prinsep: *Sir Pelleas Leaving the Lady Etarde*

5. John Hungerford Pollen: *King Arthur Receiving His Sword Excalibur*

6. William and Briton Reviere: *King Arthur's First Victory with the Sword*

7. William Morris: *Sir Tristram and La Belle Yseult* (JR: *Sir Palomides' Jealousy of Sir Tristram*)

8. Edward Burne-Jones: *The Death of Merlin* (JR: *Merlin Imprisoned in Stone by the Damsel of the Lake*; JC: *Merlin and Nimue*)

9. Spencer Stanhope: *Sir Gawaine and the Three Damsels at the Fountain* (JR: *Sir Gawaine Meeting Three Ladies at a Well*)

10. Arthur Hughes (variously titled): *The Death of Arthur* (WHH); *Arthur and the Weeping Queens* (Waters, p. 35); *Arthur Carried Away to Avalon and The Sword Thrown Back into the Lake* (JR); *The Passing of Arthur* (JC).

Alexander Munro: *King Arthur and His Knights at the Round Table*; stone relief after a design by DGR over the entrance to the Union.

Sir Tristram: a series of thirteen designs for stained glass windows executed by Morris & Co. for the Music Room of Harden Grange, near Bingley, Yorkshire, the home of the Bradford merchant Walter Dunlop (1862; Bradford Art Gallery):

1. Arthur Hughes: *The Birth of Tristram*

2. D. G. Rossetti: *The Fight with Sir Marhaus*

3. Valentine Prinsep: *Sir Tristram Leaving Ireland*

4. D. G. Rossetti: *The Love Potion*

5. Edward Burne-Jones: *The Marriage of Tristram and Iseude*

6. Edward Burne-Jones: *Iseude's Attempt to Kill Herself*

7. William Morris: *Sir Tristram Recognized by the* Dog

8. William Morris: *Tristram and Isoude in Arthur's Court*

9. Edward Burne-Jones: *The Madness of Tristram*

10. Ford Madox Brown: *The Death of Sir Tristram*

11. Edward Burne-Jones: *The Burial of Tristram*

12. William Morris: *The Tomb of Tristram and Iseude*

13. Ford Madox Brown and William Morris: *King Arthur and Sir Launcelot.*

A. Dante Gabriel Rossetti

(For DGR's illustrations for the Moxon *Tennyson*, see III. King Arthur and the Pre-Raphaelites. S numbers refer to Virginia Surtees' *Catalogue Raisonné* of DGR.)

Arthur's Tomb [*The Last Meeting of Launcelot and Guenevere*] (S.73, watercolor, 1854; DGR's first Arthurian subject; perhaps the source of Morris' poem in *The Defence of Guenevere*).

Studies for Moxon *Tennyson*:

King Arthur and the Weeping Queens (S.84, pen & ink, 1856-57)

The Lady of Shalott (S.85, pen & ink, 1856-57)

Sir Galahad and an Angel [*Alma Mater and Mr. Woodward*] (S.96, pen & ink, 1857; caricature made at time of the painting of the Oxford Union mural).

The Damsel of the Sanct Grael (S.91, watercolor, 1857; oil replica, 1874).

Sir Launcelot's Vision of the Sanct Grael (S.93, watercolor, 1857 + two pen & ink sketches; based on Union mural design).

Sir Galahad, Sir Bors and Sir Percival Receiving the Sanc Grael [*The Attainment of the Sanc Grael*] (S.94, pen & ink, 1857; watercolor replica, 1874: *How Sir Galahad, Sir Bors and Sir Percival were Fed with the Sanc Grael; but Sir Percival's Sister Died by the Way*).

Sir Launcelot in the Queen's Chamber (S. 95, pen & ink, 1857).

The Chapel Before the Lists (S.99, watercolor, 1857-64; based on Malory).

The Death of Breuse sans Pitie (S.101, watercolor, 1857-65).

Sir Galahad at the Ruined Chapel (S.115, watercolor, 1859).

Sir Tristram and La Belle Yseult Drinking the Love Potion (S.200, 1867; watercolor version of stained glass).

Several other works of DGR are suggestive of Arthurian themes, including *The Blue Closet* and *The Tune of the Seven Towers* (S.90, 92), which, though they inspired poems by Morris in *The Defence of Guenevere*, "don't," DGR wrote to George Rae, "tally to any purpose with them, though beautiful in themselves" (*DGR as Designer and Writer* 45).

B. Edward Burne-Jones

1. Paintings and Drawings

Sir Galahad (pen & ink on vellum, 1858; Fogg).

The Death of Merlin [Merlin Imprisoned in Stone by the Damsel of the Lake] (Oxford Union mural, 1857).

Meadow Garden, from The Flower Book (1905).

Watercolors of 1861-62:

Merlin and Nimue (1861)

Merlin and Vivien (1861)

The Marriage of Sir Tristram (1862)

King Mark Preventing Iseult from Killing Herself (1862)

The Madness of Sir Tristram (1862)

Morgan Le Fay (1862).

The Beguiling of Merlin [also known as *Merlin and Vivien*] (oil, 1870-74; Lever).

The Dream of Launcelot at the Chapel of the San Grael (oil, 1896).

The Sleep of King Arthur in Avalon (oil, 1881-98; Museo de Arte Ponce). See I.A.

The Lady of Shalott (?). Harrison and Waters reproduce a rough drawing (Plate 27) titled "an Arthurian incident, possibly "The Lady of Shalott"; Jeanine Chapel and Charlotte Gere (*The Art Collections of Great Britain and Ireland* [New York: Abrams, 1986]) identify three studies for LS (c. 1894) in Falmouth AG.

2. Other Media

The Quest of the San Grael; a series of seven designs for tapestries executed by Morris & Co. for Stanmore Hall and repeated for G. McCulloch (1891-94):

1. *The Apparition of the Damsel of the San Grael*

2. *The Departure of the Knights*

3. *The Failure of Sir Gawaine and Sir Ywaine*

4. *The Dream of Sir Launcelot*

5. *Sir Galahad, Sir Bors, and Sir Perceval at the Chapel of the San Grael*

6. *The Ship of the Knights*

7. *"Verdura" of Stags Grazing in a Wood*

Sir Degravaunt series; three designs of a projected seven tempera murals designed for Red House (1860):

1. *The Marriage*

2. *The Musicians (The Return from the Wedding)*

3. *The Wedding Feast*

King Arthur: designs for costumes and settings (armor, dresses, furniture) for J. Comyns Carr's play, produced by Henry Irving with music by Sir Arthur Sullivan at the Lyceum Theatre (Autumn 1894). The leading roles were played by Irving (Arthur), Ellen Terry (Guenevere), and Forbes Robertson (Launcelot). The props and stage settings were destroyed by fire following an American tour, but a photograph of the stage setting survives and is reproduced in Harrison and Waters (p. 157). Of this exercise, these two authors observe, "it was almost as if he had moved into one of his paintings" (pp. 155-56).

Designs for Chaucer's *Legend of Good Women*, 1863: embroidery designs for a room in Ruskin's proposed retreat: scenes from *Morte Darthur* including Merlin and Morgan le Fay and Arthur and Launcelot (Harrison and Waters: 60).

C. Arthur Hughes

(See William E. Fredeman, *A Pre-Raphaelite Gazette: The Penkill Letters of Arthur Hughes to William Bell Scott and Alice Boyd, 1886-97*, Manchester: John Rylands Library, 1967; Robin Gibson, "Arthur Hughes: Arthurian and Related Subjects of the Early 1860's," *Burlington Magazine* 112 [July 1970]: 451-65; Exhibition of *Arthur Hughes: Pre-Raphaelite Painter*, London and Cardiff, 1971. SB=Sotheby's Belgravia.)

Elaine with the Armour of Launcelot [labeled *The Knight's Guerdon* by FGS] (oil on panel, late 50's; AH Ex: 17; private collection).

The Rift in the Lute [based on the line "It is a little Rift within the Lute" in *Merlin and Vivien*] (oil on canvas, 1859; RA 1862:129); W 65; repro. in color Baden-Baden p. 142; Bottomley Bequest, Carlisle).

The Brave Geraint [Enid and Geraint] (oil, c. 1860; a "worked-up study" for *It is a little rift*; figure added and title changed in 1863; repro. in color Wood 57; private collection).

The Birth of Sir Tristram de Lyonesse (1862, design for stained glass at Bradford; Birmingham CMAG; AH Ex: 42).

Sir Galahad [The Meeting of Sir Galahad with the Grail] (oil on canvas, RA 1870:324; Walker Art Gallery).

The Lady of Shalott (RA 1873:979; repro. in color Christie's Oct. 16, 1981: 34); a smaller oil version (repro. *AJ* 1904: 237) may also date from 1873. See also a study c. 1864 (repro. b&w *LS* p. 13). Lewis Carroll records in 1864 seeing AH's *LS* in three panels for which Miss Munro modeled (*Diary* 210); this may be one panel of the triptych.

The Death of Arthur (pen & ink? version of Oxford mural, sent to Alice Boyd in 1891, unlocated.) Three small ink studies for the Oxford mural entitled *The Queens in the Barge* are in the Bottomley Bequest, Carlisle; repro. *Burlington Magazine*, July, 1870: 454. For *Morte d'Arthur*, see IA, p. 282.

The Knight of the Sun [known variously as *The Burial of the Good Knight* (W. M. Rossetti in his 1870 *Portfolio* article on AH); *Morte D'Arthur* (Cosmo Monkhouse in 1883 article on Trist collection in *Magazine of Art* 70); *The Dying Knight* (1903 Whitechapel AG Winter Ex 279); *Death of Arthur* (1953 Sotheby sale; picture consigned by Viscount Hailsham)] (oil, 1860; unlocated; repro. in Tate 1984: 110). Watercolor and oil replicas commissioned by B. G. Windus (Ashmolean) and Alice Boyd (unlocated; repro. in color SB April 18, 1978: 60). While not strictly based on Malory or Tennyson—the frame is inscribed with lines from George MacDonald: "Better a death when work is done / Than earth's most favoured birth"—the picture clearly has Arthurian overtones and affinities: it illustrates, according to F. G. Stephens, "a legend, an incident of which declared how an old knight, whose badge was a sun, and who had led a Christian life throughout his career, was borne out of his castle to see, for the last time, the setting of the luminary he loved" (*Athenaeum* 20 September, 1873: 374).

IV. Miscellaneous Works: Photographs and Curiosa

Henry Peach Robinson, *The Lady of Shalott* (composed photograph; exhibited Manchester, 1861; LS 38).

Julia Margaret Cameron. *Illustrations to Tennyson's "Idylls of the King" and Other Poems.* Illustrated by Julia Margaret

Cameron. 2 vols. London: King, 1875. Each volume contains twelve 8-x-10-inch mounted photographs plus the "Dirty Monk" portrait of Tennyson, and twelve pages of interleaved text, lithographs of Mrs. Cameron's writing. A third volume (which may be unique), containing thirteen plates selected from the first two volumes, is in the Gernsheim Collection at Texas. A "Miniature" edition (actually crown 8vo) appeared in the same year with twenty-two plates (3 1/4 x 4 3/4 inches) with accompanying lithographed text. A selection from Mrs. Cameron's plates was engraved by Tom Lewin for the Cabinet Edition (London: King, 1875). For the history of this amazing project, which grew out of the dramatic performances at Mrs. Cameron's home, Dimbola, and which was actually suggested by Tennyson himself, see Helmut Gernsheim, *Julia Margaret Cameron* (New York: Aperture, 1975), pp. 42-50. The following sonnet by Charles Tennyson Turner, written in honor of Mrs. Cameron, is printed in facsimile in the first volume.

Lo! Modern Beauty lends her lips and eyes
To tell an Ancient Story! Thou has brought
Into thy picture, all our fancy sought
In that old time; with skilful art and wise
The Sun obeys thy gestures, and allows
Thy guiding hand, when're thou hast a mind
To turn his passive light upon mankind,
And set his seal and thine on chosen brows.
Though lov`st all loveliness! and many a face
Is press'd and summon'd from the breezy shores
On thine immortal charts to take its place
While near at hand the jealous ocean roars
His noblest Tritons would thy subjects be,
And all his fairest Nereids sit to thee.
                                        —Charles Tennyson Turner

[Program of *Tableaux Vivants* at Osborne, January 8 and 10, 1891, showing scenes from the *Idylls* (Elaine and King Arthur and his Knights). Ryde, 1891.] (*Tennyson in Lincoln* 2: 3987).

V. Tennyson Live and Dead

A. Caricatures

John Tenniel. *Crossing the Bar* (engraved by Charles Swain for *Punch* October 15, 1892).

Alfred Tennyson: The Laureate of King Arthur (engraving in *Period* January 1, 1870).

B. Tennyson Dead (October 6, 1892)

A. Forestier's *The Last Idyll* (drawing, *ILN* October 22, 1892: 509). Description by G. W. Whiting, "The Artist and Tennyson," *Rice University Studies* 50 (1964): 81.

Photograph of an illustration of Tennyson on his deathbed, with Hallam and Aubrey Tennyson and Dr. Dabbs, October, 1892; reproduced in *Black and White* (1892) and in Andrew Wheatcroft, *The Tennyson Album* (London: Routledge & Kegan Paul, 1980), p. 153.

SELECTED BIBLIOGRAPHY

Tennyson's Arthurian Works

Besides *Idylls of the King* (the planning for which, first as a musical masque, later as an epic, began as early as 1830; published 1859-89), Tennyson wrote only seven poems on Arthurian themes:

1. "The Lady of Shalott": seed poem for "Lancelot and Elaine" (composed 1832; published 1833; substantially revised 1842).

2. "The Palace of Art": stanza xvii (1833); rev. stanza xxvii (1842).

3. "The Epic": composed 1835; published as frame poem to "Morte d'Arthur" 1842.

4. "Morte d'Arthur": 1842 (composed 1833-34); rewritten, with addition of 198 lines, as "The Passing of Arthur" and incorporated into *Idylls of the King* (1870).

5. "Sir Galahad": composed 1834; published 1842.

6. "Sir Launcelot and Queen Guinevere": composed 1830; published 1842.

7. "Merlin and the Gleam": composed and published 1889; autobiographical.

Editions

Barber, Richard. *The Arthurian Legends: An Illustrated Anthology*. Totowa: Littlefield Adams, 1979.

Gray, J. M., ed. *Idylls of the King*. New Haven: Yale University Press, 1983.

Pfordresher, John., ed. *A Variorum Edition of Tennyson's Idylls of the King*. New York: Columbia University Press, 1973.

Pollard, A. W., ed. *Le Morte Darthur: Sir Thomas Malory's Book of King Arthur and of His Noble Knights of the Round Table*. 2 vols. London: Macmillan, 1908. Pollard's "Bibliographic Note" provides a succinct history of the editions of Malory from Caxton (which this text follows) onward; should be supplemented with Page West Life's *Sir Thomas Malory and the Morte Darthur: A Survey of Scholarship and Annotated Bibliography* (Charlottesville: University Press of Virginia, 1980).

Ricks, Christopher, ed. *The Poems of Tennyson*. London: Longman, 1969, 2nd ed., 3 vols., 1987.

Background and Criticism

Campbell, Nancy, ed. *Tennyson in Lincoln: A Catalogue of the Collections in the Research Centre.* 2 vols. Lincoln: Tennyson Society, 1972-73.

Christian, John. *The Oxford Union Murals.* Chicago: University of Chicago Press, 1981. Text accompanies color fiche of illustrations. See also J. D. Renton, *The Oxford Union Murals* (Oxford: Privately printed, 1976).

Eggers, J. Phillip. *King Arthur's Laureate: A Study of Tennsyon's Idylls of the King.* New York: New York University Press, 1971. The Appendix, "The Arthurian Century: A Chronology of Significant Arthurian Publications in the Nineteenth Century" (pp. 215-52), is especially valuable.

Harrison, Martin, and Bill Waters. *Burne-Jones.* London: Barrie & Jenkins, 1975.

Hunt, John Dixon. "'Story Painters and Picture Writers': Tennyson's *Idylls* and Victorian Painting." *Tennyson,* ed. D. J. Palmer. Athens: Ohio University Press, 1973.

Kozicki, Henry. *Tennyson and Clio: History in the Major Poems.* Baltimore: Johns Hopkins University Press, 1979. Chapters 7 and 8, on the rise and fall of Camelot, are of special interest.

Ladies of Shalott: A Victorian Masterpiece and Its Contexts. Catalogue of an Exhibition by the Department of Art, Bell Gallery, List Art Center, Brown University. Providence: Brown University, February 23-March 23, 1985. Besides the descriptive list of sixty-six works, this profusely illustrated catalogue contains eight essays—five on William Holman Hunt and one each on illustrations for the poem, the Moxon *Tennyson,* and Pre-Raphaelitism, Art Nouveau, and Symbolism—and a detailed bibliography.

Landow, George. "Closing the Frame: Having Faith and Keeping Faith in Tennyson's "The Passing of Arthur." *BJRL* 56 (Spring 1974): 423-42.

Lang, Cecil Y. *Tennyson's Arthurian Psycho-Drama.* Lincoln: Tennyson Society, 1983.

Layard, George Somes. *Tennyson and His Pre-Raphaelite Illustrators*. London: Stock, 1894.

Loomis, Roger Sherman. "The Legend of Arthur's Survival." *Arthurian Literature in the Middle Ages: A Collaborative History*, ed. R. S. Loomis. Oxford: Oxford University Press, 1959.

[Mallock, W. H.]. "How to Make an Epic Poem like Mr. T*nn*s*n." *Every Man His Own Poet; or, The Inspired Singer's Recipe Book*. By a Newdigate Prizeman. 3rd ed. London: Simpkin, Marshall, 1877.

Rosenberg, John D. *The Fall of Camelot: A Study of Tennyson's "Idylls of the King."* Cambridge: Belknap Press, 1973. For other major secondary works on the *Idylls*, see C. Ryals, *From the Great Deep*, and J. R. Reed, *Perception and Design in Tennyson's Idylls* (both published Ohio University Press, 1969).

Staines, David. *Tennyson's Camelot: The Idylls of the King and Its Medieval Sources*. Waterloo: Wilfrid Laurier University Press, 1982.

Tillotson, Kathleen. "Tennyson's Serial Poem," *Mid-Victorian Studies*. London: Athlone Press, 1965.

Trueherz, Julian. *Pre-Raphaelite Paintings from the Manchester City Art Gallery*. London: Lund Humphries, 1980.

Wheatcroft, Andrew. *The Tennyson Album: A Biography in Original Photographs*. London: Routledge & Kegan Paul, 1980.

Whiting, George Wesley. *The Artist and Tennyson*. *Rice University Studies* 50 (Summer 1964), 1-84 (entire issue).

Wood, Christopher. *The Pre-Raphaelites*. New York: Viking, 1981.

Fig. 14.1. Dante Gabriel Rossetti. *Watched by Weeping Queens* (Moxon *Tennyson*, 1857).

Fig. 14.2. Hugh Reveley. [*Bedivere Carrying Arthur to the Barge*] (1872). Reproduced with permission of the Tennyson Research Centre, Lincoln.

Fig. 14.3. Daniel Maclise. *Arthur on the Barge to Avalon* (Moxon *Tennyson*, 1857).

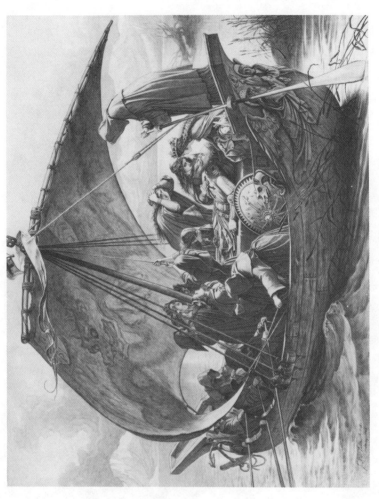

Fig. 14.4. Noel Paton. *The Death Barge of King Arthur* (1862). Reproduced with permission of the Glasgow Art Gallery.

Fig. 14.5. James Archer. *La Morte D'Arthur* (1862). Reproduced with permission of the Manchester City Art Gallery.

Fig. 14.6.   Edward Burne-Jones. *Meadow Garden* (From *The Flower Book*, 1905.)

Fig. 14.7.   Edward Burne-Jones.   Detail from *The Sleep of King Arthur in Avalon*.
The large oil in is the Museo de Arte, Ponce, Puerto Rico.

ALFRED TENNYSON——The Laureate of King Arthur.

Fig. 14.8.   Caricatures of Tennyson: *The Laureate of King Arthur* (*The Period*, 1870); *Crossing the Bar* by John Tenniel (*Punch*, 1892).

Fig. 14.9.   A. Forestier. *The Last Idyll (Illustrated London News*, 1892).

THE CONTRIBUTORS

Christopher Baswell teaches medieval literature at Barnard College and is a specialist in classical tradition in the Middle Ages. He is co-founder and director of the Women Poets at Barnard series, and a recipient of Fulbright, ACLS and NEH Fellowships. He is currently completing a book on Virgilian tradition in medieval England.

William Sharpe teaches Victorian literature at Barnard College. He has been awarded Mellon, Fulbright, and NEH Fellowships, and works primarily on the relation between art, literature and the city in the nineteenth and twentieth centuries. He is co-editor, with Leonard Wallock, of *Visions of the Modern City: Essays in History, Art, and Literature* (1987).

Judith H. Anderson is Professor and Director of Graduate Studies in the English Department at Indiana University. She has worked on Spenser throughout her career, publishing numerous articles on the subject. She is author of *The Growth of a Personal Voice: Piers Plowman and the Faerie Queene* (1976), and her most recent book is *Biographical Truth: The Representation of Historical Persons in Tudor-Stuart Writings* (1984).

Marie Borroff, Professor of English at Yale University, has not only written the influential *Sir Gawain and the Green Knight: A Stylistic and Metrical Study* (Yale, 1962) but is herself a transmitter of Arthurian tradition. Her verse translation of *Sir Gawain*, used in this volume, is standard. She is also author of *Language and the Poet: Verbal Artistry in Frost, Stevens, and Moore* (1979).

Sheila T. Cavanagh is completing her Ph.D. in English at Brown University. She also holds advanced degrees from Georgetown University and Trinity College, Dublin. Her dissertation is entitled "'That Fairest Virtue': Chastity in Spenser and Shakespeare." She has published "Practical *versus* Ideal Justice: Arthur and Arthegall in *Faerie Queene* V" (*Renaissance Papers* 1984) and "'Such Was Irena's Countenance': Ireland in Spenser's Prose and Poetry" (*Texas Studies in Language and Literature*, Spring 1986).

Sheila Fisher teaches English at Trinity College, Hartford, where she is Assistant Professor. Her recent work has focused on the role of women in medieval literature. Her thesis, *Chaucer's Poetic Alchemy: A Study of Value and Its Transformation in the Canterbury Tales*, will appear in the Outstanding Dissertation series from Garland Publishing. She is editor, with Janet Halley, of *Feminist Contextual Criticism of Late Medieval and Renaissance Writings*, forthcoming from University of Tennessee Press.

William E. Fredeman, Professor of English at the University of British Columbia, has twice been a Guggenheim Fellow. He is the author of the indispensable *Pre-Raphaelitism: A Bibliocritical Study* (1965) and numerous other monographs and essays on the Pre-Raphaelites and Tennyson. He has edited *The PRB Journal* and special double numbers of *Victorian Poetry* on Rossetti and Queen Victoria's Jubilee. He currently edits *The Journal of Pre-Raphaelite and Aesthetic Studies*.

Jonathan Freedman is Assistant Professor of English at Yale University. His specialty is British and American Aestheticism, and his 1984 Ph.D. thesis, "'The Quickened Consciousness': Aestheticism in Howells and James," won the Field Dissertation Prize of the Yale Graduate School. He is the author of "An Aestheticism of Our Own: American Writers and the Aesthetic Movement," which has been published in the catalogue of the Metropolitan Museum exhibition "In Praise of Beauty: Americans and the Aesthetic Movement."

M. Victorian Guerin is Assistant Professor of French at Iowa State University. She has also taught at the University of Paris-Sorbonne and at the University of Geneva, Switzerland. Her speciality is medieval French and English Arthurian literature, on which she has several articles forthcoming. She received her Ph.D. from Yale University in 1985, writing on "Mordred's Hidden Presence: The Skeleton in the Arthurian Closet."

A. Kent Hieatt, Professor of English at the University of Western Ontario, is a renowned Spenserian. His books include the seminal work *Short Times Endless Monument* (1960) and *Chaucer, Spenser, Milton: Mythopoeic Continuities and Transformations* (1975). He has edited works of both Chaucer and Spenser. He is the author of many articles on Renaissance thought and literature, and his recent article on the sources of Shakespeare's sonnets won the Parker Prize of the Modern Language Association.

Roberta L. Krueger is Associate Professor of French at Hamilton College. She has published a number of articles on medieval French literature and is writing a book on the problem of the female audience in Old French romance. With E. Jane Burns, she edited and wrote the "Introduction" to *Courtly Ideology and Women's Place in Medieval French Literature, Romance Notes* 25 (Spring 1985). She is an editor of *The Medieval Feminist Newsletter.*

Charles Méla is Professor of French Language and Literature at the University of Geneva, Switzerland. He is an alumnus of the Ecole Normale Supérieure and holds the Doctorat d'Etat from the University of Paris-Sorbonne. His books include *Blanchefleur et le Saint Homme, ou la Semblance des reliques* (Seuil, 1979), and *La Reine et le Graal: La 'Conjointure' dans les romans du Graal de Chrétien de Troyes au 'Livre de Lancelot'* (Seuil, 1984). Professor Méla is now at work on a study of *La Mort le roi Artu.*

John D. Rosenberg is Professor of English and Director of Graduate Studies in the Department of English and Comparative Literature at Columbia University. He is the author of many articles and books on the poetry and non-fiction prose of the

Victorian period, most notably *The Darkening Glass: A Portrait of Ruskin's Genius* (1961) and *Carlyle and the Burden of History* (1985). His book on *Idylls of the King*, entitled *The Fall of Camelot* (1973), has played a major role in the critical reappraisal of Tennyson's Arthurian epic. He is currently writing on Charles Darwin.

R. Allen Shoaf, Professor of English at the University of Florida (Gainesville), has pioneered theoretical approaches to Middle English and other medieval literatures. He is author of *Dante, Chaucer, and the Currency of the Word* (Pilgrim Books, 1983), *The Poem as Green Girdle: "Commercium" in "Sir Gawain and the Green Knight"* (Florida, 1984), and *Milton, Poet of Duality: A Study of Semiosis in the Poetry and the Prose* (Yale, 1985).

Carole Silver is Professor of English at Stern College, Yeshiva University. She is the author of *The Romance of William Morris* (1982), co-author of *Kind Words: A Thesaurus of Euphemisms* (1983), and editor of *The Golden Chain: Essays on William Morris and Pre-Raphaelitism* (1982). She has written a number of articles on Morris and other Pre-Raphaelites and is presently at work on a book about the Victorian interest in preternatural creatures.

M. Alison Stones is Professor of Art History at the University of Pittsburgh. She specializes in aspects of secular illumination, especially of Vincent of Beauvais, Alexander, Pseudo-Turpin, and the earlier Arthurian cycle texts, on which she has published numerous articles and monographs, including the article on "Arthurian Illuminated Manuscripts" in *The Arthurian Encyclopedia*. Professor Stones is currently completing a volume on thirteenth-century illuminated manuscripts from Cambrai and Tournai.

INDEX